Memoirs of a]

The Danny Mal

Danny Malloy and Andy Malloy

Vertical Editions

www.verticaleditions.com

First published in the United Kingdom in 2013 by Vertical Editions, Unit
4a, Snaygill Industrial Estate, Skipton, North Yorkshire BD23 2QR

www.verticaleditions.com

ISBN 978-1-904091-72-1

A CIP catalogue record for this book is available from the British Library

Cover design by HBA, York

Printed and bound by MPG Printgroup, Bodmin

Contents

For Margaret (1936-1993)

Acknowledgements

Special thanks go to Richard Shepherd at Cardiff City FC and Dave Forbes at Dundee FC. Extra special thanks to Richard and journalist Terry Grandin for very kindly agreeing to compose the forewords.

And many thanks to the likes of Tommy Docherty, Craig Brown, Doug Cowie, Graham Moore, Alan Harrington, Colin Baker and Barrie Hole for their kind words.

Also to Karl Waddicor and the good people at Vertical Editions for all their hard work in bringing a grey manuscript to life.

Finally, to my author son, Andrew D. Malloy, for transforming my ramblings in a way I never thought possible.

Danny Malloy, February 2013

Cardiff City Foreword by Richard Shepherd

A former BBC Radio Wales and independent radio football commentator, Richard has been part of Cardiff City's media department since 2002, although his connections with the club as spectator, broadcaster and programme-editor go back much further. He now provides match-commentary in the club's internet station, is a member of the match-programme editorial team, and is the Cardiff City archivist/historian.

It was 25th April 2009 – Cardiff City v Ipswich Town – the very last Football League match to be played at Cardiff City's Ninian Park which they had occupied since it was built in 1910. A new stadium was almost complete across the road, and the Bluebirds would soon be moving home. And present at that Ipswich match was a former player, memories of whom took me back to the mid-1950s when, as a young boy, I was first taken by my father to watch Cardiff City in action. It was in April 1956 against Portsmouth and in City's side that day was central defender Danny Malloy without whom no City line-up would be complete from December 1955 to April 1961, my formative years of watching the Bluebirds.

Clearly those near-six years left a lasting impression on Danny and his family, and here he was, at the age of 78, having made the long journey from his home at Denny near Stirling in Scotland, to be present at Ninian Park's finale. What a great reception he received from young and old, most of whom had probably never seen him play for City but were well aware that he was the last Cardiff City player to captain the side to the top level (the old First Division) in 1960. The season after he left in the summer of 1961, the club were relegated (1961-62) and at the time of writing have yet to get back to the highest status.

Danny's story makes fascinating reading, his time before and after his Ninian Park days, but especially his spell with Cardiff City. I had often heard over the years from the late Ron Stitfall (Cardiff City and Wales full-back) about how Danny had 'laid out' Brian Clough at Middlesborough's Ayresome Park in January 1958. He must be the only person in football to have 'silenced' Cloughie, and it was very interesting to read about it in Danny's own words.

I was delighted to be able to assist in this autobiography by providing Cardiff City's playing-records from his time with the Club. At the age of 82 he still closely follows City's fortunes from his home in Scotland. If he does have any remaining football ambitions, it would perhaps be to see Cardiff City competing at the highest level as they did during his time with the Club.

Richard Shepherd

Supporters Foreword by
Terry Grandin

Publicist and football journalist, Terry Grandin, has followed Cardiff City since the 1950s – originally from the Grange End and more latterly the press box. An author of several books on the club, his favourite memory is the promotion of the Bluebirds to Division One in 1960 led by the inimitable Danny Malloy.

It was the last day of 1955 and my schoolpal and I made our way to Wolverhampton Station after watching the Bluebirds beat the world-famous Wolves 2-0 at Molineux.

The reason why we spent all our pocket money on a train trip to the Midlands was probably because this fixture was one of the nearest Cardiff City came to a derby match in those heady far-off days of First Division football.

It certainly wasn't because we thought two points were in the bag. At the start of the season in the home match against the Wanderers I was in the boys' enclosure behind the goals at the Grange End when Johnny Hancocks scored after 15 seconds. Wolves were 5-0 up at half-time and went on to win 9-1, equalling the heaviest top flight home defeat ever recorded at the time. Even the City goal was scored by a former Wolves player called Ron Stockin.

They had been unbeaten at Molineux all year so you can imagine how happy we were with those winning goals from Trevor Ford and Gerry Hitchens as we climbed on board for the journey back home to Cardiff.

Now remember, this was during the days of steam engines when all carriages had corridors, so after a short while I decided to go for a walk along the length of the train. Off I went and you can imagine my surprise when I eventually came across the City players who were also travelling home by rail.

A few of them were stretching their legs in the corridor and as I gingerly approached, a big man looked down at me and said, 'Have you been to the game?'

At least I think that is what he said because he had a thick Scottish accent. It was none other than Danny Malloy.

Now I knew almost everyone else by sight in the City side but Danny had only been at the club for a few weeks, even so he soon put this fourteen-year-old lad at ease by asking what I thought of the match.

After such a time I cannot remember exactly what was said on that train journey back to Cardiff only that, despite being so young, I was welcomed in amongst the players thanks to Danny's kindness in introducing me to everyone. Of course from then on there was only one player for me, and Danny became my all-time favourite as he went on to tame all the top centre-forwards of the day.

The first home game of the following season saw Newcastle United bring their star-studded side to Ninian Park. I was there as the 'big man' never gave England international Jackie Milburn a kick all game, although I cannot say the same for Milburn's strike partner, Vic Keeble. If I remember rightly, Jimmy Scoular was also in the Newcastle side that day.

Once again I was behind the goal at the Grange End when Keeble charged into City keeper Graham Vearncombe after a Newcastle corner. Danny was on the case straightaway threatening to sort him out if he did that again. As the Newcastle man walked away with a grin on his face, Danny kneed him up the backside so hard that I don't think he ventured into Cardiff's half for the rest of the match.

The Brian Clough incident happened in an away match at Middlesbrough in January, 1958 but only went to show that Danny had by now truly earned his hard man status. The story went that Clough had been giving Danny the 'verbals' all through the game until the 'big man's' patience ran out and he decked Clough when the ball was in the Middlesbrough penalty area.

Danny soon had a reputation for not only looking after himself but also his team-mates and it was not long before he captained the Bluebirds.

Mind you, he also earned a reputation for 'Ogies' and I was at Ninian Park in glorious sunshine during August 1959 when he scored two own goals against Liverpool. Both came within ten minutes of the interval to put the visitors 2-1 ahead at the break. The first came when Danny chested a cross from Jimmy Melia back to Graham Vearncombe but it crept inside the post. Four minutes later a low centre from Alan A'Court was diverted into the net by Danny. Fortunately for City, Graham Moore and Johnny Watkins scored in the second half for a well deserved 3-2 win and the double over Bill Shankly's side.

Two games involving the 'big man' that I was lucky enough to see stand out for me. When City beat Aston Villa 1-0 in April 1960 to clinch promotion to Division One he was superb at the back organising the defence as Villa went looking for the equaliser that never came.

The other match was in the top flight the following season against Tottenham Hotspur who would go on to become double winners. The match was played under floodlights at Ninian Park on a Saturday evening in March and after falling behind early on, Danny marshalled his troops to a superb 3-2 victory over a world-class outfit.

The start of season 1961-62 caused a shock to most clubs after the ban on maximum wages was lifted. All City's players were retained on the same money except for Danny who, as captain, reckoned he was rightly entitled to a little extra. It was a black day when he was refused a small increase and allowed to leave the club as the end result for Cardiff City was relegation from Division One that very season.

No doubt Danny has something to say on that subject and many others in his excellent biography, and I look forward to reading all those previously untold stories about Cardiff City by the last player to skipper the Bluebirds to promotion to Division One.

Good luck with the book Danny, and thanks for all those great memories.

Terry Grandin

1

In the Beginning

It was 6th November, 1930. The doctor is heard to remark on the size of the Malloy family's latest addition. To be fair, thirteen pounds does sound more like the weight of a new born calf than a baby boy! Daniel Malloy (Danny to you), fourth child and first son of Andy and Annie Roy Malloy, comes kicking and screaming into the world in the small Stirlingshire hamlet known as Longcroft. House births were very much the norm back then and the rest of the clan – Nan, May, Annie, James, Andy and Ian – would each take his or her bow in that house in the area known locally as 'The Block.'

It was home to a number of large families and consisted of a perimeter of old fashioned, two-storey tenement buildings with a square in the centre. My grandfather – also Danny – and grandmother used to own a tiny wooden grocer's shop which sat slap bang in the middle of the square. The block kids, including me, used to torment the living daylights out of them as we relentlessly slammed our football against the back of the shop. Or 'the goals' as they used to double as. It cost me a few warm backsides I'll tell you! The houses were tiny and wholly inadequate, but for me, the outside toilets and wash houses failed to diminish the indomitable community spirit felt at the time.

The Block was a vibrant and exciting place to live. At least I thought so. From kicking around a makeshift football made out of rags (when we'd burst our super-duper plastic one!), to nicking exotic fruits like bananas, (yes bananas!), from under the tarpaulin of the local trader's horse-drawn cart as it stood in the square. All good fun. Families were closer then and friendships really did last a lifetime.

The Malloys became really friendly with a remarkable family who also lived beside us in The Block. The Gourlays were a large family as well and I became best friends with big Tam Gourlay who was around the same age. He was a gem of a lad and I had a lot of time for him and his brothers and sisters. The remarkable thing about them was how well they coped, given that both parents were born deaf and dumb. Of course the Gourlays had been brought up communicating using sign language, but it was sad to see other people shunning the parents, treating them as though they were imbeciles. My father being my father would have none of this and insisted we all learn to sign. I knew enough to get by as did the rest of us, but my father became something of an expert. In no time at all he was holding full conversations using signing. It was a skill that never left him and he would often delight in entertaining his many grandchildren down the years. He would marvel at the way their faces lit up as he went through his well-worn routines.

Speaking of the Gourlay family – daughter Thia later became a bit of a celebrity, but almost lost her life in the process. I was there when she made newspaper headlines at a travelling funfair which had stopped over in Longcroft. Thia went flying through the air in one of those chair-a-plane contraptions! The only problem was the chair had detached itself from the equipment and landed with an almighty crash in a field some twenty yards away. Thankfully, all was well for Thia in the end and she recovered well from her ordeal.

Of course, it could be said that time clouds memories and adds sentimentality, but I firmly believe that those were indeed happier times. The reason? Simple, everyone had the same; not an awful lot, but enough. Unless you happened to be the local doctor, or a university educated product of a well-heeled family. Then again, these people were always fair game when it came to pinching crab apples, turnips, and potatoes!

There was one wee man just up the road from us who used to have a couple of apple trees in his back yard. The main attraction with nicking 'his' apples was obvious: he could run like the wind and this made it much more of a challenge to get away with the booty. We'd put somebody on sentry duty while the rest gathered the fruit. 'Get ready, he's at the door,' was the early warning alert. This was followed by, 'he's opening the door.' By the time it got to 'here he comes!' we'd be high-tailing it up the street with our haul, giggling as we ran.

I often recall many profound memories – most good, some not so good – from my early childhood; memories that remain stark and vivid to this day. Of course, there were no computers or televisions in those days and the kids used to have to find other ways to amuse themselves. 'Chap door run' was a particular favourite among the neighbourhood kids and the way The Block building was designed was perfect for an advanced version. The doors on each landing were on a slant and facing each other. The handles were only about two feet apart and a little rope, strategically placed, could provide endless fun. The handles were tied tightly together and the two doors 'chapped.' The air would turn blue as each would try in vain to open his door. We would stand at the top of the stairs laughing, ready to take off, until one of them eventually managed to slip a knife out of a tiny gap in the door. 'Ah know who ye are! Ah'll tell yer mither and faither!' they'd shout as we pelted down the stairs.

There was a small abattoir next door to The Block. The local urchins would stand on tiptoes, and could easily peer over the wall into the yard of Tom Miller's butchery. I can still smell the stench of death in the air, even now. The poor beasts were dragged in for slaughter. What a fight they would put up. They dug their hooves in as if clinging on to dear life. Now I know the experts say they're just dumb animals, but the beasts knew what was happening. I'm certain they knew. In fact, I would go as far as saying that these early experiences left me with a little emotional scar; to this day I abhor any kind of cruelty to animals. I'm not a vegetarian or a vegan, nothing as exotic as that, but I definitely do not eat my share of beef, lamb, or pork. I mean, killing cute little lambs! What the hell is that all about? I hope that last statement dispels the myth that used to do the rounds – no, I certainly did 'not' eat raw meat at any time during my playing career!

During the early forties, I remember a new Prime Minister being driven through Longcroft on his way to some kind of war council in Glasgow or wherever. Although Winston Churchill was not a popular figure in the area following his ruthless treatment of the miners, I remember a huge crowd thronging the streets for miles to see him. I would guess maybe people showed up just to be able to say, 'I was there!' Who knows? I also remember my father refusing to be tempted by such trivialities. There was no way he would have stood among the 'welcoming committee' for Mr Churchill. My father had his stoical political beliefs and I admired him for them. I'll bet he was curious as hell though! I still recall the black, hearse-like car, the bowler hat, the cigar. And, the regal wave!

Ah yes, the war! I was too young to serve, but old enough to remember the first night of the infamous 'blitz' on Clydebank, near

Glasgow. It was a crystal clear evening complete with the brightest moon, and the story went that the German bombers simply followed the moonlight reflecting from the still waters of the Forth and Clyde canal, right to Clydebank. The canal, literally, ran just yards from our house and I can still hear the low murmurings of the German aircraft as they passed overhead. Indeed, a number of bombs were dropped all around the Stirlingshire area, the pilots presumably confused and losing their bearings. People who lived during that era will remember well the 'blackout rules' when wardens used to prowl the streets searching for chinks of light coming from improperly covered windows. 'These effing Jerry bombers will pit yer lights oot, permanently,' they would scold. Somehow, my father thought we'd all be safe from the stray incendiaries by huddling together in the cupboard below the stairs! How does that saying go? How many fat people can you fit in a Mini ...?

I must've been about six when I remember the trauma of my grandfather's death and my big sister May and I somehow being left alone together in the room with the body. 'There's your Papa, Danny,' May announced calmly, before pulling the sheet back. I was out the door in a flash and don't think I stopped running till I hit Haggs Parish church, half a mile up the road.

Academically, the Malloy family all did very well, especially my sister, Annie. Annie was very intelligent, quick-witted and extremely funny, with a dry sense of humour. I'm sure if she were growing up today she would have gone to university and worked herself into a top job somewhere.

All three of my sisters – Nan, May and Annie – ended up working on the buses as 'clippies.' Anyone who remembers the old bus services of the time will, no doubt be able to tell his or her own hilarious encounter with 'the boss of the bus.' Whilst the drivers, with a few exceptions, appeared to be cut from the same surly and bad tempered cloth, the clippies were like their alter-egos. Well, at least most of them were! Bright, breezy and funny, these ladies were like theatre dames, with a comment for every occasion and a solution for all the world's ills. But heaven help anyone with a smart mouth or a stray finger on the bell. They would soon be sent crashing earthwards by the boss of the bus. Mind you, from time to time, even my sisters would be left red-faced and unable to speak. On one occasion Annie certainly didn't have her troubles to seek on a really busy, smoke-filled journey from Denny to Falkirk. She was working the bus from the back, checking tickets, moving stray bags from the aisle, when she came upon what she thought was a small boy of about eight with his back to her, blocking her progress. Sighing loudly, Annie reached under his arms, whisked him up onto a vacant seat. 'Come on now, Son. You sit up here out the way,' she said. The wizened face of a little old man destroyed my sister with an icy stare!

My brother James also had a run in with the boss of the bus when he made to jump off an open-backed, double-decker as it stopped at traffic lights in Falkirk town centre. The clippie saw the move, spread her arms across the poles, knuckles white as snow. 'This isnae a recognised stop,' she barked, her crabbit expression daring him to go for it. James did indeed have a go and reached over to try and prise the dragon's claws apart. He failed miserably. Unfortunately the bus just happened to be full of sniggering travellers and my brother was left red-faced, muttering oaths all the way to the next stop.

My own brush with the bus company came when I was about seventeen. I was in the town of Larbert, near The Cross, waiting for a ride to Falkirk to meet a pal, maybe play a little snooker. As I was walking up to the bus stop, I could see the bus coming in the distance. I was about twenty yards from the stop when it reached me. I stood in the road with my hand out and the bus appeared to slow a little, before the driver, sporting a wide smile, floored the pedal when I stepped onto the pavement. I was stunned at first, then angry. When the bus was stopped in traffic about a quarter of a mile along the road, I ran like a hare and laughed out loud when I realised I was going to make it. I skipped in the open back and darted upstairs, before it took off again. I plonked down on a seat near the front, still laughing. The next thing I heard was the bell ringing and the bus shuddering to a halt around the corner. Heavy footsteps hit the stairs before the clippie appeared on the top deck, hands on hips. 'You'll need tae get off,' she spat, the most deadpan of expressions on her face.

'Why?' I held out my hands.

'You got on between stops. It's no' allowed. You'll need tae get off.'

'I'll just pay from the last stop. What's the problem?'

'It's no' a recognised stop. Get off, now!' She raised her voice, at the same time jerking her thumb over her shoulder, towards the stairs.

'I'm not moving. I said I'll pay from the last stop and that's it.' I folded my arms in defiance.

Next thing, I heard the driver slam his door, trudge up the stairs as if he had the weight of the world on his shoulders. The stupid git stood side-by-side with his accomplice. 'You'll need tae get off,' he droned.

'Look. I'm going to tell you the same as I told her. I'm not moving.'

I glanced around at the other passengers, smiled at them as they struggled to contain their mirth.

'I'm phonin' the polis,' the driver continued.

'Phone the Queen if you like,' I said. 'The bus can sit here all night. I'm … not … moving.' I turned to face the front.

A brief, whispered exchange between the two, before … 'Gie 'im his ticket,' the driver said. He sighed, took off his hat and scratched his thick head before sloping away.

The clippie rattled off the ticket, threw it into my lap and snatched the money out of my hand before we carried on our way. I had a big smile on my face all the way to Falkirk.

Close-knit communities resulted in small, compact classes at Longcroft School and pupils were certainly given the opportunity to learn. Not all pupils took that opportunity, however, either through lack of ability, or lack of ambition. One in particular, big Jock Fraser, a member of the former group, provided the cabaret one Friday afternoon. Now I say big Jock only because he was much bigger than everyone else at the school, including all the teachers. And, more significantly, the headmaster. I'd like to point out that there was absolutely no badness in Jock Fraser. He was a big, level-headed guy who was well liked by everyone at school.

I have no idea why he snapped that day, but I can tell you it turned out to be the funniest thing I had ever seen. The big fellow took umbrage at being told off by Miss Ramsey, our teacher, a frail, middle-aged spinster. Unfortunately, Jock reacted furiously by hurling the biggest, weightiest, hardback textbook I had ever seen at her. Miss Ramsey had turned her back on the hulk, was writing something on the blackboard, when the book crashed against the wall millimetres from her head. I kid you not, but a direct hit would definitely have killed her stone dead!

After her – and the initial shock of the rest of the class – Miss Ramsey summoned up enough energy to instruct one of the boys to go and fetch the Headmaster. The excited lad took off like a hare. Two or three minutes later Hughie Stark appeared and after a short dialogue with Miss Ramsey, they came to the mutual agreement that the only solution would be to remove big Jock Fraser from the class.

Everyone watched in anticipation as Mr Stark took a deep breath and walked up the aisle to where Jock was sitting. The look of apprehension on Hughie Stark's face was only matched by the deep determination registering on the face of big Jock; something would have to give.

A couple of reasonable requests for Jock to get up were met with bellows of 'NAW!' and before we knew it, the pair of them were grappling with each other. Everybody just sat there, open-mouthed.

Picture the scene, big Jock Fraser, arms wrapped around the body of his desk, giant fingers on both hands interlocked like two bunches of bananas, hanging on doggedly; Mr Stark, his right arm around the big fella's neck, the other arm across his chest. He's got his feet up on the desk, hauling and pulling with all his might, while wee, frail Miss Ramsey is on her knees under the desk trying to prise Jock's thick fingers apart. It was like watching a slapstick comedy as the classroom erupted.

The whole thing probably only lasted a couple of minutes, but no doubt, provided many hours of belly laughs for the friends and families of everyone present that day.

In a funny little twist of fate, I later discovered that Jock Fraser's little sister, Mary, was best friends with my future wife, Margaret.

I was lucky enough to win the coveted 'Dux' medal at school and when I was fourteen and ready to leave, I remember the headmaster dropping in at our house to try and talk me into staying on. It was a no-brainer. The family just couldn't afford to have a fit and healthy young lad sitting about on his behind all day. In any case, the last thing I wanted was to be perceived differently from my pals. In those days you left school to become a miner, or to go work in one of the local factories or foundries that peppered the area. Money wasn't plentiful in the forties, but low paid jobs were as the country was in the grip of a recession following the war effort. In fact, as people who were around at the time would recall, food-rationing persisted well into the fifties. Times were certainly tough, but I will say one thing that made them semi-bearable – I don't know why, but I just loved the powdered eggs! Anyway, the upshot was I left school at fourteen and went to work in the biggest foundry in Bonnybridge, Smith and Wellstood, as an apprentice fitter. My father also worked there and put a word in for me. That was the way it worked.

The iron foundry at that time was also one of the biggest in Britain and specialised in making fireplaces, ranges, and cookers. The products were so expertly constructed there that demand was high, resulting in thousands of orders from all over the world. George Ure's original company, prior to the collaboration between James Smith and Stephen Wellstood, made parts for Singer sewing machines in Clydebank. As both companies, literally, sat on the banks of the Forth and Clyde canal, the transportation between them was easy. Unfortunately, one day Singer's decided they could manufacture their own parts and the contract was lost. In 1858, George Ure then decided to take up an option to go into business with Smith and Wellstood, and the resultant company changed direction, trading successfully for over 140 years, until its products, sadly, went out of vogue.

Foundry work, like mining, was hard and dirty and an exclusively male occupation. My father had told me to get in, get my head down and that's exactly what I did.

'If you let them see you're a worker you'll do just fine, Danny.' His words rang in my ears as I walked through the doors into the 'dressing shop.' Of course, Health and Safety was almost non-existent in the workplace in those days and with the dearth of safety guards, gloves and goggles, many of the locals suffered nasty injuries during the course of their employment in the foundries, mills and mines in the area. Dozens of people of a certain age had various parts of their bodies either missing or injured, including fingers, toes and, in the more serious cases, arms, legs and eyes.

The main problem with the type of work I signed up for was the danger to the eye. Tiny metal filings flying around were a constant menace in the dressing shop, the lack of eye protection leading to a lot of lost time as, nine times out of ten, victims were forced to go to hospital for treatment to remove debris.

Smith and Wellstood had their very own 'witch doctor' for such emergencies; a fellow called Rab Bellingham. Rab had the knack of being able to remove even the most microscopic of iron filing from an injured eye. This would keep production going, by allowing the patient to return to his post without the need for a hospital visit. Perfect vision, a rock steady hand, and a long, lethal looking needle, were all Rab needed. Oh, and a bean can for flicking the filings into!

I remember watching a television programme a few years back, which charted the formative years of Scottish comedian, Billy Connolly. Connolly went to work as a welder in the Govan shipyards after he left school, and on the programme, he described a man who might just have been as valuable to John Brown's as Rab Bellingham was to Smith and Wellstood. The pair's methods were slightly different, however, the shipyard's man developing an exclusive solution to clearing debris from an eye. Apparently, this man would, firstly, stretch the eye wide open using thumb and forefinger, before turning away to swig a mouthful of water. The unsuspecting victim would then be bombarded by a powerful jet of water and spit, guaranteed to flush out the offending material As the years rolled on, I believe John Brown's man was 'persuaded' to use a type of water pistol instead, a few of the tough Glasgow tradesmen taking exception to being spat at in the face!

My brief stint at Smith and Wellstood went well and I enjoyed the camaraderie among the men. I already knew most of the locals and also made friends with lads from farther afield; Smith and Wellstood employed people from the likes of Banton, Kilsyth and Kirkintilloch and I was to get on well with most of them. Big Geordie Brown from Kilsyth was a jovial, outgoing type, game for a laugh and he and I became pals right away.

Despite my future reputation as a hard man on the football pitch, at fourteen, I was fairly shy and quiet. Geordie, on the other hand, would talk to the devil and the contrast between us made our friendship just right. He was a big hearted fella who would do anything for anybody, but he could also look after himself. If he thought somebody was messing him about, he wouldn't be slow in letting them have it.

An argument broke out in the canteen one day, when Geordie and this new start squared up. Apparently, Geordie knew the lad, had identified him straight away as a wrong 'un. His perceptions were proved right, when following heated exchanges between them, the new man drew a blade and speared it into the wooden table as a post of his intentions. The other lads stood up, horror-stricken, and jumped back in unison as the knife quivered back and forth between the pair. The guy was just about to reach for the blade again when I leaned across and pulled it first. You should have seen the colour drain from his face!

'I'll take charge of this for now!' I said as firmly as my nerves would allow.

A huge smile broke out on big Geordie's face just before he went on to batter the living daylights out of the new guy. I had made a friend for life.

I was to meet Geordie Brown from time to time, for years afterwards, as we both became members of Falkirk Golf Club. He would recount the knife incident at almost every meeting! Ironically, Geordie went on to form friendships with my brother, Andy, while working beside him as a heavy goods driver with Calor Gas in Grangemouth, and my cousin, also called Danny Malloy.

Cousin Danny was a year or so older than me, son of my Uncle Tam who was later killed in a pit accident in the early 1950s. There were a number of Danny Malloys in the family around the same time, and someone, I cannot recall who, had the bright idea of making up different names to identify them. I was 'Footballer Danny'; my cousin was known as 'Boxer Danny', after he became a professional fighter; there was another cousin, 'Joiner Danny', for obvious reasons. Finally, 'Big Danny', was an uncle, my father's youngest brother.

Boxer Danny and Geordie Brown actually became best friends for a spell, and the pair of them used to appear at the odd Dundee game. As well as becoming a Scottish champion in the professional boxing ring, Danny was also a useful footballer. A centre-forward, he played for a few of the local teams. Danny was especially adept at, ahem, challenging goalies for the ball. And centre-halves! I remember playing against him at youth level. In fact, I'm sure I still have the bruises. Seriously, Danny was as hard as nails and would face up to Goliath. Geordie Brown would often recount a story about the day he and Danny decided to come and see me play for Dundee, at Brockville Park, Falkirk. Now, for some reason the Falkirk fans used to really have it in for me. I never knew why. Maybe it was because I was a local boy coming back to play against them. Anyway, according to Geordie, I was coming in for some serious stick from this one man in particular. Even the people standing in his vicinity were getting really fed up with him. Unfortunately for this guy, he also happened to be standing next to Danny and Geordie. The story goes that after four or five 'polite requests' from Danny for this man to clam up, he still insisted on spouting his venom. As the crowd howled at some incident on the park, the sudden roar masked the sound of Danny's huge fist against the man's jaw. Geordie swore that the blow was so swift that nobody else stood a chance of seeing it. The loudmouth went down like a sack of spuds, before being propped up at the back of the enclosure to sleep it off.

'What's happened to the Billy Steels or the Jimmy Johnstones these days? Where's the next Jim Baxter or Lawrie Reilly going to come from?' These are just a couple of questions I've been asked over the last twenty years or so. My answer? Usually a shrug and a shake of the head. Of course, people are always willing to air their particular take on the problem and I think I've heard them all; from the computer and the television, to other sports, lack of facilities, and modern attitudes. I've even heard some blame the government! Now, I'm not exactly a huge fan of governments and politics in general, but I cannot for the life of me see how that argument could possibly hold water. For me, I think the main reasons for the current lack of emerging footballing talent are due to a combination of things: television, and/or computer, and attitude. When I was young every little boy wanted to become the next Willie Woodburn or Patsy Gallagher. Kids didn't just walk along the pavement or the road. They kicked a ball as they went. Jimmy Johnstone could play keepy-uppy all day with an object the size of a tennis ball. Now that kind of talent doesn't come easily to anybody, even someone with the extraordinary skills of Johnstone. It takes practice.

Only a select few actually make it to the professional stage, of course, and I have only one person to thank for getting me there in the first place. My father was a big influence on my career and I guess he must have seen the potential in me right away, as all I can remember from my early life is being with him, and a ball. He'd throw the ball at me from every angle, sharpening and honing my ball control skills and giving me a confidence in the air that was to last my whole career. I was to come up against some of the finest headers of the ball in the business and can honestly say that I was never bested in that department; Wille Bauld, John Charles, Nat Lofthouse, Tommy Taylor; all four were brilliant in the air, but I cannot recall any of them getting the better of me during a match.

My father had also played football, although only to junior level. I later heard that he turned down the chance of a trial with Hearts, a young family and the journey to Edinburgh during the twenties, contributory factors in his decision. The old timers used to tell me stories of my father in the Denny Hibs forward line, hammering them in from fifty yards and the like! What I do know is that my old man was an accomplished centre-forward with a rocket shot in each foot. Down 4-0 with fifteen minutes to go in a local junior cup game, it was the stuff of legend when Andy Malloy rattled in four goals to earn a replay, and an eventual place in the next round.

Denny Hibs was known as a Catholic team and this notion was borne out by the usual forward line of the time: Coyle, Boyle, Malloy, Doyle and Docherty. Although my old man was Catholic and a Celtic fan, the family was brought up as Protestant, supporting Rangers, and I loved nothing better than jumping on a bus on a Saturday and heading off with my pals to Ibrox. The Rangers team of the forties was formidable, sweeping away everything in its path. Watching from the sidelines, I was convinced these players were gods. Little did I know, a few short years later, I would be playing on the same park as some of my heroes, pitting my wits against them. Me, a skinny kid from Longcroft! Jerry Dawson, George Young, Jimmy Smith, Willie Thornton, Dougie Gray, Willie Woodburn, Tiger Shaw, Willie Waddell, Jimmy Duncanson, Torry Gillick, Jimmy Caskie, Sammy Cox, Bobby Brown, Alex Venters ... the list is endless. Nowadays, on occasion, the old memory tends to give up on me, but I can still see all of these players in my mind's eye. I memorised every thunderbolt shot, every magnificent save, inch perfect cross, every twist and turn and sure footed tackle. And the sweetest thing for every Rangers supporter during and just after the war years must surely have been the considerable gap in ability between us and bitter rivals, Celtic. I was lucky enough to witness a right few hammerings for the team from the East End of Glasgow during those years. In fact, I cannot recall ever attending an Old Firm encounter in the forties when the Hoops came out on top. Jimmy Duncanson was a particular thorn in Celtic's flesh, scoring an incredible twenty two goals in Old Firm clashes.

One match should stand out for me for obvious reasons and took place on Ne'erday, 1943. 'Rangers 8 Celtic 1', must sound like heaven on earth to the most ardent, dyed-in-the-wool, Gers fan. Strangely, I can't recall any incident of note or any fine detail about the game, apart from the final scoreline. A case of being far too easy, I suspect.

Now the 5-3 match of September 1945 does remain vivid in my memory as it contained some quite breathtaking football from both sides. The outcome was still in doubt until the very end, Alex Venters eventually putting the game to bed with the fifth goal in the very last minute.

On the subject of Old Firm games in the forties, I recall a famous encounter in the Victory Cup semi-final of 1946. This tournament was set up as a temporary competition and didn't really stand for much in the grand scheme of things. But then, this was The Old Firm, where a game of tiddlywinks would be fought to the death!

After a terrible 0-0 draw in the first leg in front of 90,000 supporters, the teams again went head-to-head the following midweek, this time before a more modest crowd of 50,000. Willie Waddell fired Gers in front with a rocket shot. Torry Gillick then rattled the bar before Jimmy Duncanson missed a sitter right on half-time. In typical Celtic fashion, they regrouped, roaring out of the blocks after half-time, a strong wind at their backs. Rangers managed to weather the storm, though only just, before they were awarded a penalty kick and a chance to double the lead with twenty minutes to go. My buddies and I stood open-mouthed as we watched bizarre events unfold in front of our eyes. Firstly, the Celtic players, unhappy with the decision to award the spot kick, crowded the referee, pushed and jostled him, trying to get him to change his mind. To be honest it did look like a penalty to me, through my blue tinted specs. Celtic captain George Paterson obviously didn't agree. He'd already been booked and was then sent off for not giving the ball up for the penalty.

As Paterson was going off, the rest of the Celtic players were still venting their frustration at the hapless referee, and as they continued to argue, someone noticed left-back Jimmy Mallan trying desperately to rub the penalty spot away with the sole of his boot. I can only assume his way of thinking was, 'no spot, no kick.' Mallan was then sent packing for his troubles, leaving the Hoops with only nine men on the park. George Young stepped up to smash the penalty into the net to make the game safe at 2-0. As if that wasn't enough, a crazed Celtic fan then took to the field, bottle in hand, and tried to attack the referee with it. Bedlam, or simply a normal day in the life of an Old Firm fan?

At 2pm on Wednesday, 28th November, 1945, the world and its wife seemed to be heading for Ibrox. It was peacetime at last and Rangers readied themselves for the visit of all-conquering Russian crack team, Moscow Dynamo. The Muscovites had already taken care of Cardiff City (10-1) in demoralising style, as well as Arsenal (4-3), before drawing 3-3 at Chelsea. Even though the matches had been labelled 'friendlies', the Russians meant business all right. They wanted to win at all costs and when Rangers included recently acquired right-winger Jimmy Caskie from Everton in their team for the match, Dynamo protested so much that Bill Struth was forced to change his intended line-up for fear of them withdrawing. The Dynamo players and officials were taken on a boat trip down the Clyde past the famous shipyards, and when they enquired as to the reason for a number of slogans that were scrawled across half built ships on the docks, they were promptly told the slogans said, 'WHO'S AFRAID OF CASKIE?'

I was one of the 95,000 work-dodging souls at Ibrox that November afternoon and watched in awe as Moscow Dynamo played with a pace and power rarely seen in Scotland, to race into an early 2-0 lead. Uncharacteristically, Willie Waddell then missed a penalty before prolific centre-forward Jimmy Smith reduced the deficit to 2-1 right on half-time. Rangers powered into the second-half all guns blazing and, as the Russians wilted under the pressure, the Gers were awarded another spot kick. This time George Young took the penalty, making no mistake, to ensure the match ended in a draw.

It was a cracker of a game and when the Russians left for home enthusing about their trip to Scotland, the Rangers players, especially Torry Gillick, could perhaps be forgiven for not reciprocating their enthusiasm. At one point in the second-half Gillick asked the referee to stop the game and count how many Dynamo players were on the pitch. He counted twelve. The Russians had made a substitution five minutes beforehand, inadvertently forgetting to withdraw the exiting player. Aye right, cheating Russians! Whoever heard of such a thing? Own up, how many of you immediately thought of the 1966 World Cup Final?

My first recollection of playing an actual organised game of football was at around twelve, for a curiously named team by the name of LBH. A local worthy called Jock Black came up with the idea of starting a team made up entirely of residents from three neighbouring villages: Longcroft, Banknock and Haggs. Later, at fourteen, I went right into my works team – Wellstood Juveniles. By the time I was fifteen I was tall and gangly and able to play in a variety of positions – at the back, up front, and on the wing. I couldn't seem to find the right position, but I must've shown something because one of the local junior scouts saw me playing with Wellstood and offered me a trial with Camelon Juniors. Camelon is a little village on the outskirts of Falkirk, easy to get to by bus, so I agreed. From that point on things seemed to move at an alarming rate.

I walked right into the Camelon team and settled in well at centre-half. It's funny, but I always felt that it was the kind of position that would do for now, until I found my true calling. I really loved either wing-half position and covered for injury there a number of times throughout my career. I certainly was confident I had the necessary speed required to make the switch to half-back. However, it was never to become reality. I was to be stuck with the number five shirt, like it or lump it!

A few months after I'd signed for Camelon we were playing a cup final at Brockville Park, Falkirk FC's old stadium. As we were coming off at full-time, this man jumped a barrier and ran over to me just as I reached the tunnel. He was a scout from East Fife and he wanted to offer me a trial there. The Bayview outfit were a good side with a lot of good players at that time and to say I was well chuffed would be understating the mark. Just as I was getting ready to shake his hand, the scout hit me with another bombshell. He was forced to tell me that someone else was waiting for me in the dressing room. He had done his bit for East Fife, selling the club to me as well as he possibly could, but when he mentioned that Andy McCall, chief scout for the mighty Dundee FC, was in our dressing room waiting to see yours truly, there was no contest.

I remember feeling light headed, giddy. As I mentioned earlier, I had grown up a Rangers fan and had seen Dundee play a few times at Ibrox. I knew they were a top side who liked to play football. In fact, only the season before they had won the league.

As I spoke to Andy, I just kept thinking how my father would react to the news. He had been a huge influence on my game, encouraging me, pushing me on to greater things. I hoped he would be really proud of me. Then another big thought hit home. In those days people didn't travel much outside their local area. Hardly anyone had a car and a trip to the likes of Glasgow or Edinburgh was regarded by most as a major excursion. I had been used to hopping on the bus to Glasgow to go and see Rangers, but I knew absolutely nothing about Dundee as a city, let alone travel to it.

It might as well have been on the dark side of the moon!

2

The Dundee Years

It was 1948 and I was nearly eighteen. Representatives from Dundee FC visited the house armed with their proposals; I was to spend a week's trial in Dundee, staying there with a landlady.

I had never been away from home before. At least I would have my own bed, even my own room. The club would feed me, put me up, and pay my lost wages for the week. I was happy. My mother and father were happy.

The time came for me to go. I had the route sorted – bus to Stirling, train to Dundee, short walk to Dens Park. I felt good on the way to Stirling, brimming with confidence. By the time I was on the old bone rattler through Perth, my tummy was fluttering with nerves. At Dundee train station I began to feel physically sick. It became so bad that I had to run to the toilet at Dens Park. I often reflect on that morning and what the young girl in the office must have thought when she saw this apparition in a borrowed suit flash past her on the way to the toilet. Don't get me wrong, I had faith in my own ability. I was not normally prone to suffering nerves on such a scale and haven't since. Maybe it was the thought of that fine line between success and failure. What if a manager or coach gets out of bed on the wrong side? What if he misses the good bits, turns up for the howler of all howlers? What if the other players don't like me, give me a hard time? I had it fixed in my mind that I was somehow not going to get a fair crack of the whip. In the end I needn't have worried. A quick briefing with some fatherly encouragement and advice from team manager George 'Toffee' Anderson and coach Reggie Smith and I was taken through to the dressing room to get ready.

I must say the Dundee players were fantastic with me and the first trial match went like a dream. Every one of them, without exception, went out of his way to encourage me. And these were players who had seen and done it all; the same players who were to miss out on winning back-to-back league titles by a single point on the very last day of the season to the mighty Rangers. Why should they care a jot about the career of a kid from Stirlingshire? Gerry Follon, Alfie Boyd, Doug Cowie, George 'Pud' Hill, Andy Irvine, Johnny Pattillo, Bobby Ancell, Tommy Gallacher, Ronnie Turnbull, Reuben Bennett, Ernie Ewen, Tommy Gray, Alistair Gunn, Albert Juliussen. Sadly, most of these great players have passed away. I remain indebted to all of them.

Bobby Ancell was one of the older players at Dens at that time. He was coming to the end of his career and had seen and done it all. After he packed in playing, Bobby enjoyed a spell as manager of Motherwell before returning to Dens Park during the mid-sixties. Bobby took the time and possessed the patience to help a young lad starting out. He went above and beyond the call of duty in making sure I was all right and I will never forget him for it.

At the end of the week Mr Anderson called me into his office and told me he'd like to have a word. Trainer Reggie Smith was there and Mr Anderson sat me down, made me sweat a little before he delivered his verdict. I glanced to the side and caught Reggie with a smirk on his face. I knew there and then I was to become a Dundee player. It was an unbelievable feeling. In fact, had Mr Anderson had the papers in front of him, I would have signed there and then, in a heartbeat. No shrewd agents brokering multi-million pound deals in those days, I'm afraid!

Mr Anderson explained that the contracts were still to be drawn up and that somebody would come down the following weekend to take care of business. Before I left he pulled out a wad of notes that would have choked a horse and peeled off two, dropping one on the floor as he passed them to me. I bent down to pick the note up, immediately noticed it was a tenner and stood up to protest.

'Mr Anderson,' I said, 'you've been really great to me, putting me up for a week, paying my wages and giving me this fantastic chance. I can't take this. It's too much.'

Little did I know George Anderson was to set a new world record transfer fee not long afterwards when he brought Billy Steel from Derby County to Dundee for £23,500. And I was handing twenty quid back to him! He must've had a real chuckle to himself after I'd left.

'Just take it, Danny. You deserve it. You've done well. Tell the lad to take it, Reggie.' George Anderson said.

'Do as you're told, son. Stick it in your tail and I'll give you a lift down to the station,' Reggie Smith said in his distinctive Cockney accent.

Reggie was small in stature, but was, without doubt, the hardest man I've ever encountered. Heaven help you if you kicked him in training! One of Reggie's early pearls of wisdom was a rather simple piece of advice and called for the right circumstances and a brave centre-forward: 'If he puts his head down, Danny, don't disappoint him. Kick it!' Mind you, sometimes even Reggie Smith could get it very wrong.

I recall an early training session where he was giving some 'friendly' advice to a young apprentice goalkeeper who had just joined the club. After a particularly brutal training session played in quagmire conditions, Reggie grabbed first team goalie Bobby Henderson's jersey and held it up in front of him like first prize in a raffle. 'See this.' He swung the top towards the young goalkeeper. 'This is what you call a goalie's jersey.' The shirt was fairly clean with a neat, muddy ball mark emblazoned into the gut. Obviously, this called for fair degrees of skill and positioning techniques, attributes which were less evident in the younger man, judging by the state of *his* jersey. He looked as if he had spent the entire training session rolling around in the heavier areas of the pitch. The young fella stood there sheepishly, to be told: 'you'll never make a goalie, son!' Bill Brown, former Dundee, Spurs and Scotland goalkeeper, obviously had other ideas!

Although Reggie was outspoken and forthright, he was also very likeable. Reggie Smith was destined to be a big influence on my career.

My father stood proudly looking on as a deputation from Dundee turned up at Camelon Juniors next home game. I finally signed the contract at half-time to become part of the Dundee family. Over the next few months, I played centre-half ... for the B team, at the likes of Brechin, Montrose and Forfar. The first eleven included a world class half-back line of Gallacher, Cowie and Boyd and I knew I'd have to bide my time to get my chance among the big boys. I didn't mind. I knew my moment would come. In the meantime I was loving life in Dundee. My landlady, Mrs. Taylor, and her family were spot on. The city was powerful, vibrant and full of life and I had a lot of time for the Dundonians. They were ordinary, working-class folk who loved their football and they would do for me. Even now I make regular runs up to Tayside in the car and spend a few hours walking around the place. More often than not, I end up in the Hilltown area heading for Dens.

The letter I had been dreading hit the mat at my parents' house in Haggs, Stirlingshire. My father decided to hold off telling me until I arrived home from the B team's game on the Saturday. His Majesty's British Army had requested the pleasure of my company for the next eighteen months, on National Service. I was to spend the first three months training in Rhyl, North Wales, before being posted to somewhere exotic, or so I'd hoped. At that time recruits were allowed to apply for a particular posting of their choice and I had my heart set on a spell in the Middle East. I had heard a couple of the local lads rave about serving in Cairo, and if I had to do my stint at National Service, I wanted it to be there. Unfortunately, the fact that I was now a registered professional footballer had not gone unnoticed and I was told that my first choice of destination had been turned down. My dreams of visiting the Pyramids and taking snaps of the Sphinx were dashed in one telephone call. But why? How should my being a footballer make any difference? Apparently, professional sportsmen were kept close at hand in case they were needed to play in exhibition games against other regiments.

Great! I was to see out my time in Salisbury, Wiltshire. How exotic! And to make matters worse, during my time as Gunner Malloy they kindly decided to extend the length of the National Service programme by six months. Home was to be Wiltshire for another twenty-one months. Surely there were only so many times a guy could visit Stonehenge!

I remember a very funny incident on my last day's training at Rhyl, just before my posting south. In typical army fashion they held you responsible for everything, even down to the cutlery, plates and cups you would use. At the start of the three month training stint you were expected to pay £1 for a cup. This would be your cup and you had to love and cherish it. Heaven help anyone who dared to lose or break their cup! The plan was simple; if you returned the cup to the kitchen in pristine condition after your training was up, the army would refund your £1. Fair enough. Now a quid was a lot of money in those days, so there would be little chance of anybody forgetting to take up the army's offer of a refund. At the end of dinner on the last day a line formed at the entrance to the kitchen as everyone queued to collect their cash. There were about a hundred people in the canteen and I was standing in line about thirty back, when an almighty row broke out at the head of the queue. News began to filter along the line and it soon became clear exactly what the problem was. The kitchen staff knew nothing about the refund and when a snooty officer was asked about it, he just threw his head back and laughed.

We'd all been had! The officers scoffed at the suggestion. But I'm happy to report we got our own back as we left the canteen.

There was a tiny stone fireplace near the exit door and someone came up with the brilliant idea of making a Greek-style exit from the camp. Every cup on the premises, bar none, ended up crashing into the fireplace. It was hilarious! Deafening cheers went up with every smashed cup as the kitchen staff and the NCOs scurried about red-faced, trying to put a stop to the mayhem. It was great fun but luckily, top brass had a sense of humour, everyone escaping a charge for his indiscretion.

Despite my early concerns the Wiltshire countryside was lovely and things didn't turn out too badly in the army. The NCOs, especially the sergeant-majors, worked hard to try and keep everyone on their toes. They were the crabbiest, most bad-tempered men I had ever come across, before or since. Looking back years later, I suppose I could understand their behaviour. Most of them were in it for the long haul and the last thing these hard bitten individuals needed was to have their barracks bulging at the seams, full of snotty, unruly kids who'd spend most of their time wishing they were somewhere else. Anywhere else!

One particular sergeant-major fascinated me almost as much as he scared me. He was what you might term an 'unconscious comedian,' although I'm sure he never meant to be. He was also the type who hated absolutely everybody, especially those wet-behind-the-ears, public schoolboy captains and majors who, to a man, were devoid of any common sense. Many a time the guys in the barracks struggled to subdue sniggers when they caught a venomous look boring its way like a laser into the back of a young captain's head. The sergeant-major must have upturned everybody's bunk at one time or another, usually when the sum total of the victim's belongings were lying on top of it. The sadist would take great delight in scattering your stuff into the four corners.

And there was one thing that really seemed to infuriate the miserable sod more than anything else; he simply hated 'louts with long hair.' Anyone sporting more than an inch on top would be fair game and the sergeant-major would stand behind them barking, 'I can nearly stand on your f***ing hair! Get it f***ing cut!'

I was convinced the army barbers were sadists as well. I must admit, it was funny when you came across a new recruit desperate to hold on to at least a little of his mane. Bare-faced bribery never cut any ice with these guys and they would even go as far as sympathising with the newbie before flicking the number one gauge trimmer's switch and scything the poor bloke's hair right into his skull.

I had the privilege of making a couple of great friends along the way during National Service. Tommy Henderson was a Birmingham lad, and as my home was a million miles away in another country, he used to kindly invite me to stay at his parents' house during periods of leave. Tommy was a brilliant guy and his parents were smashing people who couldn't do enough for me. Years later when I played for Cardiff City, Tommy and his family would come and watch me when we faced the likes of Aston Villa, West Brom, Wolves or Birmingham. The club would always have some free tickets and, after the match, I'd invite them in to meet the team and have some tea. It was the least I could do. After I returned to Scotland, Tommy and I lost touch. I often wonder if he is still with us and how his life turned out.

Derek Green was another smashing lad who became a close friend. Derek hailed from Doncaster and, some years later, I eventually travelled there with Cardiff City. I wondered if Derek would come to the game and was thrilled when I got a shout from one of the lads that there was somebody to see me at the dressing room door. I bounded round the corner expecting to see Derek Green's wide smile. Instead, a rather sombre looking couple stood in the doorway. I hadn't met Derek's parents until then, but they were just as I had expected them to be. Kind faces, soft, polite, good people. The sadness which was evident in their expressions told me all I needed to know. Derek Green had died of cancer a couple of years earlier at the age of only twenty-three. I hugged his parents, told them how shocked and sorry I was. We said our goodbyes before I got ready to play.

I can't remember much about the game. I only know that we lost and I played badly.

*****

I came back from National Service during the latter part of 1950. I felt good, like I could hurdle the moon. As I walked up to the front door at Dens, I recalled the choice parting words from Dundee trainer Reggie Smith just before I was due to leave for training in Rhyl two years before: 'Now you remember and get yourself back here in good shape, or else!' he barked, shaking a fist. To be honest, I wasn't prone to putting on weight, at least not back then. Maybe I hadn't seen out my time in one of the most exotic locations in the world, but I'd readily concede that the choice of posting must've helped me to stay lean and fit. Had I landed in Hong Kong or the Middle East, I dare say I might have found it hard to resist enjoying a more 'relaxing' time. At least that was the somewhat heady impression of army life in such places I'd formed in my mind. Maybe I had watched too many Hollywood movies!

One thing was sure; I had particularly enjoyed the football side of the army and the many training sessions and endless games the pros were ordered to play suited me just fine. I was looking forward to playing even more games when I got back – a lot more games! Thanks to Messrs Gallacher, Cowie and Boyd, I swept right back into the team – the B team. The finest half-back line Dundee had ever seen! And everyone was still saying: 'bide your time, Danny. You'll get your chance.'

I had no choice but to be patient. I threw myself into the football, played hard, trained well. The coaches tried me in other positions away from the usual centre-half – on the wing; right and left-half; even centre-forward. In all truth I would have played anywhere. I just loved playing.

I scored a right few goals at centre-forward for the second string and really began to fancy the position until I stupidly got myself sent off for the one and only time in my career. It was at Montrose one rainy afternoon. I never liked the position after that and instead began to settle in well at half-back. I loved the freedom of that role, especially right-half, but I could play either side. It was fair to say I had my heart set on a half-back position in the big team. The only problem with that notion was that Tommy Gallacher and Alfie Boyd were doing quite nicely in both positions, thank you very much. And the centre-half spot was also occupied. Doug Cowie was one helluva player, a true Dundee legend, and still young. He was to play in the team for many years to come. And there was another small problem; all three of them were genuinely nice people and, although I'd heard stories of unscrupulous reserve team players firing into heavy tackles in training to try and put first team members out of the game, I could never have done that to anybody in a million years, let alone these guys.

The finest half-back line Dundee had ever seen; I just kept telling myself I'd get my chance.

Later, I learned from one of my team-mates that the great Alfie Boyd had confided in him. Apparently, Alfie told him he was certain that once Danny Malloy made his first team debut, he would never again be left out of the line-up. Little did I know, but Alfie had been contemplating early retirement for some time. He was still young enough to have played on for a few years more, but he had strong South African connections and had made up his mind to move there. I remember meeting Alfie for the last time in early 1953, in Glasgow's city-centre of all places. We spoke for a bit and he told me then of his decision to move to South Africa. Before we parted he wished me well in the first team. I replied jokingly that I'd have to hang on until big Doug Cowie died. Alfie smiled and advised me to 'wait and see.' I wondered what he meant.

I found out later that, like me, Doug Cowie hated the centre-half position with a passion and had put himself forward, following Alfie Boyd's departure, for the vacant left-half role. There was an opening at centre-half and, as I'd said before, I would've played anywhere. I just wanted to play. Gallacher, Cowie and Boyd would become Gallacher, Malloy and Cowie. Bliss!

It was 1953 and there had been talk of a high profile, pre-season tour of South Africa. Dundee's links with the country had been forged over decades. I never really found out the reason for these links, but as a result, many great South African players had come and gone over the years. I was privileged to play with a couple during my time at Dundee and, apart from their undoubted skills on the football field, the one thing that struck me about Gordon Frew and Ken Ziesing was how polite and well-mannered they were. I came to the conclusion that it must be a South African trait after I met golfers Ernie Els and Retief Goosen at a pro-am event in Scotland a few years ago. Quietly spoken, but good company; genuinely nice lads.

I had just been told that I would be in the team for the coming season and was preparing for the all expenses paid, dream trip to South Africa when I picked up an ankle injury. I had to stay at home for treatment while the rest of the lads enjoyed the experience. Great! Things didn't turn out too badly after all though when, during the close season, I met the love of my life. Bonnybridge lass Margaret Fisher was beautiful and flame-haired like Maureen O'Hara. I was in love!

The summer of 1953 was to introduce me to another great passion of mine, although I did not fully realise it until I stopped playing football. The British Open Golf Championship that year was to be held, as luck would have it, at Carnoustie, a few miles up the road from Dundee. My good pal, inside-forward Albert Henderson, was also on the injury list and was to miss the South African trip as well. Albert had recently bought himself a half set of old clubs. He'd been badly bitten by the golf bug and was itching to go to Carnoustie. Golf? Nowadays of course, almost anyone can have the chance to play, but at that time only the privileged few managed to swing a driver. Suffice to say, the Malloy family wasn't big on golf.

We did a little light training and some physiotherapy at Dens on the morning of the first round of The Open, before Albert managed to cadge us a lift to the course with a journalist friend. The guy was going there to report on the tournament and during the short journey all he could talk about was the prospect of seeing the great Ben Hogan play over here. 'Who?' I asked. I'd never heard of him. 'Danny's not a golfer,' Albert said, almost apologetically. The hack rolled his eyes before filling me in on the life story of the diminutive American.

In 1949 Hogan and his wife Valerie had survived a horrific accident, their car colliding with a truck. Hogan was left with terrible injuries and told that he may never walk again, let alone play golf. Eighteen months later he was playing in the US Open! Incredibly, he went on to win the tournament. Some reporter then had the audacity to suggest Hogan 'go play in the British Open,' to which he replied: 'nobody tells me where to play.'

When Ben Hogan did finally decide to play in our Open Championship it was only after he had bagged the first two majors of 1953 – the Masters and the US Open. At the press gathering following that US Open win the inevitable question of Hogan coming to play in our tournament was once again posed. 'You could even combine it with a holiday, Ben,' a voice suggested from the back of the room.

'I don't play golf on holiday.' Hogan replied tersely. I sat back, grinned. Maybe this would not be so bad after all!

We arrived at the course early afternoon and the first thing that struck me was the size of the galleries. This game must be more popular than I thought, I mused. Bobby Locke (the defending champion), Dai Rees, Eric Brown and Peter Alliss all passed by. Eventually, Ben Hogan strode into view. We stood directly behind him as he tipped his hat in response to some warm applause before lining up a drive. A couple of waggles of the club later and the ball speared like an arrow into the distance. Sweet as a nut! Hogan handed his caddy the driver, tipped his hat once again, and strode off.

Apart from the sense of effortless ease with which the shot was executed, the other thing that struck me was the look of sheer determination on the face of the little American. At that moment I just wanted to do the same. I was already hooked even before I'd swung a club for the first time. History records a famous win at Carnoustie for the legendary Ben Hogan with rounds of 73, 71, 70 and 68. It would be his one and only visit to these shores.

Not long afterwards, I played golf for the first time in my life. I'll say one thing. Football is a whole lot easier! Although I spent a little time on the golf course after that, it was not until I retired from football that I became really keen on the game. I was never going to be a Hogan or a Palmer, but getting down to a seven handicap felt like a big achievement. My son, Andrew, managed to get his handicap down to four until marriage, kids and work commitments put paid to any thoughts of a career in golf.

Who was the greatest golfer of all-time in my humble opinion? Ben Hogan was great, but Jack Nicklaus was peerless. I had the good fortune of meeting Jack a few years back in the lead up to an Open Championship at St Andrews. He'd been out practising and was signing autographs outside the famous clubhouse when we exchanged a few pleasantries. He didn't disappoint, making sure he signed every kid's book. A true gentleman.

Later that day, I was watching some of the players hitting their second shots to the final green, when I did a quick double take at the man standing next to me. Tappie Toorie hat, green sweater, checked slacks and spats style golf shoes, Sean Connery couldn't have looked less like 007 if he tried!

The lads laid it on thick after they got back from their South African trip with their tall stories and bronzed bodies. I was still sick to have missed out, but as luck would have it, from that point I was to go through my career almost entirely injury free. I think I missed only a handful of games with a dodgy ankle over the next nine years or so. I suppose the sobering training sessions at a deserted Dens Park must have set me up well for the challenge ahead as I hit the road running for the start of the 1953-54 season.

Season 1953-54
12th September, 1953: My Debut as a Professional Footballer

I'd hardly had a wink of sleep the night before and I remember feeling the tight knots in my stomach as I took the field in front of a big crowd of 23,000. Fife team Raith Rovers were the opponents that day at Dens Park and I was delighted as a centre-half to troop off at the end not having lost a goal in a 0-0 stalemate. Especially since the team had lost the two previous games against Partick Thistle and Falkirk by the same scoreline – 4-0. In a nice touch Raith's long serving full-back Willie McNaught took the time to congratulate me on a fine debut. It was much appreciated.

You could feel an electric atmosphere around Dens in the lead up to our next match. Aberdeen at Pittodrie was our local derby, and as difficult a match as we could possibly face. Dons' 'keeper Fred Martin was in unbelievable form that day and we were denied a win by a late equaliser after Bobby Flavell had given us the lead.

We went on a decent run after that with victories over Clyde, Hamilton and Queen of the South, 2-0, 3-2 and 4-1 respectively.

The next match at Tynecastle against Hearts would be my first real test as a centre-half when I came up against a young striker, who it was said, was destined for great things. Willie Bauld didn't score that day, but it was plain for everyone to see that he was a special player. Alfie Conn and Jimmy Wardhaugh also looked very useful indeed and it was easy to see why a lot of people were tipping the Jambos for the league title. The result? I caught an accidental elbow from Bauld, and as well as losing two teeth, we also lost the match, by 2-1.

Things didn't get any easier as we were scheduled to play the team I supported as a boy, defending champions Rangers in the next match. I had to pinch myself. I couldn't believe that I was walking out to play on the same pitch as the likes of Jerry Dawson, Ian McColl, George Young, Willie Waddell, Willie Thornton (who was to become my boss the following year at Dundee), and one of the best centre halves I had ever seen, the legendary Willie Woodburn. I don't know if it was because I was facing my heroes and I was desperate to impress, but I didn't put a foot wrong all afternoon. A bumper crowd of 34,000 packed into Dens Park to see us triumph by one goal to nil, Albert Henderson netting a beauty in the second-half. And I was thrilled when Willie Woodburn made a beeline for me at the end of the match to congratulate me on a fine performance. Willie was in his mid-thirties and coming towards the end of an illustrious career when, the following season, a reckless tackle by a Stirling Albion player during a cup tie provoked a retaliation which would result in the Gers' centre-half being hit with an unbelievable 'sine die' ban. Apparently, the SFA bigwigs took just four minutes to come to the decision when it convened the next month. It took a further three years for the 'beaks' to revoke the ridiculous decision, but by that time it was too late for Willie, at the ripe old age of thirty seven, to make a comeback. Later, Willie Woodburn was to become a top sportswriter with *The News of the World*.

The other half of the Old Firm lay in wait for me in the next game, also at Dens Park where 27,000 witnessed a 1-1 draw, big Doug Cowie scoring our goal with a great header. Like Rangers, Celtic were packed with an abundance of talent; players such as Jock Stein, Bobby Evans, Bertie Peacock, Neil Mochan, Charlie Tully and Willie Fernie. I got on really well with Willie Fernie and our paths were later to cross when Willie moved to Middlesborough to partner a certain Brian Clough in the 'Boro attack. More about him later.

Northern Irishman Charles Patrick Tully wouldn't score against us at Dens that day, but it was plain for all to see he was a special talent. One famous story attributed to Tully actually took place later that season. Celtic had drawn Falkirk at Brockville Park in a Scottish Cup tie and when Tully swung in a vicious corner kick which went straight into the net, the linesman flagged to disallow the goal. The official maintained the ball was outside the arc at the corner flag when Charlie took the kick. Legend has it Tully merely shook his head, replaced the ball – this time taking care to ensure it sat inside the arc – and whipped it straight in once again. This time it *was* a goal!

A couple of weeks before I broke into the first team, Dundee had travelled to Firhill Stadium in Glasgow for a League Cup tie against Partick Thistle. We'd lost heavily by 4-0 and hopes were high we could do a lot better there in our next league match. Thistle had a good side in those days and they were difficult to beat, especially at Firhill. Rangers' legend Davie Meiklejohn had spent six years as manager there, the team gaining a reputation for playing good football. With the likes of Davie McParland, Jimmy McGowan, John Harvey, George Smith, Jimmy Walker, John MacKenzie, Jimmy Davidson and the prolific Willie Sharpe on their books, Thistle were a formidable side. Most of these guys were long term servants of the club, some notching well over 500 appearances.

Jimmy Davidson was a fine centre-half, later to become a rival of mine for a place in the full Scotland team in the aftermath of the World Cup of 1954. I seemed to just hit the road running in my career at Dundee and by the end of 1954, I was firmly in the frame for full international honours. My solid performances had not gone unnoticed by the selectors and my efforts were finally rewarded when I was picked to play in an international warm up match against Falkirk at Brockville Park. The reward for a successful showing was to be a mouth-watering match against probably the number one international team in the world. Not long before, they had scored six goals in the demolition of Billy Wright's England side.

Hungary were coming to town with Hidekguti, Czibor, Kocsis, Bozsik and the incomparable Ferenc Puskas. What a side! There was just the small matter of the Falkirk match to be put to bed first. A poor crowd welcomed the teams onto the field at Brockville on a cold November night. I hardly felt the chill as I waited eagerly for the first whistle.

The Scotland select side lined up like this: Fred Martin (Aberdeen), in goal; Willie Cunningham (Preston) and Harry Haddock (Clyde), the full-backs; the half-back line was Tommy Docherty (Preston), Danny Malloy (Dundee) and John Cumming (Hearts); the forwards lined up as John Mackenzie (Partick Thistle), Bobby Johnstone (Hibs), Lawrie Reilly (Hibs), Jimmy Wardhaugh (Hearts) and Tommy Ring (Clyde).

Teenage fullback Alex Parker was in the Falkirk ranks and stood head and shoulders above every other Falkirk player that night. It was no surprise to me when the young Ayrshireman later secured a move to English giants Everton as well as cementing a regular starting slot in the national team. Parker aside, the other Falkirk lads were fairly ordinary and I was in dreamland when we raced into an impressive 4-1 lead. Ten minutes to go and we were still 4-1 to the good. I'd played well until that point, hardly broken sweat if truth be told.

Then, calamity! We proceeded to lose three goals – one a penalty – and the match ended 4-4. We seemed to just switch off. The game had been in the bag, no question. Hard to explain.

Although I remember trudging off at the end, deflated, I really felt that the goals Falkirk scored weren't down to me. A couple came about via the flanks and I didn't give away the penalty for the other goal. How would the selectors see it? Well, I did feel a little more confident about my position following the after match meeting; the general feeling was that the late aberration was due to some bad luck mixed with a little complacency.

The following week I looked forward to lining up in front of 120,000 frenzied Scotland supporters at Hampden against Hungary. The squad gathered together on the Tuesday morning at Largs on the Ayrshire coast. We enjoyed a light training session, discussed some tactics, and went for a stroll along the beach. We would be told the line-up the next morning, the day of the match.

The team lines were pinned up first thing and showed the same team as for the Falkirk match ... with one exception. You guessed it. Partick Thistle's Jimmy Davidson would play at number five and I would watch the match from the bench. Nightmare!

Scotland lost 4-2 to the talented Hungarians, but I would still have loved to have played.

In a nice touch the Hungarians presented every Scotland squad member with a gift as they were leaving Hampden that night. I was thrilled when the great Ferenc Puskas hugged me, slapped my back and carefully handed me a wrapped present. 'Be very gentle weeth thees,' he said in broken English. 'Can break,' he nodded.

I didn't open the present until I got home later that night, but the wait was well worth it. The very beautiful piece of Hungarian china depicting a boy sitting on a white swan takes pride of place in a glass cabinet in my daughter's lounge. Linda had always been fascinated by the ornament, even as a young child, and dropped one or two unsubtle hints about 'future inheritances' when setting up home with husband Derek.

The league match at Partick ended in a 1-0 reverse. We played well enough, but once again, some bad luck and poor finishing cost us dear. Thistle would go from strength to strength that season, eventually finishing a very creditable third in the table.

Ronnie Turnbull and George Christie picked up knocks at Firhill and both missed the next match away at Airdrie. South African Ken Ziesing and ex-Shettleston Juniors player George Carmichael came in for them and did well. We should have had the game wrapped up when we went in two nil to the good at half-time, goals from Billy Steel and Bert Henderson putting us on easy street. However, a late goal saw us surrendering a point in disappointing fashion.

It was nice to meet up with a good friend of mine once again at Airdrie. I had met inside-right Ian McMillan, later known as 'The Wee Prime Minister' after his move to Rangers, at Scotland get-togethers. We were about the same age and just seemed to hit it off. Ian was a very good player and a guy for whom I had a lot of time. His goal scoring record during his first spell at Airdrie was phenomenal, especially for an inside-forward, averaging almost a goal every two games over a ten year period.

Struggling Stirling Albion came to Dens the following week. We tore into them like a whirlwind with goals from Bert Henderson and Ron Turnbull putting us in control until a late strike from them had us sweating. We held on for a good win in the end.

Billy Steel had missed the game against Albion due to a niggling foot injury, but it was hoped that he would be fit for the big game against Hibs the following week. Everybody felt we would need all our best players for the challenge. After all, this was Hibs and they boasted the most potent forward line in the game; the famous five were in town with the mercurial Lawrie Reilly at the spearhead. What a player he was! Mind you Gordon Smith, Bobby Johnstone, Eddie Turnbull and Willie Ormond could all play a bit as well!

The upshot of it all was that Billy Steel didn't play, but we still managed to pull off a great 1-0 win, Doug Cowie heading a beauty.

Personally, I was delighted. I got stuck in – as usual – and felt I'd given a really good account of myself against Lawrie Reilly. In a nice postscript the great man took me aside at the end and congratulated me on a fine performance. Lawrie was a real gentleman and I was well chuffed to hear it straight from him. In fact I would say everyone played their part in keeping the Famous Five quiet that day. Only Willie Ormond on the left managed to threaten a couple of times during the match until big Gordon Frew eventually got to grips with him. Willie was very quick, but then Gordon was no slouch either. It was an excellent head to head. The fans went wild at the final whistle and everyone went home happy.

I am often asked about the Famous Five by people of that era, usually Hibs fans and lovers of fine football. What were they like? Was it the best forward line I ever played against? In reply to the first question:

Gordon Smith

I didn't really get to know this quiet lad, but there was no doubting his ability. He was sheer class; quick and skilful. A total of 359 goals in 544 games for the Easter Road outfit is a quite incredible statistic. Smith then made the unenviable switch to the other side of Edinburgh after being released by Hibs. I didn't know this, but apparently a recurring ankle injury threatened to end his career on many occasions. Gordon joined Dundee after I'd left and was fortunate enough to be able to play on when everyone thought he was finished. He holds the unique distinction of winning the league with three different clubs, all outside of the Old Firm. Now that's some going, and the way things have panned out in recent years in the SPL with Rangers and Celtic enjoying exclusive spells of glory, it's a record that will never be surpassed.

Bobby Johnstone

'Nicker' later became a good friend. The only one of the five to play in England, Bobby joined Manchester City about the same time as I moved to Cardiff City and we enjoyed some juicy battles over the years. Bobby was a cracking lad, always armed with a joke for any occasion. He was prone to putting on a little weight, and as a result, it used to slow him down a little. Pity, but he kind of made up for the lack of pace with his football brain; as sharp as a tack and ideal for an inside-forward. If Bobby had played today he would have been a superb attacking midfielder and I'm convinced could have walked into any team in the world.

Lawrie Reilly

The gentleman of the five. Hardly a word from him on the park, but as soon as the game was finished Lawrie was happy to shake hands, regardless of the result. Lightning quick, he wasn't tall as you'd expect one of Scotland's best ever centre-forwards to be, but he had a great spring and was a terrific header of the ball. I firmly believe that the best headers in the game are identified not by their height, but by their timing. They seem to be able to just hang in the air and wait for the ball to reach them. Okay, being 6' 7" in the mould of a Peter Crouch does help, of that there is no doubt. But I've witnessed great headers of the ball up close and on the telly who have stood nowhere near as tall as Crouch, but who were, and are, better in the air. Lawrie Reilly was one. Modern players like Swede, Henrik Larsson and Australian, Tim Cahill are also perfect examples. Was Lawrie Reilly the best centre-forward Scotland has ever produced? I think he was right up there. He had a better strike rate – a 61% goal to game ratio – for the national team than Dalglish, Law and Jordan. Enough said!

Eddie Turnbull

Eddie, like Willie Ormond, hailed from Falkirk. He was the strong man of the side, a kind of enforcer type. The rest were better known for their silky skills, although Eddie was also a fine footballer in his own right. He took on the job of looking after the others and would not be slow in putting the boot in where it hurts. And it usually did! I didn't mind that though as Eddie could dish it out, but he could also take it. I met Eddie purely by chance about fifteen years ago while he was walking along a quiet street on the outskirts of Edinburgh. I'd stopped to ask for directions and couldn't believe it when I saw the familiar face. We shook hands, had a wee blether about the old days before going our separate ways. Eddie Turnbull was one of the good guys and I was sorry to hear of his recent passing. And not a lot of people know that Eddie holds the unique distinction of being the first British player – in 1955 – to score in a European competition.

Willie Ormond

Although he was a local lad from Falkirk, Willie was a bit older than me and I never really got to know him that well. Playing-wise, he was quick with a great left foot. He also had the knack of being able to curl his boot around the ball and deliver deadly crosses into the box that were a nightmare to defend. Willie was the main reason for so many of Lawrie Reilly's goals.

Later, Willie Ormond enjoyed the most successful World Cup finals campaign of all the Scotland managers. We still didn't make the final stages (as usual!), but ended up as the only unbeaten side in the tournament. Sadly, some of the occasion's gloss was taken off by an ongoing spat between the press and the manager and squad.

Willie didn't take too kindly to some media reports during the lead up to the 1974 World Cup tournament. Stories of drinking and high jinks made their way to the front pages and it was inferred that he was a little too soft on the players. And it was no great secret that Willie Ormond liked a wee dram now and again. I heard a funny story that did the rounds some years after his Scotland exploits, when Willie was manager of Perth side, St Johnstone. In those days most of the managers were suit, shirt and tie men, leaving most of the coaching and training to the staff. In more recent times bosses were encouraged to get the kit on and train along with the players, taking a more hands-on approach to the job. Willie Ormond was very much a suit, shirt and tie boss in the same mould as George Anderson and Willie Thornton were at Dundee. Dens' coaches Reggie Smith and Reuben Bennett would take the full blown training sessions with the boss only popping out for brief spells before retreating into his office. As far as I could make out the manager's main roles, apart from transfer dealings and press interviews, were to pick the side and hold the pre- and post-match team talks. It wasn't uncommon for some bosses to harbour a little stash of alcohol – usually whisky – in a desk drawer, to keep out the cold on a winter's day. Or so they would tell people! The St Johnstone chairman at the time had noticed Willie sliding the drawer open a little too often for his liking and decided one day to tell him so.

'D'you no' think yer overdoin' it a bit there, Willie? Wi' the drink, I mean?' the chairman asked as Ormond plonked a glass and bottle down on the desk in front of him.

Willie frowned as he unscrewed the top of the bottle. He nodded towards the window outside which the team was being put through its paces. 'You'd take a drink an a' if you'd tae watch that lot every week,' he said, without even a hint of a smile.

*****

Into December 1953 and our next two matches were in front of our own fans, Bert Henderson scoring a goal in each in a 1-1 draw with East Fife and a 1-0 victory over Falkirk.

Boxing Day saw us make the journey to Kirkcaldy to take on Raith Rovers. Inside-forward Jimmy Toner scored twice in a 2-1 win which set us up perfectly for a derby day match against Aberdeen on New Year's Day. Jimmy Toner was a very good player, a late developer who'd joined the club from crack junior side, Fauldhouse

United. He was a popular lad among the other players and he and I were to become good friends. Jimmy moved to Leeds United in 1954 and although I moved to Cardiff City the following year, I didn't get the chance to play against him. There were no mobile phones or motorways in those days and players weren't paid nearly enough to be able to hop on and off planes willy-nilly, so our friendship kind of tailed off. I found out later Jimmy had moved back to the Dundee area after he'd finished playing, taking up a part-time coaching position with the club between 1966 and 1978. Sadly, I also later read that Jimmy had been badly injured and his wife Christine killed in a horrific coach crash in England, in early 2007. I felt really sick for Jimmy and couldn't begin to imagine the hell he must have gone through. It was nice to learn that he'd recovered and is still very much alive and well and living in Monifeith, just up the road from Dundee.

My son, Andrew, and I were recently invited to a supporters' morning get-together in the Andy Penman suite at Dens and I'd hoped to meet Jimmy Toner there. Unfortunately, he was unable to make it that day. Doug Cowie and George Merchant were also supposed to be on the bill, but for one reason or another, were unable to attend. Pity, it would've been nice to pore over old times with some old timers. Like Jimmy, Doug and George were genuinely nice guys and it would have been an honour to meet them once again.

Although the three ex-players I've mentioned couldn't attend the event, I did get the chance to meet another two from slightly different eras as well as organiser Dave Forbes and around forty dyed-in-the-wool supporters. Ex-goalkeeper Pat Liney, ex-striker Kenny Cameron and I spent an extremely enjoyable hour or so speaking about our experiences at the club and answering questions from an eager audience. We also took the chance to have a wee blether before and after the event and it was genuinely humbling to meet the people who make the whole thing possible – the people without whom the club could not exist. I even found out that day I was an early fifties fashion icon well before the likes of David Beckham and George Best strutted their stuff! Maybe I should explain. One of the supporters – a man in his sixties – confided in me that he started going to watch Dundee with his father around the same time as I broke into the team. Apparently, I was his favourite player and he used to annoy the hell out of his old man to take him to the barber's to 'get ma hair cut like Danny Malloy's!' Another man around the same age asked me if I remembered kicking a ball about in the afternoons with a bunch of kids after training.

'Aye, I do,' I said. 'In the park near the old bandstand. By the river.'

'That's right. Well I was one of those kids,' he said, a wide smile on his face.

Yet another supporter remembered an early game against Hibs when he reckoned I'd put the great Lawrie Reilly in my pocket as we went on to win 1-0. I don't know so much about that, but it did feel great to be appreciated.

Afterwards, Dave Forbes and Pat Liney took us on a tour of the main stand, taking in the various lounges, bars, offices and dressing rooms. I have to say the layout has certainly changed since the last time I saw it, way back in 1955. I was most impressed. All in all it was a great day, one I'll never forget, and I'd like to thank Dave Forbes for making it possible.

Mr Anderson treated us to a meal on the Hogmanay evening of 1953, before our annual derby battle against Aberdeen. No expense was spared and we were even given licence to have a couple of shandies at a city centre hotel before bedtime. Good man management? Well, that's part of it, but I'm sure the sly old fox's main aim was to ensure everyone stayed sober and fresh for the game. The coaches were warned to stay vigilant after Mr Anderson left for the night around nine o'clock. We'd heard through the grapevine his instructions were that there was to be no more drink from that point on and everybody had to be in bed asleep by eleven. Luckily for the plotters, Reggie Smith had a touch of flu and he was easily persuaded to head home for the night, to get some sleep for the day ahead. 'On ye go, Reg. I'll make sure the lads are in bed before eleven.'

I can still hear Andy Irvine's reassuring voice in my head, just before he reached into his bag to pull out a half bottle of whisky! The lookouts made sure Reggie was well on his way before the jungle drums rang out, and everyone gathered in Andy's room for a wee snifter before bed. I'd made a promise to myself to always do the best I could on the park and I didn't feel that I could do that with a drink in me, so I politely refused to indulge in the whisky drinking session. Some of the older guys had other ideas though, and, before we knew it, most of them were half cut, recounting stories from the old days. I bet you can't guess who turned out to be the life and soul of the party that night? None other than Billy Steel, that's who! It was the first time anybody had seen Steely with a drink and it seemed to bring out the best in him as he pored over his many experiences in the game. My sides were splitting at some of the stories and couldn't believe it when I glanced at my watch. What had happened to the time? It was two in the morning!

Now I don't know what happens these days in football, but in my day a wee nip before a match or at half-time was a common occurrence among players at football clubs up and down the country. Personally, I never felt the need, but I wouldn't have criticised anybody for doing it. As long as it's only the one. I remember reading about an incident a few years back between former Rangers manager Walter Smith and English international, Paul Gascoigne. Rangers were playing Hearts in a cup semi-final at Celtic Park when an on-field argument broke out between team-mates Gazza and Ally McCoist, just before half-time. The argument carried on into the dressing room and it culminated in Walter pinning the Geordie genius up against a wall.

'Have you been drinking?' Walter asked.

'No, boss. I haven't touched a drop, I swear.' Gazza replied.

'Well away and f****** get one then and get out there and win this match for us!' Smith insisted. Gazza then marched into the upstairs players' lounge at Celtic Park in full kit and ordered a double whisky. He necked it quickly before producing a scintillating second-half performance, scoring two great goals to put the Ibrox side into the final.

Our game against Aberdeen on New Year's Day 1954 could have gone two ways given the amount of drink and lack of sleep. And it was of extra significance to me due to an incident near the end. In an enthralling encounter in front of a bumper 30,000 crowd, we were leading 3-2 with about five minutes left. Our goals had come from Jimmy Toner (two) and Billy Steel when we were awarded a penalty which would extend the lead.

I think I speak for every player in our side in that we sighed with relief when Steely, who had just been fouled for the penalty, bent to pick up the ball. You could have cut the tension with a knife. The Dons were our bitterest rivals; we were leading by a goal with little time left; if we scored with the penalty, there would be no way back for them. Surely the wee man would stick it away, wouldn't he?

What exactly did Steely do then? Stroke the ball into the corner? Blast it high into the roof of the net? Well no, he strolled over to me as I stood at the edge of the penalty box, hands on hips, in anticipation of him bursting the net.

'There you go, big man,' he said, grinning. 'Stick it away for us.'

I felt my heart sink to the soles of my feet as I took the ball from Billy. I was in a daze! I remember thinking, why me? Then it struck me. Reggie Smith had asked me to stay behind after a couple of training sessions in the lead up to the game, to give keepers Henderson and Brown a little practice saving penalty kicks.

I'd played some reserve games at centre-forward, scored a few goals as well and I actually enjoyed my wee spell at the sharp end, even if it was only for a few matches. Having said that I shouldn't have thought Messrs Steel and Flavell would have any cause for concern that they might lose their places in the team to a converted defender! Anyway, I cracked in a fair few past Bobby and Billy that first session and as I clowned around, punching the air when a penalty hit the net, something caught my eye at the far end of the pitch. Billy Steel had found a wee dry area and was dribbling a ball around one of the corner flags. Well he did need the practice! Aye right! Steely was a bit of a loner, as I'm sure everyone who knew him would concede. Sometimes he just liked to get out the way, give himself a little space. Everyone else had gone inside to get showered and Steely had taken the chance to wind down on his own. The wee bugger was standing, foot on the ball, watching the shenanigans at the other end. He stood for another minute or two, taking everything in as we wrapped up the session. I don't know if Billy had said anything to the manager or trainers about my taking spot kicks. Not that it would make any difference to Billy, mind you. He would make the decision anyway!

The first thing I did when Steely handed me the ball was look at their goalkeeper. He was already prowling along his line like a tom cat ready to pounce on an unsuspecting bird. Fred Martin was a great keeper, and well established as Scotland's number one. I swallowed hard as I stooped to place the ball on the spot. A hush fell over the place. I'd already made up my mind as to where the ball was going. I was going to put my foot through it, keep my head down and strike it firmly. Bang! The ball exploded into the net behind Martin and the crowd erupted. What an incredible din! It was the most thrilling moment of my career to date. I was mobbed by the rest of the team and even got a pat on the back from Billy Steel. I was walking on air!

I went on to take the penalties at Dundee right up until I moved on. I can't recall missing from the spot for the Tayside club. My philosophy for taking spot kicks was simple – get it on target and make sure you bang it in. If the goalie saves it, fine. But at least make him save it. Alan Shearer, Wayne Rooney, Frank Lampard, Kris Boyd, Jorg Albertz; all excellent modern day strikers of the ball who would score nine penalties out of ten. From my era, Nat Lofthouse, Tommy Lawton, Tom Finney and Bobby Smith were all experts in their field.

It was 2nd January, the day after the Aberdeen match, and we travelled to Glasgow to face Clyde. Now I don't know if it was anything to do with the effort we put in against the Dons, or the fact that Jimmy Toner, who had scored doubles in his last two games, was missing after having picked up a little knock, but we stuttered to a poor 2-0 reverse.

We scraped a narrow 3-2 win at Dens against Hamilton on 9th January, before going on a nightmare run of three games, three defeats. Going down to Hearts and Rangers was perhaps understandable, but a heavy defeat away to Queen of the South? Not good. Don't know what happened that day, but we capitulated big-style, losing by 5-1. The one bright spot on the horizon for the club on that icy cold day in Dumfries was the scoring debut of big George Merchant. George, from Falkirk, had joined the club around the same time. His preferred position was centre-half and we had both been in the frame for the role after Alfie Boyd's retirement. Up front, Englishman Ronnie Turnbull had suffered a loss of form and Bobby Flavell had unfortunately sustained a long term injury, so we were light in that department. Somebody had the bright idea of trying big George in the centre-forward position beside Billy Steel and it paid off! George himself would agree that he wasn't the most gifted footballer in the world, but what he did have was a big heart, height and speed; and one other priceless asset – the knack of scoring goals. He would go on to notch a fantastic eleven goals in thirteen matches from then until the end of the season. George Merchant had another vital use during training. The coaches used to pair him off with players who were in need of, shall we say, a little speed training? It was hoped that the big man's pace would draw the best out of his partners in the sprints. I recall full-back Andy Irvine – a very funny man – speak about trying to catch George Merchant and his 'butterskelpers!' George was very tall and had feet that slapped the ground as he ran. Everybody fell about the place laughing when Andy shared his analogy.

We'd drawn lowly Albion Rovers in the Scottish Cup second round and travelled down to Coatbridge armed with plenty of confidence. Rovers gave us the fright of our lives that day, George Merchant earning us an undeserved draw and a replay at Dens. We got back on track in that replay as George went daft, cracking in all four goals in a 4-0 win.

The draw for the third round of the cup had us drawn away again, this time at Berwick. There was the little matter of a league match against Celtic to negotiate before we took on the wee Rangers. Big George scored again, this time at Celtic Park, but it was to no avail as we went down by five goals to one. Not good enough by half! Worse, we also crashed out the cup, 3-0 at Berwick. In our defence we suffered a horrendous injury crisis around the same time and it didn't help that many of the players were asked to play in unfamiliar positions.

Again, we somehow managed to steady the ship with a couple of good wins at home to Airdrie and away at Stirling before Hibs gained revenge for our win earlier in the season, beating us 2-0. A couple of Jekyll and Hyde performances against St Mirren – 2-0 at home and 0-3 away – sandwiched a nondescript 1-1 draw at Bayview against East Fife. I say nondescript, but a little pre-match dirty trick by the home side certainly spiced things up a bit. We'd been out doing our stretching routines when a raging Reggie Smith gathered us together before the usual kick about. He told us not to try shooting or heading before the kick-off. 'Just pass the ball about lads,' he advised. Why? Well Reggie had forgotten something back in the dressing room and on his way past the home team's changing area he caught a couple of the coaches soaking a number of footballs in a deep sink in the corner. Now anybody who remembers the old-style, bladder balls will never forget the sheer weight of them, especially on a wet day. I recall seeing stars on a number of occasions when heading balls dropping out of the sky. And if you managed to catch the lace it felt almost like a punch from a heavyweight boxer! I can only assume they were hoping one or two of us would pick up an injury kicking or heading the 'curling stones.' Not nice!

Our final league match of the season came at home on 17th April and was against one of the toughest teams in the league. In fact Partick Thistle had humbled us 4-0 in the League Cup at Firhill on 29th August, mere days before I broke into the first team. Thistle were either going to finish second or third in the table, depending on their result at Dens and the outcome of Hearts' game against St Mirren. Just before we took the field one of the coaching staff came into the dressing room and said they'd heard one or two of the Thistle players talking as they were coming into the stadium. They were giving it 'how they would do this and how they would do that' and 'how easy this would be,' as well as 'if St Mirren can do us a favour, we can finish second.' We had played things low key all week in any case. We were going to go out and enjoy it, whatever the result. We hadn't exactly set the heather on fire all season, but were still going to finish seventh or eighth. 'Nothing at stake so just go out and enjoy the game lads,' was the sum total of the pre-match team talk. Things had changed of course after the comments and we went out determined to spoil any party Thistle had planned. We absolutely tore them to ribbons, George Merchant and Bert Henderson grabbing a hat trick apiece as we destroyed the stunned Jags 6-0. In all honesty it could have been twice that score, such was our superiority. As well as Merchant and Henderson, Pud Hill, Billy Steel and Bert Walker were all immense as we gave the fans a real treat, showing everyone what we were really capable of when the circumstances were right.

The result was enough to secure seventh spot in the league, same as last term, but the win was soured a few days later by the announcement of the departure of arguably the greatest player to have played for the club. Now I don't know if it was Billy's decision to quit or whether Mr Anderson eventually got fed up with the wee man's antics. In either case, at the end of season 1953-54, Billy Steel was on his way.

Detailed below are a few of my memories of the great man and his time at Dundee.

Billy Steel

The fact that Dundee had one or two influential players who rated me must've helped my cause. They had always been known as a side who liked to get the ball down and move it around. The only recurring criticism they'd received was that they sometimes lacked a wee bit of devilment. They needed someone who could put their foot in where it hurts. I was to find out later that Billy Steel had campaigned for quite a while to get me into the team.

Steely was known as a 'moaner' and would constantly harp on about getting kicked up and down the place by opposition defenders while their attackers were given a relatively easy time by our defence. Billy and his strike partner, Bobby Flavell, were small men who used to endure a lot of punishment during a match. While Billy was known for uttering a swear word or two, Bobby never ever cursed. Following a brutal encounter with Motherwell, in particular their centre-half, Andy Paton, Bobby was heard to mutter the immortal line: 'Sufferin' jings! I need shin pads on the backs of my legs as well,' on the way off the park at full-time.

I remember a game at Dens where I'd gone in hard on several occasions, leaving 'lasting impressions,' shall we say, on the opposition forwards. Bobby, and especially Billy, played the game that day with big smiles on their faces. 'How'd you like yer eggs boiled now, eh mate?' Steely was heard to shout at an opposing attacker who'd faced the 'wrath of Malloy.' Mind you, if a defender happened to wander up the park with designs on taking a pot shot at goal, Steely wouldn't be slow in making his feelings known. 'Gie' the baw tae us. You get back! We're the forwards.' It was a favourite saying.

What can I say about Billy Steel that hasn't been said a thousand times? The man was an absolute genius on a football field! George Anderson had bought him from Derby County for a Scottish record fee at that time – £23,500 in 1950. I often wonder what he would have been worth in today's market. Torres, Henry, Rooney. Steely was every bit as good, if not better. A class act. Billy was a huge Rangers fan and I always wondered why they hadn't made an attempt to get him. Then I sat and analysed it one day. As I'd said Billy had been signed from English giants Derby County. After my move down south to Cardiff it wasn't long before we came up against Derby in the league and after the match I spoke to a former team mate of Billy's who was still there. Apparently, Billy caused a fair bit of bother at the club and it became common knowledge that the other players resented him, thought of him as a bit of a big time Charlie. Billy was both opinionated and forthright, of that there was no doubt, but he was also as fly as a jailer and it did not go unnoticed among the other players that he was moonlighting as a journalist, feeding his paper with inside stories of life at Derby. Billy didn't care a jot He was being well paid and of the opinion that, if the other players didn't like it, well stuff them! Eventually, much to everyone's delight – well, except maybe his adoring fans – Billy was shipped out before he was run out of town.

As I mentioned earlier, Billy rated me as a player and was instrumental in getting me in the team. Although he was too miserable to tell me himself. Overall, I did not have one problem with him and I saw every side during my time at Dens Park. Maybe he tolerated me because we came from working class areas within two miles of each other – Billy was a Dunipace lad from the famous 'Gangways' area. Or maybe he knew that I would not be slow in telling him to f*** off if he started his nonsense! Interestingly, the first memory I have of Billy was well before he became famous as a footballer. He used to go round the houses where I came from emptying the gas meters. He would be a popular man at that time as most of the meters were rated high, which would mean decent rebates left behind in the form of little piles of shillings sitting neatly on kitchen tables everywhere.

Most of the lads at Dundee seemed to be permanently in awe of Billy Steel and he didn't go out of his way to change that perception – aloof, petulant, rude, arrogant; add to that, argumentative, irritating, bossy. Every one of these could be used to describe the little genius. Steely was never happy until he had everyone at each other's throats and it wasn't an irregular occurrence to hear him cruelly slag off players from both sides. Wee George Christie in particular was one who regularly felt a stinging lash from the Steel tongue. George was a good player, a typical Scottish type winger, quick and tricky with a good shot. Every Dundee side, past and present, played the game in a certain style, and that style demanded an incredible work rate from both wingers. From the team I played in with Christie and wee George 'Pud' Hill, to the likes of Hughie Robertson, Charlie Cooke, Neil McCann, Georg Nemsadze and Nacho Novo. Every one of them was expected to run a million miles for the team.

I remember playing against Rangers at Dens Park in a Scottish Cup replay. Billy Steel was coming to the end of his time at Dundee and he knew that his chances of getting a move to Rangers were becoming slimmer by the day. Steely being Steely was desperate to get one over on the Ibrox side to show them how much of a mistake it had been to ignore him. We played a great game that day and I remember big Dougie Cowie congratulating me in particular for 'the best display I've ever seen from a centre-half.' I was particularly touched by the compliment as I considered big Dougie to be the best centre-half (along with Rangers' Willie Woodburn) I'd ever seen. A fantastic player. We pounded Rangers from start to finish that day, a mixture of bad luck, terrific goalkeeping and a glaring miss costing us dear. Steely played inside-left beside George Christie and, not long before time up, George was fed in by a terrific pass from Billy. George danced round the Gers goalkeeper, George Niven, and coolly rolled the ball towards goal before turning to celebrate. Unfortunately, it had been raining for most of the second-half and the penalty box at the Rangers end was pretty heavy, especially around the goal line. Big George Young, the Rangers centre-half, refused to give it up and collided with a post after sweeping the ball off the line in the nick of time. There was a stunned silence from the Dundee fans. It was nothing compared to the look on wee George's face. He looked as if he wanted the ground to swallow him up. Steely stood, hands on hips, glaring at Christie as if he wanted to commit murder by strangulation. If it hadn't been so tragic, it would have been hilarious. To compound matters Rangers went right up the other end. Winger Willie Waddell fired the ball across, at midriff height. I was at the far post waiting to deal with it when Tommy Gallacher flew past between players and threw himself at the ball. One spectacular diving header into the roof of the net later, and all was lost. Tommy, son of Celtic legend Patsy Gallacher and a fanatical Hoops fan, was strangely philosophical about it after the game. 'It's a good job we weren't playing Celtic and I'd just done that,' he maintained.

There was an intense rivalry between Dundee and Aberdeen in the forties and fifties. I suppose the pairing could be loosely termed a local derby due to Dundee United languishing somewhere in the lower reaches. The only time we would play United was in the Forfarshire Cup and the outcome was usually embarrassing – for them. Billy Steel, true to type, often used to get himself involved in games against Aberdeen. He would get so pumped up he'd almost explode with energy and drive. I often wonder how good he would have been in a Rangers jersey against Celtic. The bigger and pricklier the occasion, the more Billy loved it. At training before matches against Aberdeen, Steely would even tease the Aberdonians who played in our side, just to engineer an edge. One particular morning on the training field had Billy against the rest, as per usual. He was at the wind up, stating that, as far as he was concerned, there had *never* been any decent Aberdonian footballers. When somebody offered the name Doug Cowie in response, there was a poignant silence, followed by a conciliatory, 'aye, all right, I'll give you that. Who else, though?'

As well as George Christie, Johnny Pattillo was another Aberdeen lad who often fell foul of the Steel temper. One time during a match Johnny received a through ball from Steely and took a couple of touches before lashing an unstoppable shot into the roof of the net. Johnny ran back to the centre circle and winked at Billy on the way past. 'Christ almighty! You took yer time hitting that, did ye no?'' Billy shot the big man down with his cutting comment.

Billy was also extremely vociferous when offered pain killing injections to help him get through a game. 'Get yourself to f***,' he'd tell the trainer. 'I'd rather come off the park.' Steel maintained, perhaps rightly so, that as no pain could be felt, there was no way of knowing exactly what damage was being done. 'F***ing Russian Roulette!' was how he would often put it.

Billy's quarrels with boss 'Toffee' Anderson were legendary. I remember one particularly nasty exchange following a defeat. Steely, Bobby Flavell and I were the only ones in the dressing room, hurrying to get ready to catch a train down the road when Mr Anderson sauntered in.

'Nae wonder you get annoyed wi' them, Billy,' Anderson said, sitting down on the bench next to me.

'I don't know what you're on about!' Steely replied boldly. 'Just because you paid ten grand for a player, you think you have tae play them!'

He was referring to Ronnie Turnbull who had returned to the club for an unsuccessful second period. Englishman Ronnie was a good player and a top bloke, but it just didn't work out for him after his return. It happens sometimes. Billy, of course, had no mercy and wanted Ronnie out the team – pronto. The only problem, as usual, was the way he went about it.

Another time, not long after I'd broken into the first team, there was some unrest about the place regarding unpaid win bonuses and the like. The rumblings became so strong that there was even talk of a strike. Unsurprisingly, Billy Steel was one of the ringleaders and had plenty to say on the matter. There was to be a clear-the-air meeting among the players in the home dressing room following training the next day. Of course, Mr Anderson had got wind of the meeting and surprised everybody by turning up unannounced armed with little brown pay packets.

'It didnae need to come to this,' he said, playing the martyr. 'I thought you were ma boys. Very disappointing. Very disappointing.' He shook his head as he tossed the packets around the room. I couldn't believe it when one hurtled my way. I had only played a couple of games and didn't expect anything. I remembered the time before when Mr Anderson had given me cash at the end of my trial period and I decided to keep quiet. He'd made a big fuss about me deserving it and I knew that he could certainly afford it. I stuck the cash in my pocket.

The rest of them sat shamefaced until the boss left, doffing his hat on the way out. They were too embarrassed to open the packets until they got home but I disappeared into the toilet to tear into mine. I was delighted with the few quid I got, but as I found out the next day, the other guys only got about half of what they were expecting. The fly old bugger had conned them. His ploy had worked. And they couldn't go back. They'd lost the moment.

Not long after that the enigmatic Billy Steel was on his way to Los Angeles and a brief spell in US soccer before settling into a marketing career. Later, I heard he had died a young man. Very sad.

*****

In a nice postscript to my first season in the top team at Dundee I received some great press from *The Daily Express*, more specifically Rangers' winger, Willie Waddell. In an end of season article he listed me and John Cumming of Hearts as his two top players of the season. Willie went on to tip me as the natural successor for the Scotland centre-half position to Rangers' teammate, Willie Woodburn, who was close to retirement. It certainly put an extra spring in my step to be so highly rated by one of the legends of the game.

Season 1954-55

The football season in Scotland at that time always used to start with the League Cup. It was a four team, mini-league with the winners of each section progressing to the quarter-finals. Hearts, Falkirk and Celtic lay in wait for us in the sections with the first game scheduled to take place at Tynecastle. We lined up with three new signings in the side: Davie Gray at left-back, Bert Walker at outside-right and Joe Roy at inside-left. South Africans Gordon Frew and Ken Ziesing left to return home with all the very best wishes of the players going along with them. Both were true gentlemen. Andy Irvine covered for the injured Doug Cowie and Pud Hill switched to the left wing to replace George Christie who had suffered a slight ankle knock during pre-season training. Bobby Flavell had missed the last few games of the previous season, but he was re-installed at centre-forward for the Hearts game with my pal Bert Henderson moving to inside-right.

30,000 packed into Tynecastle to witness us start well and take the lead after only eight minutes through Pud Hill. We spurned a few chances and felt really hard done by when we reached half-time only one goal up. In the proverbial game of two halves, Hearts got a right grip of proceedings, eventually running out winners by 3-1.

The next three matches were at Dens and we managed to win them all, really hitting the goal trail with three in each against Celtic and Falkirk, and four in the return fixture against Hearts. George Merchant carried on from where he left off the previous season, notching five goals, while new lad Joe Roy hit three. The games against Celtic and Hearts both attracted 30,000 spectators with almost 20,000 roaring us to victory against Falkirk.

The following Wednesday evening we travelled to Celtic Park looking for another victory which would put us in a great position to qualify for the quarter-finals. Our goal difference was better than the other teams and we figured that if we could beat Celtic, we'd have no trouble taking care of Falkirk in our last match. I don't know if it was because Celtic had already blown their chances of qualifying, but they were strangely lacklustre that night and we really should have scored a hatful of goals. Our front men had left their shooting boots at home and when we were awarded a spot kick early in the second-half, there was only one name in the frame to take it – yours truly! Somebody remarked after the game that I looked like calmness personified, but really I was shaking like a leaf. Just as against Aberdeen I made up my mind before I ran up, kept my head down and rifled the ball into the corner. Easy! We held out for the win without too much trouble and looked forward to facing Falkirk the next Saturday for a place in the quarter-finals.

As you would have expected, Dundee didn't have too many

fans attending the Celtic game and when the goal went in I heard a couple of shouts coming from the direction of the main stand. I later found out that my father and my sister Annie were sitting in that stand. They had got so wrapped up in the match, and the fact that I had a chance to score, that they forgot where they were for a moment and leapt out of their seats to cheer my goal. 'If looks could kill!' My old man explained after the match.

We travelled to Falkirk bursting with confidence. And why not? We'd just beaten Hearts and Celtic, good teams packed with star players. In fact, they were to finish fourth and second, respectively, in the league table that season. We started like a whirlwind at Brockville and should have been four up within the first ten minutes, a combination of poor finishing and good goalkeeping preventing us from putting the game to bed in the first-half. As the game rolled on the pendulum began to swing Falkirk's way and a wee guy called James 'Javo' Davidson began to run riot. He'd just signed from Cattofield Juniors and he was so small I think he could just about have run through my legs without having to duck. We lost two quick goals at the start of the second-half, and as we laid siege to the Falkirk goal to retrieve the situation, Davidson struck another two within a minute, effectively killing the game. With Hearts winning their last sectional match against Celtic, they would progress into the quarter-finals. Disappointing.

As I mentioned earlier in the book, I liked playing at Brockville and it hurt to lose so heavily there. Luckily, the 4-0 defeat Dundee suffered there last season came the week before I broke into the team. One consolation was that the League Cup game I've just detailed would be the only time I was on a losing side at Brockville. Bob Shankly, brother of the great Bill, was Bairns' boss at the time of that match and he would move on to great success at Dundee some years later, winning the championship in the early sixties. At the same time as Shankly moved to Dundee, Dens coach Reggie Smith made the switch to Falkirk as manager for a couple of seasons. Reggie would write his name into club folklore by guiding them to a famous Scottish Cup win in 1957. I was down at Cardiff at the time of Falkirk's triumph, but kept in touch with what was happening at home. I was well chuffed for wee Reggie. It couldn't have happened to a nicer guy.

The mini-hangover at the tail end of the League Cup sections spilled into our league campaign and we lost away to Raith Rovers in the opening match before going down to bitter rivals, and eventual champions Aberdeen, by 2-0 at Dens in the next.

The team managed to rally round after that, coming away from Kilmarnock with a terrific 2-0 scoreline.

We continued our good form with a fine 3-2 win at home to Hearts, new signing Davie Dunsmuir grabbing the first of the goals. It was a terrific match with Hearts winger Jim Souness hitting two to put them in front early in the second-half. Once again we were awarded a penalty and, once again, I stepped up to stick it away for the equaliser. Who'd have thought it? Me, a penalty kick specialist! The game swung from end to end after that, both sides having chances to win it, before Albert Henderson popped up with the last kick of the match to send the big crowd into raptures. What a brilliant game!

The next few games were a bit of a mixed bag, a 2-0 reverse at Clyde, followed by a little revenge for the cup defeat at home to Falkirk by the same score.

We travelled to Ibrox next with more than a little trepidation. Our concerns were two-fold; Rangers had had a great start to the season and were sitting top of the pile; at the same time we could never be sure which Dundee team would turn up on the day. As it happened, the Mr Hyde team appeared and we were turned over 3-0. The game was notable for two reasons – a couple of big policemen bustled their way into our dressing room at full-time and were about to arrest Reggie Smith for an incident that happened just inside the tunnel on our way off the park. Reggie had reacted to some idiot leaning over the tunnel wall. The guy was spitting and shouting foul abuse at us and Reggie reacted by grabbing a soaking wet sponge and slapping it into his face. I was walking in behind Reggie and witnessed the whole thing. I don't think I would have handled the situation any differently had it been me. Except, I might just have seized the offender's arm and pulled him over the wall to straighten him out. Unbelievably, some do-gooder then made a complaint against Reggie and the cops were called in to investigate. I couldn't believe it and was one of about six players prepared to vent his feelings on the matter. Even Rangers manager Scot Symon called the complaint a load of nonsense and the matter was dropped before it became plain stupid.

On the football side, I experienced both the friendly and the not so friendly from a fine Rangers side on the day. Firstly, I was facing my own goal and guiding the ball back to goalie Bill Brown when Rangers' centre Billy Simpson came in a week late and raked his studs down the back of my leg. As I've said, I believe the term is 'posting your intentions'. I know it's hard to believe but I'd been known to post some intentions of my own and I could also be very patient in finding the right moment. That perfect riposte came about ten minutes later. Willie Waddell swung in a corner from the right. Instead of making contact with the ball, the back of my head somehow found the bridge of Billy Simpson's nose. It was unfortunate but that's how things go sometimes.

A seventeen-year-old right-winger called Alex Scott played a blinder for Rangers that day. It was the first time I'd come across the Falkirk born lad but it was clear he was going to be a very good player. In fact, he was already a very good player. Our left-back, Andy Irvine, half dead and glad to be in the dressing room after the game, agreed with my analysis. Alex Scott was a nice lad who would go on to enjoy a great career with Rangers, Everton and Falkirk, winning a total of sixteen Scottish caps. I got to know him pretty well after I finished with the game and often used to drop into his pub, The Hurlet, in the Hallglen area of Falkirk, for a pint. Years later my son met Alex Scott at a wedding in Falkirk, not long before Alex's tragic death at only sixty-three.

Alex described Danny Malloy as one of the best centre-halves in the game. In his view Danny played for all the wrong teams and, had he been at Rangers, he'd have walked into the international side. Danny was quick, peerless in the air, more than comfortable on the deck and his ball distribution was better even than Terry Butcher.

Don't know about any of that, but wherever you are, thanks Alex.

Queen of the South at home were next up and we got back on track with a good 3-1 win against a useful side. The games against East Fife and St Mirren were unremarkable in that both finished in defeat. However, they were also significant as they signalled Bobby Flavell's last goal and final game before his move back to Hearts. I have included my experiences in the company of the great man at the end of this section.

I was mostly getting good press for my performances up until that point, but I was still shocked and surprised to hear I'd been picked to take part in a Scotland select match against South Africa at Ibrox Stadium.

Some 80,000 spectators turned up for the midweek match and, though I wasn't one for suffering too much from nerves, I must admit to a few wobbles walking down the tunnel. Directly opposing me at centre-forward was one of the most ferocious looking characters I had ever seen. Word had it that Don Kitchenbrand was on Rangers' radar. The man dubbed 'The Rhino' at Ibrox after his eventual move looked as if he had been chiselled out of volcanic rock. And he played the way he looked, all flying elbows and wild swings. He'd also a reputation for charging goalies although he had his work cut out that day against another tough guy, Hibs and Scotland keeper Tommy Younger. Anyway, the game kicked off and I caught a couple of dull ones early on from Kitchenbrand, gave him a couple back and we were off and running.

Kitchenbrand wasn't the most gifted of players, but he certainly gave the fans their money's worth. The thing I liked about him was the way he could take the rough treatment as well as dish it out. And it wasn't only me who was dishing it out. Rangers' South African winger Johnny Hubbard prepared to take a corner kick when Tommy Younger gave me a shout to step out of the way when the ball swung in. As I said, Tommy was a real tough guy and he gave Kitchenbrand a clatter that would have halved most players in two. Don simply shook his head like a dazed fighter and sprang to his feet, eager for more. The Rhino would score twenty-four goals in twenty-five games in his first season at Ibrox.

Years later, after all the furore caused by Mo Johnston's decision to jump ship and ditch Celtic for Rangers to become their first Catholic signing, a story was leaked to the media concerning Kitchenbrand's transfer to Glasgow. Apparently, one of Rangers' representatives had met Kitchenbrand at Glasgow airport and was making small talk on the drive to Ibrox to complete the signing formality, when he somehow unearthed the fact that Don was born a Catholic. After almost crashing his car, the guy advised Kitchenbrand to keep that information firmly under his hat and his spell in Glasgow passed without detection.

The match against the South Africans finished in a 2-0 victory for Scotland and I hoped I'd done well enough to be considered for future international honours. Time would tell.

Hibs were our next opponents at Easter Road on 20th November. Although we went down 3-1, I felt that it was a sort of false scoreline as we had played well that day. I think we'd been right in the game until the last minute, Bobby Johnstone finally killing it off.

Stirling Albion were points adrift at the bottom of the league and we enjoyed a fairly comfortable victory at their place with George Merchant and Albert Henderson notching the goals. This had been my second visit to Annfield Stadium, the first coming right at the end of the previous season. We'd eventually overcome a spirited Albion side by 3-2 and I'd kind of taken a liking to the place. The stadium was small and compact but modern, neat and clean. The football team had been known as King's Park until July 1940 when their original ground, Forthbank, was badly damaged by the only German bomb to fall on Stirling.

Stirling Albion rose like a phoenix from the ashes after the war, moving to Annfield where they were to remain until the early 1990s when a benevolent council stepped in to build the team a brand new stadium almost on the site of the original.

Albion were cruelly dubbed the 'yo-yo' team of the forties and fifties, too good for the second tier, but not good enough to survive in the top flight for more than a season or two at a time.

The beginning of December saw us return to Dens Park for the next couple of games. Motherwell had been relegated for the first time in their history two seasons before, but had made an immediate return to the top flight. They were struggling at the wrong end of the table, however, and we fancied our chances of turning them over. And there was the small matter of revenge for a Scottish Cup Final hammering a couple of years before which still prickled among the rank and file at Dundee. We'd played them a couple of times in the league since the cup defeat, coming away with one solitary point for our efforts. Mind you, I wouldn't have traded those results against Motherwell for the one that rivals Dundee United suffered earlier in the League Cup in 1954. 12-1 would be the Lanarkshire club's biggest ever win over anybody, a record that remains to this day. Some of the older guys in the side had warned us about the sheer physical aspect of that Motherwell side and Bobby Flavell, especially, had come in for some really rough treatment from 'Well centre-half, Andy Paton, which I'll describe in a later section of the book. Paton was crude by any standards and, along with brick shithouse full-backs Kilmarnock and Shaw, the 'Well defence tended to take no prisoners during games. Don't get me wrong, they were good players – but they could put the boot in. Yes, I know! I'm a hypocrite of the highest order!

Willie Kilmarnock, in particular, was typical of most of the full-backs of that era: huge ... and brutal! I couldn't swear to it but I'm almost certain Dundee left-winger George Christie delayed a return from injury until after the Motherwell match. George had suffered at Willie Kilmarnock's hands – or boots – on a couple of occasions prior to the game and wasn't keen to repeat the experience! Pud Hill was in the firing line for the latest encounter. Pud didn't stand a chance and hobbled off at the end, missing the rest of the season through injury.

Motherwell left-half Willie Redpath was probably the most skilled footballer in their defence. A clever player, I had met Willie on Scotland squad get-togethers. He was a nice guy and we took our chance to enjoy a quick chat after the match. Even he admitted that he often cringed when he witnessed one of his teammates prepare to make a challenge.

In what was probably our best match thus far that season, we went on to hammer Motherwell 4-1 to exact some revenge for that Cup Final defeat. Big George Merchant was on fire that day, cracking in a fantastic hat trick. The other goal? That's right! Another perfectly executed penalty kick. Well, maybe not. I lost my footing on the heavy ground in my run up and scuffed the ball off the spot and into the net – off a post!

Partick Thistle had finished third the previous term and we expected a tough test at Firhill in our next match. And Thistle had been a sort of jinx side for us in recent times. Winger George Carmichael fired in two goals in quick succession to put us on easy street and when George Merchant added a third not long after, we realised that the monkey was coming off our back at long last. It was a bright purple patch for big Merchant as he would go on to score an incredible eight goals in just five matches.

We'd beaten Celtic twice in the League Cup competition at the start of the season, but there was to be no repeat of that scoreline at Parkhead on 18th December. It was a bad day at the office and we lost 4-1.

The thought of a scrumptious late evening dinner on Christmas Day must have spurred us on as we roared out of the traps at home against Raith Rovers. It was 4-1, the right way this time! A good day was had by all at Dens.

The New Year's Day derby fixture was at Pittodrie and this time we stayed over at an Aberdeen hotel with no access to drink, no late night stories or anecdotes. It was early to bed for everybody. The result? A 1-0 defeat, although, given the chances we created, it should have been an easy victory.

Two days later and we were lining up at home against Kilmarnock. We'd beaten them fairly comfortably at their place earlier in the season and were quietly confident of taking a few goals off them at our place. Killie hadn't been in the top flight for about seven years, finally winning promotion under the stewardship of former Celtic player, Malky McDonald. They'd hit the headlines three years before by unexpectedly beating Rangers in the League Cup semi-final when bottom of the B Division. We'd beaten them in the final that year, Bobby Flavell notching both goals in a 2-0 win.

Kilmarnock were to go on to enjoy the most successful spell in their history under McDonald and then Willie Waddell, winning a couple of cups and gaining top five finishes in the league. They gave us a real roasting that day. To be fair I think that the 5-2 result came about due to a mix of complacency by us and youthful exuberance on their part. Killie had a few young players on the field that day: – Bertie Black, Frank Beattie and Matt Watson stood out alongside old timers Bob Thyne and Jimmy Middlemass. And they had just signed a terrific goalie in Jimmy Brown from Hearts.

The Kilmarnock game signalled the end of the line for right-back, Gerry Follon. Gerry had been a terrific player for Dundee, signing way back in late 1945 as an inside-forward. The next season he'd found his true calling at right-back, only missing a mere handful of games over a period of eight years. In fact, Gerry was only just reaching the twilight of his career as I was breaking into the side. I'm so glad I did get the chance to play with the man I considered to be the consummate professional. The only part-time player at the club, Gerry was a highly intelligent and articulate man. A teacher at the local high school, he would concentrate fully on his calling when his playing days were over.

We played much better at Tynecastle in our next match, unluckily going down 2-1 to a late Jimmy Wardhaugh strike. The man had thunderbolts in both feet! I found out later that ex-Hibs and Newcastle United wing half Bob Fraser, now chief scout for the Magpies, had attended the match. Apparently, Newcastle were on the lookout for a centre-half and I was on their radar. Although I was flattered by the Geordies' attentions, I was enjoying my run in the Dundee first team and wasn't looking to move anywhere at that time. It all kind of fizzled out anyway and I was left to get on with the football. It suited me just fine.

A bumper crowd of 25,000 at Dens roared us on to a great victory over Rangers at the end of January 1955. The two Georges – Christie and Merchant – did the damage in a brilliant 2-1 win. The match was the first of three-in-a-row against the Ibrox outfit. The second instalment was a Scottish Cup fifth round tie in Glasgow and, according to the press, I had played an absolute blinder in a 0-0 draw, snuffing out the Rangers attack. The headline went something like this:

MALLOY TO BLAME FOR THE MOST BORING GAME SEEN AT IBROX FOR MANY A DAY

I can only apologise to anybody who attended that match.

Gers players John Prentice from Shotts and Ulsterman Billy Simpson were not exactly big buddies of mine for one reason or another. As the match wore on I think they were a little annoyed that their comments and dirty tricks weren't working as our defence hardly gave them a sniff. Exactly what was their problem with Danny Malloy? Well I suppose it was all about flawed assumptions and jumping to the wrong conclusions. I'll let you work that one out for yourselves!

I've covered the ill-fated replay at Dens in the Billy Steel section earlier in the book.

It was the middle of February and we went on a decent unbeaten run from then, finally succumbing to Partick Thistle at Firhill – only just – by 2-1.

On the 25th of March, 1955 my life changed forever when Margaret and I were married in her home town of Bonnybridge, Stirlingshire. I was delighted when my two Dundee pals, Bill Brown and Bert Henderson, turned up for the wedding. The celebrations afterwards couldn't have affected us too much as we all played against Motherwell the next day and won easily by two goals to nil.

Our defence had been chopped and changed through injury in the early part of the season and it was only towards the latter part that we were able to send out a settled line up. My first full season and the team had finished top half again, though only just! I must've been doing something right as I'd been the only player to play in every game. And I was on the Scotland selectors' radar for international honours. Better still, I'd heard strong rumours that Rangers were interested in signing me. I didn't want to leave Dundee. I was loving my time there. I'd become a fans' favourite and I got on well with everyone at the club, from the kitman and the ground staff to the players, the management and the office workers. Yes, I could do a lot worse ... but if Rangers were to come in for me? Now that would be hard to resist!

Here's the section I promised earlier on Dundee legend, Bobby Flavell:

Bobby Flavell

Bobby reminded me a little of that great actor, Charles Laughton. Now I don't mean that in a derogatory way. It's just that, well, some people don't look like footballers. Bobby was one of those; a character actor, maybe; a footballer? Not a chance! That said Bobby Flavell was one helluva footballer, and a bit of a celebrity at the time. I didn't know a whole lot about it, but began to piece together the story during journeys to and from Dundee. Bobby was one of the few people to own a car in those days and he was good enough to pick me up on his way to training. I didn't know why at the time, but training was all he was allowed to do.

Bobby hailed from Annethill in North Lanarkshire and began his career with his local club Airdrie, moving on to Hearts in the late 1940s. In early 1950, a group of British players upped and left to take part in a pirate league set up in Colombia, South America. Bankrolled by cattle barons, this league was unrecognised by FIFA. Bobby Flavell, Stoke City centre-half, Neil Franklin, and Manchester United's Charlie Mitten, all decided to head for South America.

Due to maximum wage restrictions in Britain money was undoubtedly the main draw for top European players, but a close second was the chance to play with some of the best players in the world. Flavell lined up alongside Alfredo Di Stefano for the Bogota-based Millionarios. The side became renowned for their artistry and were nicknamed the Ballet Azul (Blue Ballet). There, Bobby and Di Stefano began a friendship that was maintained throughout their careers and beyond. A few years ago, I read that Bobby met Di Stefano one last time, when Real Madrid arrived in Glasgow for the Champions League Final against Bayer Leverkusen. It was the match that featured a famous wonder strike from Zinedine Zidane.

Bobby would go on and on about Di Stefano this and Di Stefano that during our car journeys, but it would not be until the European Cup Final at Hampden Park in 1960 that I would see for myself just how good he was. Alfredo's Real Madrid team slammed Eintracht Frankfurt 7-3 in an unforgettable match with Ferenc Puskas and Di Stefano utterly sensational. What a game! And the Germans were no Joe Palookas either. Eintracht had humbled Rangers 12-4 on aggregate in the semi-final.

I remember Bobby telling me that he and his wife Pearl were treated like royalty in Colombia. A five grand signing on fee and another five per year were some of the amounts that were being bandied about. Now that may not seem like much nowadays, but to give you some idea of the deals that were on offer, back in 1950 £5,000 probably worked out at around fifteen years' wages for most folk.

Like all good things, they usually come to an end, and in 1950, after Millionairos had wrapped up the league title, the Colombian FA announced they were coming back under FIFA jurisdiction. This meant a return to the restrictive wage clause and the mercenaries were duly shipped back to their respective countries.

The players were banned for six months and fined £150. Hearts still held Bobby's registration, but surprisingly, wanted nothing more to do with him at that time, so he took up an offer to train with Dundee until his ban was lifted. At the end of the ban, Dundee stepped in to buy Bobby's registration from Hearts for £6,000 and he went straight into the team beside Billy Steel. The pair had already played together for Scotland and they went on to form one of the most potent partnerships in the league over the next few years.

I recall a good friend of mine, ex-Rangers and Airdrie great, Ian McMillan, speaking at Bobby Flavell's funeral in 2005. He said: 'My father used to take me to Airdrie's home games. One day he leaned in close to say, "if you want to be a footballer, watch that player." He was talking about Bobby Flavell.'

Bobby Flavell was a popular, well liked and respected figure at Dundee FC. I found him to be a really nice man who always took the time to be positive and encouraging towards the younger players. His skills on a football field were without question, but I am sure Bobby himself would be the first to hold up his hand and say that he could never have been described as an expert driver. Whilst I was glad of the lifts, many a time I feared for my life sitting beside Bobby.

Of course there were no motorways or even dual carriageways at that time, and there were a few accident blackspots on the road to Dundee, especially around Perth and beyond. I knew the danger signs. Bobby would be chatty and quite relaxed for the early part of the journey until he reached the other side of Stirling, around Dunblane. He would then fall silent and lean in close to the windscreen. He would grip the wheel really tightly, hunch over with his foot heavy on the accelerator pedal. By the time we reached Perth he would be driving too fast for the road conditions. We had one or two near misses at, or close to, a small bridge across a river just short of Perth.

One day in particular, a handful of men were working on the bridge. There were no fancy traffic light systems in those days just a man standing with two flags – red for stop and green for go. That was it! I can still see the look of panic in the man's eyes when Bobby's car hurtled towards him and his red flag, which was frantically flapping in front of us. Bobby had gone into some kind of a trance and it was only my last minute cry that had brought him round in the nick of time. Mind you, the workman and his red flag still had to leap into a ditch at the side of the road to avoid serious injury. The man's obscene gesticulations visible in Bobby's rear view mirror provoked the comment: 'Sufferin' jings! I wasnae that close to him!' Priceless.

Another time, in Dundee city centre, we had finished training and were heading for lunch at D W Brown's when Bobby somehow ended up stalling the car across tram lines. For those of you too young to remember the city tram drivers, you only have to picture today's bus drivers, only ten times more territorial. Anyway, this guy had an even shorter fuse than normal and it wasn't long before he was out of the tram, and heading in our direction with a face like fury. Unfortunately, in his haste, he hadn't applied the brake properly and the tram started to roll down the hill at his back. By the time he heard his passengers' cries and realised what was happening, he was unable to jump back in. The tram slipped past him and Bobby almost ended up on my knee as the hulk slowly nosed into his car, trapping it against a traffic island. I suppose you could say the car turned into a kind of metal banana. One of the local shop owners then called the police. It turned out the two coppers were big Dundee FC fans, instantly recognising us. After the obligatory taking of statements and signing of autographs, the policemen kindly asked us if we needed a lift. You should've seen their faces when Bobby jumped into his car and made to start her up. 'It's all right. We'll be fine,' he said, despite both wheels on the driver's side lying almost at right angles. Pale faced, one of the officers reached in Bobby's window, removed the keys and thrust them in his pocket.

After Billy Steel left the club for the US, Bobby wasn't long behind him, ironically heading back to Hearts, the club who had earlier discarded him. Obviously, his exploits at Dundee had put Bobby back on Hearts' radar, and he enjoyed a brief spell there before retiring. Later, Bobby became manager and then director at Albion Rovers.

Season 1955-56

Rumours were rife all close season about my going to all sorts of places; as well as Newcastle the season before, Rangers, Celtic, Blackpool and Wolves were all mentioned in dispatches. And, the Scottish newspapers were touting me as the natural replacement to George Young of Rangers in the international set up. I had a feeling my time at Dundee was coming to an end. More rumours circulated about financial troubles within the club. As Dundee had signed me for nothing, I was an asset to them; a saleable asset.

On the playing side, a slight knock made me sit out the very first match of the season, a League Cup tie away at Airdrie, and we went down 4-0. It was the first match I had missed since breaking into the team in September 1953. I recall wanting to give it a go but Reggie Smith, probably rightly, vetoed that idea. If I felt ok for the next match on Wednesday I'd be back in.

I missed very few games throughout my career, but any time I was out I absolutely hated it. I just wanted to play, whatever the situation. I'd received rave reviews from all and sundry for some of my performances at the club, but I still feared being left out of the team.

I came back into the side for the game against Kilmarnock, the first of eighteen in a row at the start of that season. My last game before my move to Cardiff City, was at home on 3rd December, 1955, as we beat Queen of the South 3-0.

I'd scored three penalties, one as we hit Raith Rovers for six at Dens. The other two came against Clyde in a 2-1 win and Celtic, as we lost by the same score.

I remember someone telling me about the fans venting their fury at manager Willie Thornton and the board during the match away at Hibs after my transfer south, I assume for taking Cardiff's £17,500. To make matters worse, the team lost six goals that day. All would be forgiven, however, the following game where they roared to a tremendous 5-1 win against St Mirren at Dens. I was delighted to see Dundee get right back on the rails. The club will always have a special place in my heart. The centre-half berth was in good hands after my departure, a succession of good and great players ably filling the role; guys such as Ralph McKenzie, Jimmy Gabriel and Billy Smith, culminating in a fantastic league championship win in season 1961-62 under the captaincy of Ian Ure. Alan Cousin was still a young player when I was at Dens. An Alloa lad, Alan and I used to take the train together up to Dundee. Even at such a young age he had tremendous potential, and I wasn't surprised to see him play a pivotal role in Dundee's league winning squad, before helping the team reach the dizzy heights of a European Cup semi-final the following year. A superb achievement! I rated Alan Cousin's partnership with the fantastic Alan Gilzean as right up there with the best in the business.

I'd like to finish the Dundee years with a heartfelt tribute to one of my favourite players of all-time. I missed Tommy Gallacher most of all when I left Dens, and still do.

Tommy Gallacher

Tommy Gallacher's was one of the first faces I saw when I walked through the gates at Dens Park.

'You up for a trial, son?' he asked, pausing at the door to the dressing room, bag over his shoulder.

Before I could answer he followed up with, 'what's your name?'

I told him.

'Right, Danny.' He shook my hand. 'Don't you worry about a thing. We'll look out for you. You just enjoy yourself and play your game.'

That gesture summed Tommy up perfectly. He was a gentleman to everyone and I feel privileged to have considered him a great friend.

Tommy came from Clydebank, near Glasgow, and was the son of the legendary Celtic forward, Patsy Gallacher. Later, nephew Kevin would also become a top player with Dundee United, Blackburn and Scotland. After I eventually broke into the first team at Dens, my old man Andy would travel to every game I played for Dundee. Before the home games he would drop into Tommy's pub at the bottom of the Hilltown area for a quick couple of drams before walking up to Dens. Tommy would call in to the pub on his way up to the ground to check everything was ok and spend ten minutes or so chewing the fat with my dad.

As it turned out, Tommy's dad Patsy was my father's all-time favourite player and he would recount stories of the winger's legendary exploits at the drop of a hat. I well remember the newspaper clippings pasted into a scrapbook in the house. Tommy was well chuffed. I always wondered if the old man laid it on a bit thick with Tommy in an effort to cadge a couple of free drinks!

Tommy was also a kind hearted guy who would do anything for anybody and he had a thing about helping old pro boxers who had hit the skids. One particular Glasgow fighter – a huge guy, a heavyweight – was a friend of Tommy's family. He had taken a little too much punishment over the years and it had left him a bit punchy and slow. Rather than see the guy slogging his guts out in a gym for peanuts and tips, Tommy took him up to Dundee to work in the pub, changing barrels, pulling pints and the like. Of course, this man mountain felt so indebted to Tommy that he would have done anything for him.

Tommy chuckled when he told the guys at training about an incident in the pub the previous night. He had been getting a bit of a ribbing from one of his regulars – an Aberdeen fan – about the result of a Dundee v Aberdeen game the previous Saturday. Tommy being Tommy was giving as good as he was getting and the Aberdonian had to intensify his efforts to try and keep the wind up going. Apparently, the big ex-fighter stood behind the bar next to Tommy, face like thunder. 'D'ye want me to chin him the now, boss?'

Like all good players Tommy Gallacher also had a tough side and I remember an altercation between him and Billy Steel near the end of a match at Dens. Steely had been on his high horse that day and everyone was getting the sharp end of his tongue. George Christie had been getting dog's abuse from the wee man about this and that and when Tommy stepped in to stick up for George, Steely told him to mind his own business. Well, maybe not in quite so polite a manner! I don't know if Billy saw a look on Tommy's face that he didn't fancy, but he turned on his heels to get back into position just as the whistle went for full-time. Luckily for Billy, he was only yards from the ramp to the dressing rooms and he hardly broke stride as he trotted to safety. Or so he thought. Little did Steely know, but Tommy was right behind him on that ramp. I'd seen the fury in Tommy's face as he passed me on the park and I knew what was in his mind. I managed to get a hold of him just as he reached the dressing room door. Tommy ranted like a man possessed as the rest of the players poured into the mayhem, forming a barrier between the pair. The look on Billy's face was a picture as Tommy began to launch stuff around the place. I think Billy realised that he'd overstepped the mark and stammered an apology before Tommy wrecked the dressing room. Eventually, Tommy started to calm down and the pair actually shook hands before leaving the ground. Disaster averted! It certainly made me look at Tommy Gallacher in a different light. I'd thought he was an easy going kind of guy, but then, what did I know?

As I mentioned earlier, Tommy Gallacher would have walked to the other side of the world to follow in his illustrious father's footsteps and play for Celtic. And, if he had, I'm certain he would have been massive for them. He was that good! Maybe the fact that the Hoops already had a world class wing-half in the shape of Bobby Evans prevented them from approaching Dundee for Tommy's signature. I played beside both men in a half-back line (Bobby and I played together for the Scottish League v the English League), and honestly couldn't split them, ability-wise.

People have asked me many times if players of provincial teams raise their game when they come up against either half of the Old Firm. Of course, I can only speak for myself, but I can honestly say it did not matter a hoot who the opposition was – I wanted to win. The only time I can recall going a little easier was during Jimmy Toner's testimonial match against Dundee United in April 1954. At that time we would only ever face United either in friendlies or competitions like the Forfarshire Cup as, more often than not, they'd be languishing in the lower reaches of the bottom division.

The Tannadice outfit were often cruelly described by Dundee fans in the forties and fifties as the 'Ragged Arse Rovers' of Tayside. In fact, their main stand could best be described as a 'hen hut' and when we played them away we preferred to change at our own place and walk across the road. Anyway, at something like 9-1 in front in the derby match, the Dundee team, collectively, took things a bit easier, and played out the final few minutes of the game.

I recall the United centre-forward at that time. He was a useful player called Peter McKay, a Fifer, I believe. I think McKay took the hammering to heart more than his team-mates as he refused to speak to or even shake the hands of any of our players at the final whistle and walked straight off the park. Mind you, I might have been a little annoyed myself had I been on the receiving end of our relentless onslaught that night, both physically and verbally. There was nothing sweeter than stuffing it right up your closest rivals. And, it had been our easiest game for years! I felt at the time Mackay was too good for that United side, but wouldn't dream of telling him so. I was not surprised to hear he had later moved down south. Not only that, Burnley FC were one of the top teams in England at that time. Our paths were again to cross ...

Sorry to digress! Now where were we? Ah yes, do I think players of provincial teams try harder against the Old Firm? Maybe. Probably. In Tommy Gallacher's case I've already said he was a huge Celtic fan. You'd think then that he'd have fire in his belly when he turned out against Rangers? Yes, that was true. I remember one particular altercation at Ibrox between Tommy and the Rangers manager at that time, Scot Symon. We were winning and the game was going into the final few minutes. Tommy was on the touchline near the dugouts waiting to take a throw in. He was blatantly wasting time and Symon's frustration was boiling over by the second. Symon leapt out of the dugout and, partly restrained by their trainer, began shouting a few unmentionables at Tommy. Now Tommy was a particularly dark skinned, swarthy looking character and when Symon bellowed the immortal line, 'throw the baw in ya Tally bastard!' we all fell about the place, even the Rangers players who happened to be within earshot. Funnier still, Tommy glanced over his shoulder, grinning, and replied just as the referee blew for full-time. 'Aye, an' a very happy Tally bastard at that!'

I recall meeting Tommy Gallacher years later at a Dundee v Hearts match in the late seventies or early eighties. He was a sports reporter for *The Courier*, and I met him after travelling up for the match with an old friend of mine, Duncan Sinclair. Duncan was the father of former Dens centre-forward, Eric. Tommy and I had a ball going over the old times. So much so that I can't even remember anything about the game. The following week, courtesy of Tommy Gallacher, I received a copy of the latest edition of *The Courier* through the post. Emblazoned on the back page was a full size spread on how a Dundee legend had returned to the scene of his past triumphs. That was Tommy Gallacher for you!

To clear up the issue of whether I think players try as hard against their favourites, I believe that if you support either Rangers or Celtic you'll try just as hard against your team to show them exactly what they're missing – that they should be signing you without delay.

Personally, on the subject of playing for Rangers, it was to be three times unlucky for me during my career. According to reports I'd heard, Scot Symon fancied me as a player and was keen to sign me on a number of occasions, once at Dundee and another couple of times while I was down at Cardiff City. I was told by a reliable source on Tayside that, just as Mr Symon was readying a bid to take me to Ibrox, I was off in a rush deal to Cardiff before the bid could go through. As I've said the Dens Park club had money worries at the time and decided to snap up the £17,500 Cardiff laid on the table. The story went that Cardiff originally wanted Doug Cowie. Big Doug didn't fancy moving down there and next thing I knew my name was firmly in the frame. I later found out that Doug tried to get in touch with me before I left to tell me how much the Welsh club were offering him. Maybe I could've held out for more money? Who knows?

Back in Dundee, although the supporters weren't happy at the sale, the word was that the club had no choice. I'd been an ever present since getting my chance but money talked and the decision had been made. Later, I met goalkeeper Bill Brown when I returned to pick up some gear at Dens. Bill, Bert Henderson and I were all around the same age and used to knock about together away from the football at Dundee. Bill shook my hand and thanked me for going to Cardiff. I stood bemused as he explained; evidently, some of the £17,500 fee was earmarked for Bill's benefit payment. The club had been so cash strapped that there was some doubt as to whether or not the benefit would be paid.

I didn't really want to leave Dundee but Cardiff were prepared to give me more money, a five hundred quid signing on fee, and I'd have a shot at the top division in England. Also, I'd just got married the previous March, and Margaret and I decided the extra money would come in handy just at the right time. And, just for good measure, the Welsh club threw in a spacious club house in

Llanishen, among the leafy suburbs of Cardiff. I was sold and ready for the next chapter.

On the subject of transfer talk I also recall an unsolicited approach from a member of the coaching staff at one of England's top teams. It was early on in my time at Dundee and I was having a lie-in after a particularly tiring midweek match. The landlady knocked on my door just after nine am, told me somebody was downstairs in the living room and urgently wanted to talk to me. I dragged myself downstairs and, within about two minutes, I had been told by the coach I was top of Stan Cullis's shopping list at Wolves. He was in the market for a no-nonsense centre-half and, as he had heard good things about me at Dundee during the previous months, he had had me watched on a number of occasions leading up to the visit.

Usually, players and clubs would sooner or later get to know all about such things, but Wolves must have had some special covert operation procedures in place as nobody had an earthly. Initially, I was well chuffed that such a top side would want me in their team and was prepared to take it a step further, until one important thought flashed into my brain. Who was the present incumbent at centre-half in the Wolves team? None other than England's most capped player and team captain, Billy Wright, that's who. I immediately thought 'why would they need me?' I had already served my time at Dundee and wasn't about to head south to sit in another queue. As I've said, I just wanted to play so I politely declined Wolves' offer.

Sometime later I had the chance to speak to Billy Wright following a Wolves game against Cardiff and he nearly floored me by telling me that he was fully aware of his club's move for me. He was another who hated the centre-half spot with a passion and was prepared to play alongside me in the right-half position. I often wonder what would have happened to Billy's England career, as I'm sure he won all, or at least the vast majority of his caps, playing pivot.

The Social Life at Dundee

Social entertainment played an important part of the ethos at Dundee and the club used to actively encourage the players to attend selected functions and events which took place from time to time in the city – as long as excess booze wasn't your big draw. The club had 'spies' all over the place, and any over-indulgences were quickly identified and snuffed out. Green's Playhouse in The Nethergate, (now the Mecca Bingo building), was a popular haunt among the players even though the manager, Mr Taylor, also provided digs for some of the younger players, including myself. For me the Caird Hall was a magnificent auditorium. Located in the city centre, it was Dundee's main place to be seen, and I spent many a night there enjoying everything from big bands to comedians, from international wrestling and boxing, to some good, old-fashioned variety shows. Ted Heath and Joe Loss were two prominent band leaders who used to love bringing their orchestras there, and I particularly enjoyed the memorable performances of some of the singers of the time. Lita Roza, Dennis Lotis and Dickie Valentine were all absolutely terrific. A young man called Ross McManus played trumpet for Joe Loss back then and I recall him stepping in front of the mike to perform some vocals to cover a singer who'd called in sick. His performance that night was sensational, and it wasn't until many years later I learned that his son, Declan, had become an international star. The lad's stage name was Elvis Costello.

I also loved the variety shows at The Caird, especially the comedians. Lancashire comic Frank Randle was a particular favourite of mine, my sides absolutely aching after one of his appearances. Of course, our own comedians were also excellent and I remember going to see Lex McLean and his pal, Walter Carr. Very funny. Mind you, you'd have to grow a thick skin if you dared to go to one of Lex's shows. He'd a reputation for finding out who was in the house each night, and he'd be especially adept at taking the mickey. After only a few matches, I had gained the name of being physically strong and uncompromising during games. At least that was my description. Lex would come up with a slightly different slant on it, the names dirty and b****** often used in conjunction.

Glasgow's Pavilion Theatre was another famous old variety hall and I recall going there with the rest of the Dundee lads the night before an Old Firm match to see legendary Bridgeton comedian, Tommy Morgan. Tommy was one of those people who just had to walk out on to the stage to get huge belly laughs. Very few could achieve this. In fact, the great Tommy Cooper is the only other comic who springs to mind.

Tommy Morgan was one of the funniest men I'd ever seen – flat cap, spindly walking stick, baggy trousers, tartan jacket and striped tie. His big baw face could've brought a smile to the stoniest of expressions and, by the end of his act, the place was in absolute chaos, people falling about in hysterics. Tommy rattled off joke after joke in the style of many of the old music hall comics of the time. After all, it was the age of variety, and each act only had a comparatively short time in which to make its mark. A typical Tommy Morgan joke would go something like this: 'It's the Clydebank blitz and a man and his wife are making their way to the air raid shelter. The wife shouts, "ah hiv tae go back tae the hoose, ah forgoat ma teeth!" "Fur goad's sake wummin," the man replied, "it's bombs they're drappin,' NO sandwiches!"'

The great Glasgow comic, Chic Murray, was another extremely funny man who was to go on and make a name for himself on the international circuit. Players were often invited backstage to meet the stars – usually when they were trying to mooch a couple of tickets for a game – and I got to know Chic quite well off stage. Chic and his wife, Maidie Dickson, were smashing people and used to regularly steal the show as a superb double act, known affectionately as 'The Tall Droll with The Small Doll'. They were 6' 3" and 4' 11" respectively.

It was Chic's absurd and surreal take on life which produced hundreds of classic one-liners that were to make him famous. Here are some of my favourites:

'My mother was so house-proud that when my father got up to sleepwalk, she had the bed made by the time he got back.'

'I met this cowboy with a brown paper hat, paper waistcoat and paper trousers. He was wanted for rustling.'

'I had a tragic childhood. My parents never understood me. They were Japanese.'

'You know what they say about stamp collecting. Philately will get you nowhere.'

'My wife went to a beauty parlour and got a mud pack. For two days she looked nice, then the mud fell off. She's a classy girl, though. At least all her tattoos are spelt right.'

'We were so poor, the ultimate luxury in our house at the time was ashtrays without advertisements. It was all the wolf could do to keep us away from his door. A luxury meal was prairie sandwiches – two slices of bread with wide-open spaces between them. There were so many holes in my socks I could put them on seventeen different ways.'

Scene: Chic and Maidie at Edinburgh airport, next in line to check in, festooned with luggage – en route to, let's say, Lanzarote.

Maidie: 'You're very quiet, Chic. Everything all right?'

Chic: 'Och, I'm just wishing we had our piano here ...'

Maidie: 'The piano? Why on earth would we want the piano at an airport?'

Chic: 'Because our flight tickets – and the passports – are on it!'

*****

Boxing and wrestling were big attractions at that time in Dundee and local wrestling champion George Kidd was in regular action at the Caird Hall. This was the real McCoy, nothing like that puerile, staged WWF rubbish we get on our TV screens nowadays. Guys like George Kidd were true exponents of the sport, quick, agile and strong, and the shows were so good they had to be seen to be believed. Though George was never a lover of tag matches, the public loved them and he would be forced to take part. Tag partners at that time would include Andy Robin of Hercules the Bear fame and Jimmy Savile (yes, the infamous future DJ). George Kidd retired as undefeated and undisputed World Lightweight Champion – a true legend.

Boxer Bobby Boland was another Dundee lad, a tiny bantamweight who would save his best performances for the Caird Hall. Sixteen appearances, sixteen wins there, eight by way of knockout in a record that included forty-eight wins in total. If you went to see a Boland fight at the Caird, one thing you would be guaranteed would be one helluva show. Bobby used to come in regularly to Dens for training, and we actually became quite friendly. In fact, Bobby once gave me a master class on how to lead with your head to deliberately foul an opponent. Needless to say I'd have nothing to do with that kind of nonsense!

The Kingsway rink just down the road from Dens was the home of ice hockey team, Dundee Tigers. Ice hockey was very popular with the Dundee public and the Tigers were a top team during the forties and fifties. It was widely accepted that Canada produced the top hockey players in the world and, even to this day, they make up the spine of almost every team in the UK.

The Dundee footballers used to love watching the hockey and I was no exception. I loved the rush of the game, the end to end flow. And the fights were something else. That's right, we thought *we* were tough guys. No chance! Some of the scraps used to go on for ages, the players knocking seven bells out of each other. The referee would stand back until the battle blew itself out, then simply send the offenders to the sin bin for a few minutes to cool off. There were no red cards in those days for these hockey players. To be honest football was much the same. You'd have to really do something pretty bad to get sent off when I played. Nowadays, it seems that if you sneeze the wrong way, you're liable to take an early bath.

Whilst I cannot condone the way some of today's players go out to deliberately hurt opponents by throwing elbows, going over the ball or leaving their boots in, I think that some of the red or yellow card 'offences,' such as last man foul, or over-zealous goal celebrations, are just plain ridiculous. I recall an incident during a game in the mid-nineties between Rangers and Hibs at Ibrox. Paul Gascoigne had been a huge hit in the Rangers midfield since signing from Lazio and he was absolutely immense that day as Hibs were swept aside by 7-0. However, one incident midway through the first-half took a bit of the polish off the result. The referee's yellow card dropped out of his pocket in the Hibs goalmouth and Gazza just happened to be in the vicinity. He trotted up to the halfway line and brandished the card at the startled ref. Everybody fell about the place at the look on the official's face, even the Hibs players. So what did the ref do? Well, instead of laughing it off and stuffing the card in his pocket, he proceeded to book Gascoigne. As I said, Rangers scored seven great goals that day, but the howls of displeasure directed at the little Hitler from the Ibrox faithful at half-time and full-time, even trumped the cheers that accompanied each strike.

I heard an interesting interview on the local Real Radio station the other day. Ex-Ranger Derek Johnstone suggested that the football authorities should consider changing the rules that penalise teams for having injured players. DJ put forward a case for the referee having the power to send the tackling player off the field for the same time as his unfortunate victim, thereby maintaining parity. Sounds reasonable to me!

That just about wraps up my experiences at Dundee. I hope you enjoyed reading the stories as much as I did recounting them.

3

A New Country – Flying with the Bluebirds

As I said before, Dundee FC's financial plight was no secret to the football world. Cardiff City's offer of £17,500 was a massive amount of money to them at that time and they were in no position to turn it down. I often wonder what would have happened if I'd decided to stay. Would I have ended up at Rangers? It was not that Dundee were trying to push me out the door or anything like that. And I was happy there – no question. Ex-Rangers centre-forward Willie Thornton had taken over as manager. He was a big hero of mine in my younger years and I was delighted when I heard he was coming to Dundee. Better still, we seemed to hit it off right away and I could only see good times ahead. Mr Thornton had the knack of getting the best out of his players and was well liked by everyone at the club. But did Willie Thornton possess that elusive recipe for success? Maybe not. It transpired that Dundee would not exactly scale the heights again until the early sixties with the likes of Alan Gilzean, Charlie Cooke and Ian Ure in their side.

A league title followed by a magnificent run to a European Cup semi-final lay ahead for that team and I often felt a little jealous of the fact that I had played at the wrong time – between good sides. I broke into an ageing team in 1953, part of a squad that had gone as far as it possibly could, peaked, achieved its potential, and was heading down the other side. At the time of my transfer down south I considered that maybe a change would do me good. I would soon find out ...

Part of the deal that took me to South Wales included a good look around the set up at Cardiff. I was to check out the whole caboodle, from the football ground itself, Ninian Park, to the accommodation, culture, and general feel of the place. If I didn't like what I saw, the deal was off. Of course, I would take my new wife Margaret with me. After all, she also had a right to choose where we were to spend our next few years. And she was an excellent judge of people.

In what best could be described as a military operation, the visit was meticulously organised by both sides. A couple of the local hacks had got wind of the transfer and spent their time hanging around both our house and the ground, waiting for any movements. Dundee wanted to keep everything under wraps for the time being and release the story to the press when they were ready. It was something to do with the money men and the timing of the deal.

With the help of Willie Thornton and a couple of the coaching staff, Margaret and I were soon on the sleeper heading south.

Hours later we rolled into the station at Cardiff. We were met there by Cardiff City manager, Trevor Morris. Talk about first impressions! Trevor couldn't have been nicer, making sure we got settled in at our hotel before taking us on the grand tour. Even stepping out into the main street, I realised that this was a big city, even bigger than Dundee. Just before the transfer was finalised, I paid a visit to the local library to find out all I could about the place and learn about the football club.

The club had been in two cup finals, losing the first in 1925, but recovering to beat the mighty Arsenal two years later. It was the only time the trophy had gone out of England. In season 1923 – 24, City were pipped to the First Division title on goal average by Huddersfield Town, with all-time top scorer Len Davies missing a late penalty that would have secured the championship on the final day of the season. Since then the club had slipped down the divisions, only managing to return to the top division not long before I joined up.

I had been selected to replace club legend, Stan Montgomery, who was stepping down to non-league football in his twilight years. I only met Stan a couple of times after I'd moved to Cardiff. He was a huge man with a presence about him. I instantly liked him and remember him as someone who was well thought of by everyone connected to the club.

In a strange twist of irony many years later, a little boy of around seven was playing a Saturday morning match for his local side, Marlborough Sports Club. His mother was, as usual, watching from the sidelines when she got chatting to an elderly gentleman standing beside her. 'You know, that young lad reminds me very much of someone,' he said. 'He reminds me of Danny Malloy who used to play for Cardiff City. Have you heard of him?' My niece, Angela Hart, was stunned. 'Danny Malloy is my uncle,' she said. 'And that young lad is my son, Callum.' The elderly gent was Stan Montgomery. Talk about coincidence!

Young Callum went on to play left-back and centre-back at City as a teenager before moving on to Bristol City and then Bournemouth. His fine displays for the Seasiders got him to the verge of an under-21 call up for Wales against Paraguay, but an injury crisis at his club resulted in the lad having to withdraw from the squad. Sounds like another prime example of typical Malloy luck when it comes to international honours. At present Callum Hart is playing full-time with Salisbury in the Conference South division.

*****

I began to weigh up the pros and cons of a move to Cardiff City. On the plus side it was December and City were sitting about mid table, safe from relegation; the ground was compact, had a nice feel about it; I could imagine the crowd close to the action, intimidating, encouraging; the club had around six teams as I recall, from boys and youths to reserve and the first team, with a separate training pitch and changing area just down the road. Not one of the Scottish clubs had anything even close back then, not even the Old Firm. In fact, Celtic have only just built an all-purpose training complex within the last two or three years. Cardiff had all that in place, pre-1955.

The cons? None that I could think of, at that time. Well, maybe the location. I wondered if there would be a hint of home sickness. After all, there were no motorway networks in those days. A 400 mile journey would be a major undertaking. I would just have to get over it. I was a big boy.

I also took the chance to meet my prospective team-mates during the visit. I regarded it as an important factor which would greatly influence my decision. No problems there, the players going out of their way to welcome me into the fold.

The final piece of the jigsaw would be slotted home when Margaret and I were taken to the leafy suburb of Llanishen. At the time the club owned some properties in Solva Avenue. It was perfect, a small cul-de-sac with number twenty-three earmarked for the Malloys.

Another plus point – fellow players Johnny McSeveney and

Harry Kirtley had only recently moved into the same street. Ron Stitfall was already there. Johnny, originally from Shotts in Central Scotland, not that far from my own home town, and Wearsider Harry, had both signed on the same day from Sunderland. It was a sort of standing joke among the players when they referred to the signings of Johnny and Harry as the club 'getting them on a job lot.'

Johnny was a quick, tricky winger, useful, with good pace and stamina ... and tiny! Wing-half Derrick Sullivan was the joker of the side. The pitch camber at Ninian Park was particularly severe and Sully used to kid Johnny on that if he knelt down on one touchline, he wouldn't be able to see any part of the wee man standing on the other!

Both Johnny McSeveney and Harry Kirtley became real friends of ours, especially Harry, as his wife Maureen and my missus really hit it off. We would take in shows and trips to the cinema together. I remember one time we all went to see a very young Morecambe and Wise in cabaret. Maureen laughed so loudly at the comedy duo's antics that Eric Morecambe began to refer to her as 'his mam up in the balcony' during the show. Another memorable trip to the theatre saw us enjoy an incredible debut performance by a young teenage singer from Tiger Bay. She had been tipped to become an overnight sensation. Shirley Bassey had hit the big time.

A couple of days spent having a look around Cardiff, and Margaret and I had made our minds up. We were going for it! As I'd said there were lots of things to consider about the move, but the bottom line was that I'd liked what I'd seen during the visit. I believed we could make a decent life down south, and on a personal level I'd be playing against famous players from some of the top teams at that time, clubs such as Manchester United, Wolves, Preston, Spurs, Arsenal, Aston Villa, Everton, Blackpool and many others. All that had to be organised was a removal firm to take our stuff from Dundee to Llanishen. And of course, to say our goodbyes to our families.

I used the signing-on fee to buy a car and, just as Margaret and I were getting ready to set off, someone had a surprise for us. Ian, my youngest brother, had just come back from National Service. He was around eighteen, had no ties, no job.

'Danny, Margaret! Wait there, I'm coming with you!' he boldly announced, tugging a suitcase behind him. It's strange the way fate sometimes pans out.

Ian made the move to Cardiff, stayed with us for a few months, and ended up marrying local lass, Margaret Buckley, my son's babysitter. He got a job as a lorry driver and set up home in Cottrell Road, Roath. They had two children, my niece Angela, whom I mentioned earlier, and nephew Andrew. Both are now grown up with children of their own.

Ian would often regale the family with stories of his time doing National Service, which was spent largely in Germany at the same time as a certain singer by the name of Elvis Presley. Apparently, he and Elvis had been good buddies, swapped stories, chewed the fat, even strummed a little guitar. Now it's a fact that my brother had a name for being a bit of a kidder. Do I think this story was for real? Who knows? But I like to think so.

Sadly, Ian died suddenly in November 1977, at the ridiculously young age of forty following a severe asthma attack. In a strange twist of fate his buddy Elvis had passed away only weeks before.

My first match for City:
10th December, 1955 v Charlton Athletic

Luckily enough my debut was at home. I say that because I think you've a much better chance of making a good first impression when you turn out in front of the home fans. Conversely, if you have a stinker, that notion might not make a whole lot of sense!

I must admit I did sense a fair bit of pressure on my shoulders that day. Since Stan Montgomery left at the end of the previous season, City had struggled for continuity and consistency in the centre-half position. It was felt that they needed a little grit and determination in that department and manager Trevor Morris had made a point of highlighting the fact during his pre-match team talk. Put me right on the spot, he did. Mind you, it helped a bit that local lad Neil O'Halloran was also making his debut that day. And what a debut it was! The crowd went into raptures when Neil banged in a stunning hat-trick to get himself off to a flyer. Unfortunately, he could not reproduce this form consistently enough, failing to hold down a regular starting slot.

Londoner Brian Walsh, a tricky little winger, was also early into his playing career at Cardiff. Brian was a good player and a top man, although often criticised for being a little faint of heart. I used to feel sorry for the little wingers as most of the opposing full-backs at that time were as hard as nails and built like brick shithouses

Really, could anyone blame a winger for jumping in anticipation of a brutal tackle? Would you listen to this shrinking violet? Unbelievable! Nowadays of course, full-backs, or wing-backs as they're now known, are more skilful and mobile and play more like old style wingers.

On a personal note, I had a fairly easy first match, the only black spot the loss of a goal – I hated not keeping clean sheets. On a plus point, however, although my very first touch of the ball was not until about eight or nine minutes into the match, my through pass led to the first goal. All in all, not a bad start. The game also gave me a chance to experience the atmosphere inside the ground as well as check out my new team-mates. I was well pleased. Ninian Park consisted of the Main Grandstand, the Canton End, the Grange End and a fantastic enclosure known locally as 'The Bob Bank.' The Bank was so dubbed because it cost one shilling to get in and seemed to rise up forever. The whole place raised the hairs on the back of my neck as the fans cranked up the volume. There was a good feel about the team as well. I'd enjoyed a couple of useful training sessions before the match and was most impressed by the squad and the general attitude about the place. Alf Sherwood, Gerry Hitchens, Trevor Ford and Derrick Sullivan had all really impressed me, but quite frankly, it was clear the whole squad could play a bit. I felt I was going to enjoy my time at Cardiff.

The team had had an indifferent start to the season, losing a total of eleven times up until my first game. In fact, they had gone down by the hugely embarrassing scoreline of 9-1 to Wolves at Ninian Park in the September. We managed to further steady the ship after the Charlton match, drawing 1-1 with Sunderland at Roker Park (one of my favourite grounds), and beating Aston Villa 1-0 back at Cardiff. I must say, Sunderland's inside-left Len Shackleton was a stand out for me that day in the North East. What a player! It was actually the second time I'd faced Shackleton, the first a pre-season encounter back at Dundee. What struck me about a lot of the older players I faced throughout my career was how they'd have a wee word of encouragement for me during games. Stanley Matthews and Tom Finney readily spring to mind. Len Shackleton was another. Nice man!

I certainly felt like a popular bloke at Sunderland as some members of my wife's family decided to stop by and pay a visit. Margaret's younger cousin, Jim McNab, had only recently joined

Sunderland as a fifteen-year-old apprentice, and he popped into the away dressing room for a quick chat before the match. He was a nice kid, keen as mustard, and it was no surprise when he turned out to be a great player at left-half for Sunderland over the next few years. Later, he moved to Preston before finishing up at Stockport County. Jim broke into the first team at Sunderland when he was only eighteen and we managed to play against each other at least a couple of times. As he was ten years younger than me I hadn't seen Jim play until then, but I was impressed with his reading of the game as well as that cultured left peg of his. Ironically, Jim's mother Mary only lives two doors down the road from me and I used to see Jim from time to time when he came up to visit her. Mary is still fit and going strong well into her nineties. Sadly, in 2006, Jim McNab lost his battle with cancer and passed away at the age of only sixty-six.

My other visitors the day of the Sunderland match came afterwards and I shouldn't have been surprised to see my wife's aunt and uncle at the dressing room door, given that they lived not too far away in Thornaby-on-Tees. Some years before, Jock and Mary Scott had moved south from Scotland to find work, settling in the North-East. The three of us were standing chatting just inside the dressing room door when Trevor Morris appeared.

'Come on Danny. We'd better get going,' he said. The club had some tables booked at a nearby hotel and we were heading there for some dinner before taking the train back down the road.

'This is Margaret's aunt and uncle,' I said. 'They've come down from Thornaby to see me.'

'Bring them along. We'll set up another couple of places,' Trevor said.

Jock and Mary travelled with us the short journey to the hotel before spending a hugely enjoyable hour or so chatting to the lads. Jock was a right old fashioned football man and fancied himself as a spotter of promising young talent. After two or three whiskies, he had talked himself into a job as Trevor Morris's man in the North East!

The Villa game was played on Christmas Eve and it was followed by a double header against Chelsea on 26th and 27th December. Three games in four days were not uncommon in those times, as were matches home and away on consecutive days. I wonder what today's prima-donnas would have had to say about those arrangements?

We battled to a well deserved 1-1 draw at home against Chelsea on Boxing Day before travelling back to London with them on the same train for the match the following day. I recall feeling we were unlucky to narrowly lose the Stamford Bridge encounter by 2-1. I used to love playing in London. The place just had a kind of magical feel about it and the grounds were always packed out and chockful of atmosphere. Stamford Bridge, White Hart Lane, Highbury, Upton Park and Craven Cottage – I loved every one of them.

Cardiff used to charter the same coach company to pick us up at the train station for games in London and we became friendly with the drivers, especially a lively wee Cockney called Stan. We always had a couple of hours to spare before heading to the ground and we'd fill in the time on the coach. In exchange for match tickets for him and his mates, Stan would take us on a grand tour of the capital complete with the slickest and wittiest of commentaries. I'm convinced the guy would have made a fortune on the stage.

The one thing that struck me about the majority of grounds in England was how close the fans were to the pitch. Back home in Scotland, many of the grounds were larger with wide running tracks around the playing surface. The old Ibrox Park, especially, had a huge semi-circular grass area behind each goal, big enough to accommodate full scale training sessions.

Of course some of the provincial Scottish grounds were also pretty tight for space, which made for a cracking atmosphere ... most of the time. Falkirk's previous ground, Brockville Park, was one in which I used to love playing. As I mentioned in an earlier section, the crowd there could be hostile and they weren't usually slow in spouting their venom at opposing players. I would delight in giving it straight back to them when collecting a loose ball, or taking a throw in. I'd mouth off a couple of expletives as I bent down to retrieve the ball – out of earshot of the officials, of course! I swear you could see the veins, literally, bursting out of their necks!

One afternoon I did feel sorry for a young lad in the Brockville crowd who ended up with a painful reminder of one particular visit to watch his local team. I'd slid in on the Falkirk centre-forward around the halfway line and the ball shot into the crowd, striking the kid full in the face and knocking him out cold. Thankfully, he came round quickly with the aid of some smelling salts and was able to watch the rest of the game. I still felt bad about the incident and, at the end of the match, ran over to the crowd, took off my shirt and handed it to the kid. I asked him if he could take good care of it for me.

In those days most clubs were strapped for cash and players were never ever encouraged to swap shirts. Our kit man went ballistic when he saw me come in to the dressing room without my shirt, but as we'd managed a win, I got away with my 'wilful disposal of club property.'

Many years later, I was walking round a local supermarket when I met a familiar looking man in his early sixties who asked me, 'do you want it back now?' It was the young kid who'd been hit in the face all those years ago. The shirt had been passed down to his grandson, who was an avid collector of footballing memorabilia. Ironically, due to him being given my number five shirt to start off his collection, the Falkirk born youngster had become a confirmed Dundee FC fan.

I recall speaking to Eddie Turnbull of Hibs after a match and he told me how much he loved winding up opposition fans, especially at the major clubs such as Rangers and Celtic. If he was playing at Ibrox, it would be 'Orange B******'s,' and the opposite at Celtic Park. Now there was no way Eddie was bigoted or anything like that. He just liked the wind-ups; reckoned it gave the game an edge.

Speaking of interaction with the crowd, I heard familiar shouts from the terracing at Stamford Bridge that December afternoon. 'Durty Bonnybrig!' 'Durty Bonnybrig!' It was a familiar saying back home among the locals. As I'd mentioned earlier, Bonnybridge was very much an industrial town with numerous foundries, mills and pits peppering the landscape. When I heard the shouts, I turned around to see this madman behind our goal waving at me, maybe six rows back. Will Ritchie was an old friend I'd forgotten was working in London. The Ritchies and the Malloys were large families who'd grown up, literally, a stone's throw from each other. The boys were roughly the same age and we all used to run about together. Will and I met up after the game and I promised to get him a couple of tickets each time we played in London.

From time to time some of the other lads from the village would turn up out of the blue at Cardiff on match days. It must have been a Scottish thing, much like the bi-annual pilgrimage to Wembley. If you've ever seen the film *Lost Weekend* with Ray Milland, you'll know exactly what I mean. I'd look forward to seeing the lads after a game where we would have a few beers and go over old times. They would then go on to have a good few more before heading home. Their visits certainly helped to ease any homesickness.

Next up on New Year's Eve were Wolves, managed by Stan Cullis, who of course, had tried to sign me from Dundee the previous year. As I mentioned before, Cardiff had been trounced 9-1 at home earlier in the season and we were out for revenge, big time! The team was immense that day as we triumphed 2-0, wrecking Wolves' unbeaten home record that season. Mr Cullis and I shared a few words at the end of the match. He told me of his disappointment that I had chosen not to join his team, but wished me well for the future. Nice man.

The games were coming thick and fast; next match was at Leeds in a third round FA Cup tie. The 'Terrible Twins,' Alan Harrington and Colin Baker, played most of the time each side of me in the half-back line. Alan and Colin were great lads, pals who joined the club at the same time from a local junior team. They were only a little younger than I was, and we got on famously. Interestingly, Alan and Colin continued to change for training with the youngsters, even when they'd broken into the first team. They'd get in, shower, and get ready in double-quick time, so they could get in beside us, join in the *craic* among the lads. I could identify with their thinking as I'd done exactly the same as a youngster at Dundee. Both Alan and Colin played a terrific match beside me in the half-back line at Leeds that day. They were excellent players who turned out to be fantastic servants to Cardiff City.

Leeds maybe were a second division outfit at that time, but their team had some extremely talented individuals. Centre-forward John Charles was a man-mountain set to become a Welsh legend, but even if I do say so myself, I hardly gave him a kick that day. It was one of the easiest games I had ever played. I don't think John and I ever exchanged words before, during or after any match. He wasn't exactly the talkative type. In fact, I much preferred his brother Mel who was a real gem of a lad with a brilliant personality, always laughing and joking. John, on the other hand, had nothing much to say for himself. I figured later that, as with most good players, maybe he just didn't like to lose.

Jack, the elder of the World Cup winning Charlton brothers, was playing at centre-half that day directly in opposition to Trevor Ford. Fordy had been well shackled throughout the match and it was decided midway through the second-half that he move out wide, with Gerry Hitchens switching to centre. The plan worked like a dream when Gerry cracked in the opener with fifteen minutes to go. Wee Johnny McSeveney fired home the second seven minutes later and it was all over. Leeds did manage a consolation goal with three minutes left before big John Charles managed to give me the slip for the first time in the match, leaping to meet a last minute corner kick. Unfortunately for Leeds, Jack Charlton also jumped for the ball, putting Charles off and the chance was lost. You should have heard the language from Charles as Jack stammered and stuttered an apology before tearing off up the park to safety. Priceless!

I suppose there was one advantage in defeat for Leeds; the early exit was to benefit the club in another way as it allowed them to concentrate on securing promotion at the end of that season. Incredibly, we went on to draw Leeds in the FA Cup for the following two seasons in a row, all away from home, all in the third round. The scores were also 2-1 to Cardiff each time – a fourteen million to one chance! It was fair to say the Yorkshire club were to become absolutely sick of the sight of us.

The next league game was back at Ninian Park and we trounced a good Manchester City outfit by 4-1. The team was beginning to gel and we really felt that we could have beaten anybody that day. Famous last words as we came unstuck away at bogey team Sheffield United in the next game. We went down 2-1, but were unlucky to lose, a couple of rotten breaks late on sealing our fate.

On another note, Bramall Lane was the oddest ground I had ever seen. It was entirely open on one side, conjoined with the local cricket pitch. The club employed a row of eager ball boys, all poised to scamper after the ball every time it went out of play. Of course, we didn't get ourselves into a winning position on that particular day, but I couldn't help thinking that if we did in the future, it might not be the worst tactic in the world to simply hoof the ball as far as we could onto the cricket pitch. It would be the ultimate time-wasting ploy!

It was FA Cup time again after league duty and we faced a tough game at West Ham in the fourth round. As with Leeds, the Hammers were also a second division outfit. In fact they were languishing in the lower reaches and, as such, we fancied our chances of progressing. However, things didn't go too well at the start and we lost a goal after only about four minutes. Upton Park was noisy, boasted a really tight pitch and the crowd was very close to the action. It was a really wet day in London and before too long the surface began to get really heavy, almost unplayable. Despite the conditions, as the time wore on, we started to play better and take a hold of the game. Trevor Ford wheeled inside at the edge of the box and blasted an unstoppable shot just over the bar. A minute later, Fordy latched on to a Johnny McSeveney through pass and slipped the ball under the advancing goalkeeper. A great goal! We felt really confident of going through at that point, even if it meant getting them back to Cardiff to finish the job. Then, just before half-time, disaster struck. Alfie Sherwood cleared a scoring effort off our line and when the ball came back in we were all caught flat footed as a West Ham player headed home from close range. Manager Trevor Morris gave us a right old rocket at half-time and we came roaring back in the second-half. However, despite carving out some great chances, we just couldn't get the goal we needed and tumbled out of the cup.

Huddersfield Town away was the next league match with Scot Andy Beattie in charge of The Terriers. Andy was a bit of a perfectionist and, having finished second the season before, the club had slipped to fifteenth spot. Such was the pride in his performance, he offered up his resignation to the board. Rightly, the offer was turned down flat, but after another unsuccessful spell, Andy eventually resigned the following November. Beattie decided to leave football for a couple of years after that, only returning to land a dream job as manager of the Scottish national team following a short spell at Carlisle United. Andy Beattie's assistant would take charge at Huddersfield after his departure. The great Bill Shankly was about to make his mark.

I almost forgot to mention the game – Gerry Hitchens and Trevor Ford scored for us in a 2-1 win.

There was a bumper crowd of 36,000 at the next game for the visit of high flying Blackpool. I must admit I was especially looking forward to this match. Only two years before, I was over at Andy Irvine's house in Dundee with some of the other Dens lads to watch the famous Stanley Matthews' 1953 FA Cup Final between Blackpool and Bolton Wanderers live on TV. Andy was the only one of us to have a telly in the house as we watched Blackpool triumph 4-3 in a terrific game. I remember saying to the guys in Dundee that I'd love to play against that team some day! Well, there I was, ready to look

Matthews straight in the eye! Or rather left-back Alf Sherwood, in direct opposition to the right-winger, was in the line of fire. Just as well then that Alf was one of the best left-backs in Britain – in my opinion, at least.

The great Stan Mortensen had recently moved on to Hull City so I would face fellow Scotsman, top scorer and centre-forward, Jackie Mudie. Great! I knew Jackie pretty well as he hailed from Dundee. He was a very good player, small for a centre-forward, but with the heart of a lion. He was a prolific goalscorer and his record of 144 goals in 324 games for Blackpool will always guarantee him legendary status at Bloomfield Road. Our team was on a bit of a roll and the big crowd roared us on to a famous 1-0 victory, Fordy again hitting the net. Admittedly, we hung on a bit near the end as Stanley Matthews began to weave his magic. What a fantastic player he was, and Sir Stan also proved to be a true gent when he went out of his way to congratulate each and every one of our players at the final whistle. Even better, Matthews used to write a weekly column for the local paper in Blackpool, and a couple of weeks later I received a posted copy of his next piece following our game from a friend. I was in dreamland when Sir Stan described Danny Malloy as 'the best centre-half I have seen for some time.'

Our next visitors at Ninian Park, Preston North End, included a couple of remarkable players; quite different, but remarkable nevertheless. One was a tough Scot from the infamous Gorbals area of Glasgow – Tommy Docherty. The other, the man who was to later top my list as the greatest player I'd ever played with or against – the mercurial Tom Finney. I'd met Tommy Docherty on a few occasions prior to this game, on Scotland squad sorties and the like, but this was the first time I'd played against him. The Doc was a really likeable man, larger than life, with a droll sense of humour ... and an answer for absolutely everything.

I heard later that Tommy was an outstanding personality on the after-dinner circuit when his involvement with football management came to an end. I can't say I'm surprised. He was always good company, a serial practical joker with a funny story for every occasion; walking off at half-time while playing an Old Firm reserve match at his first club, Celtic, Tommy noticed that one of his younger team-mates was a little upset. The lad was from Northern Ireland, a Protestant, and had been on the receiving end of some verbals from a couple of the Rangers players. 'They're calling me a

Fenian B******, 'was all he could say.

Tommy put a consoling arm around the youngster's shoulder. 'Ach, don't worry about it, pal. I get that all the time,' he chirped.

'Aye, but you *are* one!' The lad replied, straight-faced.

When asked to give his thoughts on a certain centre-forward who perhaps wouldn't have been on his wish list, the Doc replied, quick as you like, 'A hundred thousand wouldnae buy him. An' I'm one of them!'

One of Tommy's Preston team-mates, Willie Cunningham, could never be described by anyone as having 'Hollywood looks,' and, following one particular training session, the Doc suggested to a packed dressing room that Willie had enlisted the services of a world renowned plastic surgeon to improve his looks. The story went that he turned up for a facelift and when they saw what was below, put it back down!

Getting back to the actual game against Preston, I did get a chance to have a quick word with Tommy Docherty prior to kick off. He, like me, was a huge fan of Tom Finney and, to his credit he did his best to allay my fears of getting 'a bit of a chasing' from the great man. 'Don't you worry, Danny, just play your game. You'll do just fine.' The Doc's words of encouragement paid off as we won 3-1 with goals from Hitchens, Kirtley and Ford.

Despite one or two hairy moments, I came through the game fairly well against The Preston Plumber, limiting him to few opportunities. Finney, like Matthews before him, was a true gentleman, a genuinely nice man who took time at the end to thank me for the game and wish us well for the rest of the season. In a nice touch Tommy Docherty also congratulated me on my performance that day, adding that he was glad I hadn't suffered the same fate as the Spurs centre-half the previous week. Tom Finney had tied the poor guy up in so many knots that he came off the park at the end looking like Ben Turpin (Turpin was a silent screen comedy actor in the same mould as Charlie Chaplin, especially famous for his cross-eyed look).

Our team was superb against Preston that day and I was particularly impressed by our auxiliary left-back. Alfie Sherwood had missed the game due to a leg knock and Derrick Sullivan stepped in and took to the role like a duck to water! I used to feel sorry for players who were employed primarily in a utility role. It indicated, to me at least, that the manager thought the player wasn't good enough to hold down a starting place in a regular position. Derrick had played everywhere for Cardiff, from inside-forward to right-back, from left-winger to centre-half. I was lucky enough to have him play beside me at right-half on a number of occasions and, put simply, in that position I considered Derrick Sullivan to be world class. He was that good. My opinion was vindicated by members of the greatest team in the world a couple of years later, in 1958. The Samba stars of Brazil, including a seventeen-year-old sensation named simply, Pele, narrowly edged out Wales 1-0 in the World Cup quarter-final and right-half Sullivan was singled out for special praise that day. I was well chuffed for Sully, and envious as Hell! My green eye was eased a little by an article written later by *The South Wales Echo's* Dewi Lewis who reckoned that, 'if Danny Malloy had been Welsh we'd have won the blooming World Cup.' I don't know about that, but it was nice to feel appreciated!

You may recall an earlier chapter in the book when I mentioned a game I had played for Dundee against our local rivals, Dundee United. United were in a lower division then and the only time we used to play them in those days would be in the Forfarshire Cup. The game in question had finished 9-3 for us and the centre-forward for United, Peter McKay, had been so frustrated and annoyed that he stormed off without shaking hands or even acknowledging any of our players. You may also recall my opinion that McKay was too good for United, and that he would have to move to realise his full potential. His subsequent transfer to Burnley and mine to Cardiff meant that we were, once again, about to cross swords.

Not a word was spoken between McKay and me as we lined up at Turf Moor on 25th February, 1956. Manager Trevor Morris had stressed that a win would move us up to around tenth in the table and I had used this well placed information to get myself fired up for the match. As if I needed firing up! Looking at Peter McKay's surly face as we lined up was enough to do the job.

Now I'm not sure if it was the fourth or fifth crunching tackle that did it, but I *was* sure that he'd had enough; couldn't take anymore. Peter McKay rubbed his aching shins before turning the air blue, suddenly launching into this uncontrollable, foul-mouthed tirade. I hadn't mentioned our previous history to my Cardiff team-mates so you should have seen the looks on their faces when McKay spluttered and stammered various expletives, finally getting rid of all his pent-up frustration. Our defence, especially Ron Stitfall, fell about laughing when he realised that McKay's outburst was about to earn him a booking while I got off scot-free. You couldn't make it up!

The game finished 2-0 to City, Gerry Hitchens grabbing both goals. Peter McKay trudged off the park at the end, crestfallen, face like thunder. It had been my easiest match, thus far. And we'd just climbed to tenth position.

We were due to play Wrexham in round six of the Welsh Cup the following midweek. Meanwhile, I was heading back to Dundee. No, I hadn't re-signed for the Dens Parkers, though I would have loved to have turned out for them at least one more time. I had been called up to play in a Scotland B friendly match against the Auld Enemy.

A crowd of 11,500 turned up to see the match, and I was well chuffed to receive an extra special welcome from the Dundee fans when I ran out. And it was really nice saying hello again to some great friends. The game itself was a cracker, Manchester United's Tommy Taylor giving hot favourites England a 1-0 lead at half-time. It was the first time I had encountered the centre-forward although Cardiff were scheduled to visit Old Trafford ten days later. If the rest of the United side were anything like as good as Taylor, we were in for a real test. The match eventually finished 2-2, John Atyeo scoring in the last minute for England, and was seen as a great advert for both leagues.

It was back to Ninian Park on 7th March for the visit of Newcastle United and a face-to-face encounter with a certain Geordie legend by the name of Jackie Millburn. At Dundee, Billy Steel would delight in regaling us with stories of his time in the top flight with Derby County. 'Wor Jackie' was in Steely's all-time top eleven and, given the wee man's hard to please attitude, I'd figured the big centre-forward must have been some player. I was not to be disappointed.

Hailing from Ashington and full cousin to the Charlton brothers, Millburn was thirty-two and nearing the end of an incredible 492 game/272 goal spell at Newcastle, but as our game wore on it was plain to see that he still had it in abundance. Not a great header of the ball, Jackie's strengths were lightning-quick speed, unbelievable ball control and the ability to score from almost any angle. Aside from Matthews and Finney, Millburn was the trickiest player I had faced up until that point. And, like them, he was a quiet, modest, unassuming sort. Somehow, I managed to stop Jackie Millburn scoring, Colin Baker netting a rare goal for us in a fighting 1-1 draw. I was dead chuffed for young Colin. He and Alan Harrington were cracking lads and it was an honour to play alongside them.

Three days later we travelled to Old Trafford to face the champions-elect, Manchester United. I expected this to be my toughest match so far. 'The Busby Babes' were so named after an affable Scotsman and his band of young players who had taken British football by storm with their special brand of attacking football. Manager Matt Busby, later to become Sir Matt, came from the tiny mining village of Orbiston near Bellshill, in Lanarkshire, Scotland. He had started his football career on a part-time basis with Denny Hibs – ironically my father's first team. Mr Busby wasn't long with Denny Hibs before being given a one-year deal at Manchester City on £5 per week. He went on to play over 200 times for City before moving to another of Manchester United's fiercest rivals, Liverpool, where he went on to make another 100 appearances. In another twist Mr Busby went out of his way to help a young footballer settle in at Anfield, the two of them going on to form a lifelong friendship in and out of football. Matt Busby and Bob Paisley were to become possibly the two greatest managers the game had ever seen.

Before we ran out for the match at Old Trafford, I took the opportunity to have a quick wander around the corridors of power, drinking in the experience. I was like the proverbial kid in the candy store as I looked at hanging pictures depicting the history of the great club.

I started when I felt a strong hand on my shoulder. 'You all right, Danny? How's Willie getting on?'

The distinctive Scots accent cut the silence. I couldn't believe it! I turned to face this man, his firm handshake nearly shattering my fingers. Although I'd never met Mr Busby, I knew right away who he was. Everybody knew who Matt Busby was. But the thing that really did it for me was that he knew who I was. He was talking to me, shaking hands and calling me by my first name. But then, that was the mark of the man. Like everyone at the very top of his profession, he had taken the time to find out, to do his homework. Mr Busby was a good friend of Willie Thornton, my old boss at Dundee and had played alongside him in the forces.

I stuttered a reply, my heart going twenty to the dozen. 'H-hello, Mr Busby, very pleased to meet you. The gaffer, I mean, Mr Thornton's fine.'

'That's good, son. That's good. And how are they treating you?' He was still shaking my hand.

'It's a good club. I'm enjoying the football, that's the main thing.' I replied, red faced.

'Very true, son. And you're settling in well? Margaret all right?'

I was dumbstruck. He even knew my wife's name.

'Aye, Mr Busby. We're settling in just fine.'

'Good lad. I've been keeping an eye on you. They tell me you're doing well, son. Keep it up. You enjoy the game and I'll have a wee word with you after.'

With that he was away back into the home dressing room to prepare.

I walked out on to the 'Theatre of Dreams' as if I was walking on air and had a right belter of a game. Gerry Hitchens gave us the lead in front of 45,000 fans and, although we conceded an equaliser, I felt we deserved at least a draw out of the game. The match also gave me a chance to have a look at some of the 'Babes,' up close and personal: Dennis Viollet, Jackie Blanchflower, Tommy Taylor, Billy Whelan, Roger Byrne, Eddie Colman, Bobby Charlton and the incredible Duncan Edwards all stood out that day. Wing-half Duncan was a big, quiet laddie who must surely have been destined to become the greatest player on the planet. He had the lot; he was deceptively quick off the mark despite his stature, could shoot with either foot, tackle like a demon, was a great header of the ball. He *was* the complete player. I swear I saw the colour drain from the faces of our inside-forwards as they lined up against this giant of a man with a barrel chest and huge, tree trunk legs. Team captain Roger Byrne, one of the older players at twenty-six, was also a gem of a man for whom I had a lot of time.

In the dressing room at the end of the match Mr Busby congratulated us on playing well and asked if everybody was all right, if anybody needed treatment or a doctor. It was a nice touch! It was clear to all of us that day that United were a great side who were about to attain legendary status. Sadly, it was to be for all the wrong reasons as, two years later, the team would be decimated by events in Munich.

I don't know if everything else was an anti-climax after the Manchester game, but the wheels started to come off our season after that. We lost 2-0 to a good Everton side at Goodison Park, and followed it up with an away draw at lowly Portsmouth.

Two home games against West Bromwich Albion and Portsmouth again where we lost 3-1 and 3-2 respectively were followed by a visit to high flying Birmingham where we played better ... but still went down 2-1.

We managed to steady the ship against Luton Town, beating them 2-0 at Ninian Park before ending the league season with a couple of dull 0-0 draws, one away at Charlton and the other at home to Tottenham Hotspur.

The last game of the campaign was at home against Arsenal where we again lost by the odd goal, 2-1.

From our highest position of tenth after the Burnley game on 25th February, we had slipped dangerously close to relegation, eventually finishing seventeenth out of twenty-two.

I was mightily relieved. At least I was going to get another crack at the top flight next season.

*****

The Welsh Cup couldn't exactly be spoken about in the same way as its illustrious cousin, The FA Cup, but at least it was a bit of silverware. Cardiff had disposed of mighty teams like Pembroke (after a rather embarrassing 2-2 draw), Wrexham and Oswestry on their road to the final. Our opponents in that final were arch-rivals, Swansea Town and they were coming to Cardiff to try and claim the trophy. Now I believe the rivalry between the two sets of supporters is still intense, even to this day. They just don't like each other, never did! Maybe I shouldn't be admitting this but I always got on well with most of the Swansea players. Don't get me wrong, I'd still put the boot in to them if I had to! Seriously, guys like Mel Charles, Mel Nurse, Terry Medwin, Ivor Allchurch and Cliff Jones were all good lads and I used to enjoy playing against them.

In a hard fought match in front of an unbelievable crowd of 37,500, we won 3-2 thanks to goals from McSeveney and Walsh (two). The only black spot on the day came when inside-forward Harry Kirtley was stretchered off with a broken leg after an accidental clash in the first-half. Of course there were no substitutes at that time, and we had to soldier on with ten men. Harry's unfortunate departure seemed to spur us on and we raced to a 3-0 lead before being pegged back towards the end of the match, the iconic Ivor Allchurch pulling the strings for Swansea.

After the presentation of the trophy I made my way up to the players' lounge where I met my wife Margaret, who was standing beside Harry Kirtley's wife, Maureen. I proceeded to tell Maureen how sorry I was about what had happened to Harry and hoped that he would be all right, when I noticed the colour drain from her face. She didn't know. Nobody had thought to tell her what had happened to her husband. I just managed to catch her as she went down in a faint. Margaret and I helped her into a seat and gave her a glass of water before I tore away like a raging bull to give someone a piece of my mind.

Tragedy

Not long into my time at Cardiff, tragedy dealt the club a hammer blow. Our training ground was a short walk along the road to Coronation Park. One bright, clear morning the squad was heading for the park. I recall we were in good spirits due to a decent run of results, and the mood was really upbeat among the lads.

Some of the younger boys were allowed to train with the first team as a treat and, that morning, we had a few eager youngsters in tow. If the truth be told, the kids' main function was to carry the kit. At least it made a welcome change from polishing our boots! Seriously, they were a great bunch of lads and keen as mustard to do well.

We used to transport the balls in huge sacks and the boys were continually warned to keep the balls in the sacks when walking to the training ground. The coaches were concerned in case someone was hurt twisting an ankle on a kerb or tripping on a paving slab.

Peter Bryant from Gabalfa, which is in the north of Cardiff, was happily throwing a ball in the air, bouncing and heading it as he made his way along the pavement. He let the ball drop to his knee and on to his foot. The ball must have caught the corner of a raised slab as it left the lad's foot and was heading on to the road, when Peter instinctively reached across to catch it. Traffic at that time in fifties Cardiff was a fraction of what it is these days, and it was unusual if even one car passed during the short walk to the training ground. But one car did indeed pass that day and, as the poor lad reached out for the ball, he was struck.

I was walking just up ahead when I heard the impact. I turned around and couldn't believe what I was witnessing. We were at the lad's side in seconds. I sprinted back to the ground in panic to bring the doctor, the physio ... anybody. Of course, there were no mobile phones in those days and I tried to be as quick as I could. The image of this poor kid just lying there haunted me as I ran but I kept thinking that if I could just get professional help, maybe ...

The club doctor and I were back at the scene in minutes. I already knew by the grief-stricken faces of the other players as I approached them that my efforts had been in vain. The doctor laid down his bag, knelt beside the lad's body. He went through the motions, did his checks. We stood in silence. There were tears from the unlikeliest of sources.

Peter Bryant was sixteen when he died. He was a Welsh schoolboy international forward, tipped for the top. He had caught the eye of everyone at the club, not only because of his undoubted ability, but also because he was a popular lad among the rest of the players. Such a tragic waste of a young life.

4

Fall from Grace

Season 1956-57

During the close season, one of the clubs most iconic characters decided it was time to move on. Despite the offer of a new deal, Welsh international full-back and club captain Alf Sherwood had set his mind on a move to nearby Newport County. I guess he felt that he had just been at the club too long having joined City from his hometown team, Aberaman Athletic, in 1941. An ex-miner, Alf was one of the famous Bevin Boys, so named after Labour minister Ernest Bevin, who devised a scheme which called for young men aged between eighteen and twenty-five to be drafted in to work as miners during World War Two.

Alf was one of those people who hadn't a bad bone in his body. In an era when full-backs tended to be huge and intimidating, Alf was slight in stature, but blessed with the heart of a lion. Always polite and smiling, he was a terrific player, quick, with a demonic tackle. Famous as the 'King of the Sliding Tackles', the way he could nimbly nick the ball off the toe of an opponent was legendary. In fact, Sir Stanley Matthews identified Alf as 'the most difficult opponent I have ever played against.' Praise indeed.

I later found out from some of the other players that Alf had also been a stand-in keeper for both club and country and indeed, had saved a penalty from Liverpool's Scottish international forward Billy Liddell, effectively consigning the Merseysiders to relegation in season 1953-1954. And it was not only football at which Alf excelled. He and Trevor Ford also played cricket for Wales at youth international level. Alf played over 350 times for Cardiff City and went on to notch up a further 205 at Newport County. With forty-one full Welsh international caps, Alf Sherwood was a true legend!

Twenty-one-year-old inside-forward Brayley Reynolds was brought in from Lovell's Athletic, and we began our campaign with a creditable 0-0 draw at Arsenal in front of over 51,000 fans. In fact the result might have been even better. Welshman Jack Kelsey played in goals for the Gunners and was regarded by many as the top keeper in the league at that time. He certainly proved it that day, making top drawer saves from Trevor Ford and Gerry Hitchens.

Playing up front for Arsenal was another Welshman, the inimitable Derek Tapscott. It was my first brush with Derek and I was lucky enough to make it really hard for him that day. Not the most technically gifted of strikers, Tappy countered that with an incredible appetite for goals. Although he didn't manage to take any chances that day, I would not miss out on the scoring exploits of this talented striker as he was to join Cardiff a couple of years later. Highbury was a modern stadium at that time, one of my favourites. And what an atmosphere!

We opened our Ninian Park campaign the following Wednesday, thrashing a good Newcastle side 5-2. Trevor Ford and Cliff Nugent grabbed doubles in front of a bumper crowd of 36,000.

When we raced to a 3-1 lead at half-time in our next game at home against Burnley, we were looking at nestling near the top of the table. The next two-and-a-half games soon brought us back down to earth with a clatter. Burnley netted two late goals to earn a draw before, firstly, Newcastle gained some revenge for their earlier defeat, then Preston absolutely murdered us 6-0 at Deepdale. I think we were five down at half-time. My first game the season before against Tom Finney had gone well, as we had run out fairly comfortable winners. Not this time. I have to say Finney was absolutely fantastic, scoring two goals and setting up another two. Unfortunately, every one of the Cardiff players (including myself) had a shocker that day, especially in the first-half, but that took nothing away from Preston. I'd just played against the finest player I had ever seen. One positive note I took from the game – if there could be such a thing. I maintained my record (which was to last for the whole of my career) of never having a centre-forward score a hat-trick against me.

We licked our wounds after that, steadied the ship a little with a good home win against a very useful Sheffield Wednesday side, followed by a creditable draw against Chelsea.

The next game was the return against Sheffield Wednesday at Hillsborough, and in the most open, attacking game I have ever been involved in, we went down 5-3. To be honest, it could have ended up something like 19-17! A little midfielder by the name of Finney (Alan, not Tom) had a terrific match and was at the heart of everything good about Wednesday that day. The Cardiff full-backs looked as comedic as 'The Two Ronnies' – Davies and Stitfall this time, as a flying winger by the name of Redfern Froggatt (no, honestly) tore us to shreds. 'Red' switched wings at will and was just as effective with either foot. A nightmare!

Next up were Bolton Wanderers, complete with an intimidating English centre-forward by the name of Nat Lofthouse. 'The Lion of Vienna' didn't score in our 2-0 defeat and, even if I do say so myself, I actually played a blinder against him. It was clear that Nat was a great player, and despite his fearsome reputation he was also a nice bloke with a wicked sense of humour. We got on like a house on fire. And better still, he was to let slip to the press next day that he considered Danny Malloy to be the best centre-half he had ever played against. Somehow it seemed to make it all so worthwhile.

A funny thing happened before our next match away at St Andrew's, Birmingham. Right-winger Brian Walsh had picked up an injury against Bolton and Trevor Ford volunteered to play there instead of his usual number nine spot. Not exactly earth shattering news I hear you say, but it was when you consider that the previous season Fordy had refused to play anywhere else but centre-forward before a match.

Manager Trevor Morris was of the view that Gerry Hitchens would be better suited to a more central role, with Fordy just off him at inside-left. When Trevor suggested the switch on the morning of a match Fordy went daft, refusing point blank to play number ten. The resultant fallout led to him being left out of the squad altogether, and when he decided to storm out of the stadium in a huff, Fordy found himself in real bother. There was talk about a hefty fine, even rumours that he was to be transfer listed. The feeling in the camp was split. A few of the players who didn't think much of Trevor before the incident, thought even less of him afterwards. I believe some of the guys considered Trevor Ford to be some kind of big-time Charlie. Also, I had heard about a bit of previous between some of the older Cardiff lads and Fordy when he played with Sunderland. It was fair to say that they were less than chuffed when he signed up at Ninian Park. Personally, I got on really well with Trevor and had a lot of time for him. And I'd much rather have played with than against him any day of the week!

After all that, Trevor Ford did play, at number seven, and we lost narrowly by 2-1, Neil O'Halloran netting a rare goal.

A 0-0 draw at home to West Brom was followed by our best game of the season. Once again John Charles and Leeds would suffer, this time in the league as we humbled them 4-1 at Ninian Park. Gerry Hitchens bagged a fantastic double with Trevor Ford and Johnny McSeveney scoring the others. Ford's goal was to be his last for the club when he left under a cloud following our 1-1 draw at home against Manchester City.

A cloud of controversy quickly followed, extracts from his, as then unpublished, autobiography, entitled *I Lead the Attack*, printed by a Sunday newspaper. These extracts dealt with illegal payments to players and soon led to Trevor being banned from the Football League. It was suggested by some that Fordy had retired, but he was, in fact, banned 'sine die' on 30th January, 1957. The ban was then cut to three years following his appeal on 3rd March, 1958. Just three weeks later, Fordy signed a three year contract with Dutch giants, PSV Eindhoven. He played fifty-three times for PSV, scoring twenty-one goals before he successfully gained reinstatement to the Football League in 1960. Trevor Ford returned for a very brief spell with Newport County, eventually finishing up after a few games at non-league level with Romford.

Getting back to the subject of illegal payments to players, there were always rumours flying around concerning the shady side of football. I remember receiving a telephone call one Friday evening on the eve of a match against Wolves. The caller seemed very guarded and careful, but after a couple of minutes it became clear exactly what he was proposing. Basically, I was to give away a penalty or allow the centre-forward to get on the end of a cross. I was to turn a blind eye and I would be well rewarded. We didn't even reach the discussion on exactly how much as I politely told the guy where to shove his offer. Then I immediately vowed to do everything in my power to make sure we won the game. I decided not to say anything about the incident to the manager or the other lads, and it was just as well as we cruised to victory. But they must have wondered why I trudged off at the end exhausted, with a huge grin on my face.

I've always hated cheats and cheating, be it athletes taking performance-enhancing drugs, footballers feigning injury to get opponents sent off, or simply an amateur golfer trying to improve his lie in a Sunday morning foursome. Cheating just isn't right and I wish people would stop doing it.

I almost forgot to mention Trevor Ford's last away game prior to the City match. Or maybe it was a game I really did want to forget! We hadn't a look in as we were battered 5-0 by an outstanding Spurs side in front of 52,000 at White Hart Lane.

After the tragic demise of Busby's Babes in 1958, Spurs were to become one of the dominant teams on the domestic front over the next few seasons – Ditchburn, Baker, Henry, Norman, Blanchflower, Dyson, Smith, Medwin ... the names tripped off the tongue.

For the past few years, I have been in contact with long term Cardiff City supporter, Graham Lewis. Graham and his wife Maria always send Christmas cards and Graham likes to keep me up to date with any goings on down Cardiff way. Some time ago he wrote to me detailing a chance meeting with ex-Swansea and Spurs winger, Terry Medwin. I played against Terry a few times. He was a great player and a top man and I was glad to pass on my best regards. It was good to hear from Graham that the old fella was doing fine.

Northern Irishman Danny Blanchflower was another fine footballer and a really nice guy. Danny and I became quite friendly and he was another who would go out of his way to help younger, more inexperienced players from all teams with some sensible, solid advice. I was interested to read about his main reason for leaving Aston Villa to join Spurs. Apparently, Villa's training regime at that time involved very little work with a football. Their emphasis was placed firmly on physical fitness, strength and stamina building. The big fellow was very much an advocate of the passing game and, Danny being Danny, he wasn't usually slow in getting his point across. I don't know whether or not Villa's coaching staff felt a little intimidated, but the upshot was a big money transfer to an outfit who liked to play the Blanchflower way. And Spurs didn't do too badly after that, did they? The highlight of Danny Blanchflower's career at Tottenham Hotspur would be a memorable league and cup double in 1961.

Whilst I did believe that physical fitness, strength, speed and stamina building were essential elements of a team's training regime, I also liked to spend a lot of time with the actual football itself. I believed this was where skills could be finely tuned and bad habits eradicated. Not everybody would agree with this philosophy, however. I recall the Glasgow Rangers side of the early to mid seventies who used to spend a lot of time chucking up their breakfasts on the sand dunes at Gullane in Ayrshire, following some particularly brutal training sessions there. The simple instruction was to keep running up and down the dunes until you dropped from exhaustion! I was quite friendly with one of the players in that squad and he would tell me that the Rangers manager at the time, Jock Wallace, was such an intimidating and terrifying character that he would gladly have died on the sand rather than refuse to take part. I'm sure I would have had something to say on the matter, terrifying character or not. In fact, I'm certain of it!

Dundee FC always had the name of being a passing side, for getting the ball down and moving it around. From what I'd seen so far at Cardiff, they tried to play the same way and, although we had suffered a couple of heavy defeats, I felt that, deep down, there was a good side desperate to come out. The problem for us, as far as I was concerned, was the nemesis of many a decent side; the thing that sets good teams apart from great ones – *consistency*. In my short time at Cardiff we had beaten top sides like Wolves, Preston and Blackpool, only to slip up against some of the lesser lights such as Sheffield United, West Bromwich Albion and Luton Town. Consistency, or the lack of it, was to be our undoing that season.

The loss of Trevor Ford at such an important point of the season could have been a huge blow to the club, but we managed to keep going, battling to win our next two games against Charlton away and Sunderland at home. Players like inside-right Brayley Reynolds and winger Cliff Nugent managed to get themselves on the scoresheet, but it was Englishman Gerry Hitchens, now playing at centre-forward, who really stepped up to the plate to set the mood for the rest of the season. Big Hitch was a good player, superb in the air and quick with a good shot in either foot. His haul of twenty one league goals was a fantastic achievement, especially as it was achieved during a difficult season for Cardiff City. My wee pal Johnny McSeveney's tally of thirteen was also very good given the circumstances.

Through the rest of November and December of 1956, our only success was a 1-0 win at home against Everton. By the end of the year we had slipped dangerously close to relegation territory, defeats by Luton, Blackpool, Arsenal (narrowly), Burnley, Manchester United and Preston (again narrowly), really putting tremendous pressure on everyone.

The one bright spot for me amidst the carnage was that I would score my one and only league goal for the club. And just where did that goal come? No? Well let me ask you a question: what do Danny Malloy, Ryan Giggs, David Beckham, Cristiano Ronaldo, Wayne Rooney and Ruud van Nistleroy all have in common? Answer: they have all scored from the penalty spot at Old Trafford!

The goal itself? You may not believe this, but for the life of me, I just cannot recall scoring that goal on Boxing Day, 1956, at The Theatre of Dreams. How sad is that? They tell me it was indeed a penalty after only about two minutes. Checking back, the records show that normal penalty-taker Johnny McSeveney was not playing that day. That's all very well, but whose big idea was it to hand the ball to a centre-half to take a penalty? Don't get me wrong, I had bagged seven goals (six of them penalties), in my two and a half years in the first team at Dundee, and I distinctly remember scoring a winning penalty against Celtic at Parkhead in a League Cup tie. Once again, however, I cannot recall how I ended up with the ball in my hands, ready to place it on the spot. Anybody?

A funny thing happened on the way up to Manchester the night before the United match. It was Christmas night, and when our coach got stuck in heavy snow at Hereford, we all had to get out and walk to the train station. The players must have been full of festive cheer as we began to 'entertain' the locals by singing Christmas carols while waiting for our train. At least we thought we sounded quite good!

After the Preston game it was round three of the FA Cup and the second instalment of the Leeds United 1 Cardiff City 2 trilogy. At the end of the match I began to get the distinct impression we were really beginning to tick them off.

The cup triumph must have given the side a real lift as we went on to, firstly, beat Chelsea 2-1 at Stamford Bridge, then defeat Nat Lofthouse's Bolton Wanderers 2-0 at home. At this point of the season we had climbed to comparative safety from relegation.

City's players and officials went in to the next round of the FA Cup in confident mood, especially since we had been drawn against second division Barnsley at home. A bumper crowd of 32,000 at Ninian Park that day saw a typical 'Mr Hyde' performance as we crashed out of the cup to an incredible last minute strike. As I mentioned earlier ... *consistency.*

A few days later came the lowest point in a season of low points. In the opening round of the Welsh Cup, a 3-3 draw with Welsh League minnows Haverfordwest caused manager Trevor Morris to, uncharacteristically, blow a gasket. Everyone sat quietly as Trevor leapt into a rant, turning the air blue with language you just did not associate with the boss. There were one or two chuckles mind you, when Trevor swung a boot at a plastic cup lying on the floor. He slipped on a little wintergreen on the hard floor and thumped down on his tail bone. He must have been in considerable pain, but didn't show it. Trevor dragged himself to his feet, struggling to hide the agony, and continued with his tirade as if nothing had happened. Fair enough ... he was spot on!

The one good thing to come out of the evening was Harry Kirtley playing in his first competitive match since breaking a leg in the final of the Welsh Cup the previous season. Harry also marked his comeback with a goal. Pity we hadn't won.

The return match at home turned into the rout that the first one should have been. We ran out 8-1 winners and a little much needed pride was restored. And Harry Kirtley managed to get on the scoresheet once again. I don't know exactly how, but I could sense that he was not the same player as before the leg break. Somehow, he didn't seem to have the same stomach for it.

Not long afterwards Harry Kirtley was on his way back north to sign for Gateshead. He spent three years there before he and Maureen decided they wanted to go back to Wales. Harry played a few games for Rhyl FC before settling down for good in North Wales. Margaret and I missed the Kirtleys for a good while after they left. Lovely people!

I was the only player to have featured in every game that season until the Haverfordwest replay match. I had good reason to miss the Welsh Cup tie as I'd been chosen again for the Scotland B team to play England B at St Andrew's, Birmingham on the same night.

Nightmare! The English caught us cold and we found ourselves 3-0 down after twenty-two minutes, eventually losing the match 4-1. A young centre-forward called Brian Clough would score the second goal, his one and only against me. He was a good player and, although I was mad that we'd taken a beating, Clough and I seemed to get on all right before, during and after that game.

Half a season later and I was to become absolutely determined not to let him score against me again, whether it be at football or tiddlywinks, and I'll tell you exactly why a little later on in the book.

Sandwiched between these matches we were on league duty again, losing narrowly at home against a good Birmingham side.

The following league match was at The Hawthorns and Gerry Hitchens and Colin Baker gave us a much needed 2-1 win over West Brom. This was one of our best performances of the season, as the Midlands side had come within a whisper of completing a historic league and cup double in 1953-54, eventually losing out to fierce rivals Wolves in a close run-in. One national newspaper at the time even suggested sending the entire West Brom team *en masse* to represent England at the World Cup in 1954! The '56-57 version was definitely going down the other side, but you could see they were still a formidable outfit.

Left-half Ray Barlow stood out for me that day. He was a cultured player with an exquisite touch and was to be a great servant to his club with nearly 500 appearances. I was up against the prolific Ronnie Allen who was to go on and score 234 goals in 458 games for the Baggies. Thankfully, Ronnie did not have his shooting boots on that day!

On a bright note Ron Howells returned for us between the sticks and had a good, solid match. Big Ronnie had started off the season as number one before sustaining a nasty injury, pre-season. The inspired form of Graham Vearncombe, Ronnie's deputy, had rightly kept him in the side for a few months, until Graham himself picked up a knock in training before the Haverfordwest replay. Whilst I felt sorry for young Vearncombe, I was also happy for my big pal Ronnie who had been itching to get a game since he'd recovered full fitness. If I had to pick who was the best goalie between the two? Well, to tell the truth, I couldn't. Both guys could be brilliant on their day, Vearncombe a better shot stopper and the taller Howells stronger on the cross ball. They were most definitely completely different characters, however, Ronnie coming across as a level-headed guy, while Graham was as daft as a brush! Yes, young Vearncombe had to be watched very closely during pre-season tours and the like! I'll cover some of these later in the book.

As well as we played at West Brom, this was balanced out by a dire showing at Leeds in the next game. We just didn't show up that day as the Yorkshiremen took full revenge for their recent cup exit. Mind you, at least I still managed to stop John Charles scoring once again, though it was scant consolation.

We played out a very creditable 2-2 draw against Wolves back at Cardiff in our next match. Once again, we managed to raise our game against one of the top teams and probably should have won on the day. Definitely a point dropped.

The following Wednesday we were to play Chester at home in the next round of The Welsh Cup. They were languishing in the lower reaches of the Football League's Third Division (North) and we were very confident of scoring a hatful of goals to progress easily. Right? Wrong! We crashed out 2-0. *Consistency!*

Blackpool were pushing Manchester United for the league title and we knew that we were in for a right tough time in our next match at Ninian Park. Of course, we had no Alf Sherwood this time, and I remember chuckling at Ron Stitfall when he just happened to mention about a hundred times that he was to be in direct opposition to a certain Stanley Matthews. I believe Ron tried every dodge in the book in the run up to the game. Early on in the week he would wander around, one sock and training shoe in hand, complaining about an ankle knock or something and wanting treatment. When that didn't work Ron had a wee quiet word with Ron Davies who was to play right-back about maybe swapping sides for the game. One thing Davies wasn't was daft, and Stitfall was swiftly told where to go.

I recall a similar incident during an international match played in the early 1970s between Northern Ireland and Scotland. A young man by the name of George Best was playing on the right wing and lined up directly opposite Celtic's Tommy Gemmell. Unfortunately for Tommy, Best was destined to play one of his finest games for his country and he gave the big man a right going over in the first-half. The story goes that when they got in at half-time, Tommy begged, pleaded even, with left-back Eddie MacCreadie to swap sides with him for the second period. Now Eddie couldn't be described as the quickest footballer in the world, but he certainly wasn't slow in telling Tommy where to get off. Mercifully, George must've taken pity on the big man and eased off a bit in the second-half. I remember watching the match on TV at the time and recalled remarking on the wide smile on Tommy Gemmell's face – especially since Scotland had lost the match – as he trudged off the park at the end. It was to emerge later that the look was one of pure relief that it was all over! In a newspaper interview Tommy gave after the match he revealed to the media that he considered George Best to be the greatest player he had ever seen. It was hard to argue with his prognosis. I was of the same opinion until fairly recently, and the emergence of a diminutive genius called Lionel Messi.

Against Blackpool we were desperately unlucky to lose 4-3 in an enthralling match notable for the performance of Stanley Matthews. Ron Stitfall's nightmare became a reality as the great man gave him a bit of a chasing. Although the whole team has got to carry the can for a defeat, I felt, rightly or wrongly, that I had played my part as I managed to stop goal machine Jackie Mudie from scoring. Not every centre-half could have made the claim at the end of that particular season, Jackie hitting the net an impressive 32 times in the league alone.

Boss Trevor Morris didn't quite see it my way and ripped into every one of us at the end. The pressure certainly was beginning to tell on the manager, and it seemed the harder we tried for him, the worse the results got. Trevor was a gem of a man who, in my view at least, had simply lost his appetite for the game. It didn't stop him really hacking me off the following season, however, as I'll tell you later.

Although City were sitting down in the bottom half of the table in early March, we were still confident of edging into the top reaches by the end of the season. Looking at the eleven remaining matches, in nine of them we would be up against sides close to us in the table. Villa (twice), Manchester City, Charlton (they were firmly rooted at the bottom), Sunderland, Luton Town, Everton and Portsmouth (twice) would surely provide us with enough points to steer our way out of trouble. Two of our last three games – all of them at home – were against high-flying Spurs and eventual champions, Manchester United. The lads were confident that safety would be secured well before these final games would roll around.

How wrong we were! In classic Cardiff, self destruct style we proceeded to lose our next three games before drawing against Sunderland at Roker Park. A slim 1-0 victory over Villa again gave us some hope, before two goalless draws against Luton and Everton plunged us deeper into relegation territory. We steeled ourselves for a fighting finish, but a mixture of pure loss of form and downright rotten luck managed to seal our fate.

City lost all four remaining fixtures to slip to second bottom – three points behind Sunderland – and relegation to Division Two.

Season 1957 – 58

26th June, 1957 was when Margaret and I celebrated the safe arrival of our son, Andrew. Despite the elation of the moment, the pain and frustration following the club's drop to the second tier of English football seemed to hang around me like a bad smell. To a man every player at the club felt that we should never have gone down; that we were too good to have taken the drop. I kind of harboured that thought as well for a while, until one morning I looked in the mirror and realised there was a fraudster staring back at me. Who were we kidding? We were in the second division and we deserved to be there. We had let everyone at the club down, the supporters, the manager, the coaches, the office staff; everyone.

Understandably, the morale among the squad was at an all-time low and it was clear that things had to change in order for us to get into gear for the coming season. The former Cardiff and Wales winger, George Edwards, joined the board of directors and Bill Jones – ex-Worcester City player and Barry Town boss – was appointed to City's coaching staff prior to the start of the new season.

On the playing side we brought in former England centre-forward Johnny Nicholls from West Brom. Johnny had scored a barrow load of goals for the Baggies, but unfortunately, couldn't reproduce this form for Cardiff, scoring just twice in eight games. Six months later he was to move to Exeter for a couple of seasons, being forced to retire through injury at the ridiculously young age of twenty-eight.

Wrexham's Ron Hewitt, an inside-forward, also signed up along with mercurial Newport winger Colin 'Rock' Hudson.

On the debit side I was sorry to see my good friends and near neighbours Harry Kirtley (Gateshead) and Johnny McSeveney (Newport) leave the club. Harry had been a regular in the side until his tragic leg break during the previous season's Welsh Cup Final. He had tried really hard to come back a couple of times towards the end of the last campaign, but it was clear to me that he was still feeling the injury. I believe if he had been playing today, modern technology and procedures would have fixed him up good as new. You merely have to recall horrific injuries suffered by some players in modern times which, fifty and sixty years ago, would certainly have ended their careers; players such as Henrik Larsson (Celtic), Eduardo and Cardiff lad Aaron Ramsey (both Arsenal) and Antonio Valencia (Manchester United).

I was to witness another horrendous leg break a couple of seasons later involving a very promising young City player, Steve Gammon. I will cover this in more detail later in the book.

I recall speaking at length with Trevor Morris when it became clear that wee Johnny McSeveney was to be part of a deal which included Neil O'Halloran and Cecil Dixon also being transferred to Newport County in return for Colin Hudson coming the other way. I thought that we'd miss Johnny's energy as well as his goals. My fellow Scot had chipped in with a good few goals (fourteen in his last season) during his time at Ninian Park and I told the manager that, in my view, it would be a mistake letting him go. Trevor took my comments on board ... and sold McSeveney anyway. That decision was to come back and haunt him before too long.

There were another couple of additions to the playing staff at the start of the 1957-58 season; a young Glaswegian called Johnny Phillips and a twenty-two-year-old defender signed after a month's trial from my old junior club, Camelon FC. My kid brother Andy put pen to paper on a one-year deal as I watched on proudly.

It was fair to say that the move for my brother filled me with some trepidation. Don't get me wrong, Andy was a brilliant guy with a great love for life and I was genuinely pleased he was getting his chance at Cardiff. However, it wasn't the football that worried me. I knew how good a player Andy was, and I was sure if he got his head down and got stuck in, he'd do well. The only problem I could envisage, given that he was down in South Wales sharing the same digs as his new pal Johnny Phillips, was that my little brother was a mental case. Now by mental case I don't actually mean mental case. Maybe more of a tearaway would be closer to it. He'd always been the same, always would be. Anything for a laugh and a carry on. And, he was like ninety five per cent of young guys at that time – partial to the odd drink or two!

The Malloy family tended to be an outgoing bunch, no more so than my brother. He was always at his happiest as the life and soul of the party and became especially adept at story telling. He'd a great way with him around children and I'd marvel at how he'd hold their attention, telling tall tales of his exploits in Egypt during National Service.

Smith and Wellstood dressing shop, circa 1932. My old man, Andy, is in the middle row, far left. Can't believe how much he looks like a young Ernie Wise in this photo!

The Block Boys outside my grandfather's wee wooden shop. Guess who's hogging the football!

Gunner Malloy keeping an eye on some army cooks

An aerial duel with one of my idols, Lawrie Reilly of Hibs, during one of my first games for Dundee. We won 1-0

It was never a penalty ref! An early Dundee v Rangers match. I'm on the far right

A Spot the Ball competition? No, it's an early Dundee match. I'm third from the left

On your marks! Get set ... taking on my pal Albert Henderson at Dundee

Dundee goalie Bob Henderson races out to gather a cross. I make sure Hearts' centre Willie Bauld can't get on the end of it. Not an easy task

This was some Dundee side. Tommy Gallacher's far left, Doug Cowie's on my left shoulder and Bobby Flavell and Billy Steel are third and fourth at the front. Hard man coach Reggie Smith is on the far right

Game off at a snowbound Dens Park, but Bill Brown, Ronnie Turnbull and I soon find a use for the white stuff

That's how it's done!

A well timed tackle in my first ever game for Cardiff. We beat Charlton 3-1, co-debutant Neil O'Halloran stealing the show with a stunning hat-trick

25th March, 1955: Our wedding day. My brother James was best man. The cute wee girl front right is my niece, Diane

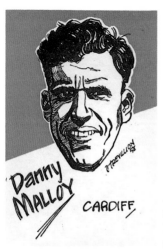

My pal, boxer Joe Erskine in typical pose. The man was not to be messed with!

A caricature of me from the 1950s. Not sure about the likeness

Me and the men with
moustaches enjoying a pint

Margaret receiving a Ninian Park shaped
cake from City director, Ron Becher. Don't
ask me why!

Derrick Sullivan, Derek Tapscott and
me showing the youngsters at Merthyr
how it's done

I guess they used to touch up the
photos even back then. Look at
my teeth!

Away at Aston Villa in 1959 and making
life difficult for Gerry Hitchens, my
former Cardiff City teammate

I watch on as my kid brother, Andy, signs on for manager Trevor Morris at Cardiff City

Keeping focussed on the opposition

Some of the guys enjoying a little down time. I look as if I'm going to tear Harry Kirtley's arm off for stealing my drink! Johnny McSeveney and Alf Sherwood are also in the pic

Pre-season in Jersey. The bottle's actually normal size – that's just pint-sized Johnny McSeveney having a 'quiet drink'

Getting ready to beat Leeds United again in the FA Cup. Three years in a row – third round away tie – 2-1 win each time

It's the Cardiff City FC promotion winning squad. And a fine bunch of lads they were

April 1960 and the aftermath of the 1-0 promotion winning match against Aston Villa in front of 54,000. That's me between the policemen. What an incredible atmosphere! Still gives me goosebumps

Cardiff v Spurs. I give goalie Ron Howells some assistance

That's me putting up a lucky horseshoe on the manager's door at Doncaster Rovers. It didn't work!

A typical Malloy wedding reception, circa 1973

Margaret and I on holiday in Corfu with my brother Andy and his wife, Hannah

Margaret and I at our son's wedding, circa 1984. Check out the brown shoes!

Andy had survived more than his fair share of scrapes over the years back in Scotland. He was as hard as nails, even as a youngster. I know I had built up a reputation as a hard man but Andy was on another planet!

A million years ago, back home in Longcroft, Andy and I were outside playing when he fell through a gap in a stairwell at our home and landed on his head. There was blood everywhere. I remember screaming, patting his cheek to try and bring him round. My brother had an enormous bump, high on the forehead. My blood ran cold. I thought he was dead. He was three-years-old and, even though I was only seven at the time, I remember vividly the visit from the doctor. I remember the worried looks and the tears of our parents and of our sisters who were that bit older and more aware of the seriousness of the situation. No fancy scans and x-rays in the thirties. It was a matter of waiting, and praying.

My wee brother was unconscious and the senior members of the family took turns sitting at his bedside. Not that anybody got much sleep that night.

The sun shone high in the sky the next morning, higher than normal, or maybe it just seemed that way. Everyone had fallen asleep through exhaustion. The star of the show's eyelids flickered, the bright blue eyes shone, and a wide smile framed the tiny face. 'Mam. I'm hungry,' he piped up.

I had already given Andy the long lecture about behaving himself at Cardiff City. To his credit he'd listened to me, agreed to be the model professional. I had done my bit, could do no more. It was up to him.

A couple of months passed with little incident. I'd heard one or two little whispers of a rowdy night out in town involving half a dozen of the younger players. By all accounts my brother had been there, but my 'mole' told me it had been good natured. And, it *had* been a Saturday night. After all, most of the lads were young and single. Fair enough.

A couple of months later the weather had put paid to a game, and someone had the bright idea of organising a night out at the Conservative Club in Cardiff. City had received the call to submit a four man team to represent the club for the evening. None of the other players really wanted to go and somehow, my brothers Andy and Ian, Johnny Phillips and myself ended up heading for a smokers' evening among the posh set. It was just as well my old man was back in Scotland! As I'd mentioned earlier, like many of the ex-miners at that time, my father harboured strong communistic ideals and beliefs and wouldn't have been too pleased to hear that three of his sons were about to socialise with the devil's disciples!

A lifelong member of The Labour Party, my father was to get a real kick out of a press cutting from *The South Wales Echo* I sent to him a couple of years later.

We were travelling by coach for the short journey to play one of our closest neighbours, Bristol City. Just before we drew away from Ninian Park, a car pulled up into a space outside the main stand. The driver jumped out and ran across to the door of the bus. 'I'm sorry I'm late. Thanks for waiting on.' He spoke in a calm, clear voice as he climbed aboard; a politician's voice.

I was sitting about half way up the bus and was sure I heard our visitor mention my name. Next thing James Callaghan, Labour MP for Cardiff and diehard City fan, was asking the player sitting next to me, Derrick Sullivan, if he could have a word with me. A future British Prime Minister was about to shake my hand and tell me how much he admired my play. Apparently, I was his favourite player.

Mr Callaghan and I chewed the fat all the way to Bristol. We talked about everything from football to families, from politics to the price of fish. The thing that struck me about him on arrival at Bristol was his vast knowledge. He seemed to be able to speak with authority about anything, and it was no surprise for me to hear that Jim Callaghan had attained the highest office in the land. He was a thoroughly decent man.

The night out at the Conservative Club went really well. At least for the most part! I was driving and had been drinking soft drinks. The others downed a few beers. We all made a point of mingling with the members and, generally, had a good time. I would say we'd done a bloody good bit of PR for Cardiff City. I should have known it was too good to last.

There was a small, tight car park around the back of the club, and when the night was over the world and its wife seemed to want to get out at the same time. Ian was in the passenger seat and Andy and Johnny were in the back. As we were trundling towards the exit, a car zoomed across from the left, half blocking our path. I slammed on the anchors and turned to look at the driver who was gesticulating that I should move back and let him through. I looked in the rear view mirror to see that there was a line of around twelve cars behind us. The next car was so tight to us that I couldn't possibly move back. I indicated to him that I had nowhere to go. As there was room behind him, I waved my hands to suggest that he reverse. I couldn't believe it when he rolled his window down and began to swear at us. Ian wound down our passenger window and explained that if he shifted back a bit, we could get out and then he could easily follow. The only explanation I could think of was that this idiot was a Swansea fan or something as he launched into a foul mouthed tirade, spouting on about 'effing Scotsmen' and 'they think they effing own the place.'

The people in the cars behind us began leaning on their horns in frustration. I got out and shrugged my shoulders. I couldn't go anywhere. I sat on the bonnet of the car, folded my arms and began to laugh. Unfortunately, this made our friend even worse as he really began to lose it, big time. Ian and I then walked over to his car and I leaned on the door as I spoke to him. 'Get your hands off my car!' he barked. I laughed again. It was insane. I walked away, shrugging at the people waiting behind.

I looked into the back seat of my car. Oh no! It was empty. The next thing I heard was a familiar phrase from a very familiar source. 'Let me have a word with him.'

'No! Andy, wait!' I shouted.

Too late. A huge fist flew in the guy's window catching him flush on the side of the face. The impact bounced him right into the passenger seat. To the guy's credit, he recovered enough to slither back across to shout something else. Bang! Another right jab shut him up for the night as he slumped down in his seat.

It was mayhem. Everyone got out of their cars and strode over to investigate. The front door of the club burst open and some men appeared brandishing bottles and glasses. We got the feeling they weren't exactly going to invite us in to have a farewell drink! I glanced over at Andy. He was in the process of taking his jacket off and rolling up his shirt sleeves. I had to act fast to avoid big trouble. I shot forward. 'Wait! Just hold it!' I shouted. 'We don't want trouble here! This man,' I pointed at the still unconscious individual, 'he was well out of order. Just ask the other guys here.'

Thankfully, two or three of them agreed with me and we somehow managed to get out unscathed with a venomous, 'don't ever darken our doorstep again' message ringing in our ears. As if! God knows what would have happened if I hadn't been able to play in the next game because of a good hiding.

Next morning I was heading for the dressing room to get changed for training when I got a shout from coach Ernie Curtis saying that Trevor Morris wanted a word with me in his office. I was a little confused when Ernie patted me on the back on the way past and muttered, 'Good for you, Danny.' I can only assume Ernie was a Labour man, like my father.

'Danny, I got a call this morning from the secretary of the Conservative Club,' Trevor said.

'I can explain, boss.' I replied, cutting him off.

'I'm disappointed, Danny. This is not how I'd expect one of our players to behave. Remember, anything you do or say here, you're representing the club.'

'I know, boss. It's just that, well, the man was out of order. He was being totally unreasonable.'

'That may well be the case but there's never an excuse for fisticuffs. Never solves anything.'

'No, I suppose not. I'm sorry for what happened.' I decided to leave it at that and take my medicine.

'Luckily enough, they're not pressing the issue. They're going to let it go.'

'That's good.'

'We were lucky. Now if it had hit the papers. Well, you know what the press are like? They would've had a field day.'

I nodded.

'I want you to go and apologise to your brother Andy and Johnny Phillips. After all, it's a bad example to set the youngsters.'

'Eh?' I said, puzzled.

'Yeah, do it, Danny. Then we'll forget about it.' He waved me away.

'So you've spoken to them already, boss?' I said.

'Yes, your brother was in at the crack of dawn. He's really keen. I like that. He couldn't wait to tell me what happened. He said I shouldn't be too hard on you though, as there was a great deal of provocation. I think he deserves a lot of credit for the way he stuck up for you.'

'Oh I'll see him about it all right, boss. In fact, I'll make a point of it!'

I reached the dressing room just in time to see Andy and Johnny sprint out the door. The walk to the training ground gave me some time to think. I suppose Andy had no choice. If he'd owned up he may have been on his way out of the club that morning. He must have figured that, since I'd been at the club for a couple of years, I'd get away with it. I suppose it all worked out well in the end.

Andy never played for the first team and left to head back up the road at the end of the season. He was bitterly disappointed and felt that he was never given a chance. I agreed with him, not because he was my brother, but I believed that he should have been given a shot. I think he would have made an excellent right-back for City at that time. He was quick, strong and sure-footed. If he had been playing nowadays I'm sure he would have got his chance coming off the bench. That was the problem in those days, no substitutes.

Andy left football soon after that and made his living as a lorry driver. He married Hannah late in life before tragically contracting throat cancer in his early fifties. He passed away on 2nd December, 1989, with his family at his bedside.

*****

The only good thing about dropping to the second division, as far as I could see, was that we would meet our arch rivals Swansea in a league match for the first time in quite a few years.

First up on a sun soaked Ninian Park on 24th August, 1957 were ... Swansea! More than 42,000 fans crammed in that day to witness a real bore of a game. Hudson, Hewitt and Nicholls all made their debuts in a flat 0-0 draw.

The next three games only yielded a solitary point against Grimsby, Johnny Nicholls grabbing a goal in a 1-1 draw. The previous game against Liverpool at Anfield had resulted in a 3-0 loss and had begun a rather unenviable series of own goals attributed to a certain Scottish centre-half!

Seriously, I always thought it grossly unfair that the record books at that time would credit an o.g. against the defender if the ball took even the slightest nick on the way past. A big part of the committed centre-half's game was to lunge in, to try and block any attempt on goal. I doubt if there was a bigger lunger or blocker in football at that time. That's my story and I'm sticking to it! I think I was credited with 14 o.g's. in total throughout my time at Cardiff, so you'll understand my wish to defend myself with something! And, at that time I was going through a rocky patch off the field as well as on it. Margaret and I were feeling a bit left out of things socially in Llanishen and, to tell the truth, I was hankering for a move up the road ... and quick. The team wasn't playing well, and I wasn't enjoying my football for the first time in my career.

As well as the own goals, I had taken a pretty severe knock on the ankle in the away game against Grimsby. I managed to soldier on against Liverpool but was then forced to pull out of the match at home to Middlesborough on 7th September. Big Alec Milne, a fellow Scot from Arbroath made his debut at left-back that day and, although he had a decent game, the team played poorly again, losing 2-0 in front of our smallest crowd for some time. Sitting helpless in the stand, I could feel the frustration of the fans as we stumbled towards the bottom of the division.

The young Middlesborough centre-forward impressed me that day. He was quick and skilful, good with either foot, and he gave our defence a tough time. Oh yes, he'd also managed to grab both goals! And, I'd played against him in a B international match at St Andrew's, Birmingham around seven months before. You'll recall that Brian Clough scored in a 4-1 win, his only goal against me.

After the match at Cardiff I met Clough in the club lounge and managed a quick word, congratulating him on an impressive performance. Again, he came across as a nice lad with good manners as he wished me well and hoped to see me in the return match in the northeast, early in the New Year. I looked forward to it.

In the next game we scraped through at home against Huddersfield by 1-0, in front of only 10,000. For me the game was more notable for the performance of a talented youngster, and future World Cup winner. Ray Wilson stuck out a mile at left-back for Huddersfield. What a player!

The lack of atmosphere was beginning to get to us and our form was suffering. The ankle was giving me serious gyp and I really should have declared myself injured after the match. Stubbornly, I decided to try and soldier on and we proceeded to lose four goals to Orient away in the next match.

I managed a word after the Huddersfield match with the irrepressible Bill Shankly, who had just taken over as manager. Bill was another old mate of Willie Thornton, my former boss at Dundee and the first thing that struck me about him was his enthusiasm for the game. He wasn't a man for small talk; didn't suffer fools gladly. Football was his life and I laughed when I later heard the famous saying attributed to him about the game being more important than life or death. That was Bill Shankly, no question. Surprisingly, Shanks had made a rather inglorious entrance into football management at unfashionable clubs, Carlisle and Grimsby, before taking over at Huddersfield. His later arrival at Liverpool was widely regarded as *the* defining moment in the recent history of the club, the catalyst that would rocket the Merseysiders into the upper echelons of European football. Shankly and his famous 'boot room' trio of Reuben Bennett, my old assistant coach at Dundee, and future Liverpool managers, Bob Paisley and Joe Fagan, were to change the face of English and European football forever.

All Bill Shankly could do that day was talk about a puny, bespectacled kid from Aberdeen the previous regime at Huddersfield had signed as a fifteen-year-old. The lad was now seventeen and had just had a bad squint corrected. He looked as if he'd blow away on a gentle breeze. He had made his debut in the first team the previous season and was already being tipped by Shankly for great things. Thankfully, the Huddersfield hierarchy had decided that they should go easy on a young Denis Law and I would not have to play against him for a while.

An undistinguished 1-1 draw in the return match at Huddersfield was followed by a 3-0 reverse at home against Charlton who had finished bottom below us in the First Division the previous season.

Still I insisted on playing on through the injury. Some days I could hardly walk between games, and had to endure pain killing injections prior to the next match. Not good! The words of Billy Steel at Dundee would come back to me every time the trainer was poised with the needle: 'you'll never know the damage you're doing.'

The team recovered enough to scrape a 1-0 win away at Doncaster, Ron Davies hitting the winner. I felt I had played better and the ankle seemed a little stronger. At least I could walk out of the ground after the match. I began to think maybe we were turning the corner. Thank God! Now all I could think of was getting the head down and pushing up the table. It was still early in the season and there was plenty of time to recover our position. Hell, we were in the top division last season. Teams should be apprehensive about facing us.

The next match was at home against Rotherham United and was one which we should have won easily. Brian Walsh and Ron Hewitt, from the penalty spot, gave us a two goal lead. The crowd was warming to us, especially those in the Bob Bank. Even the weather was kind that day. All we had to do was play out the game. We were comfortable, cruising to the finishing line when a late Rotherham goal ensured a nervy last few minutes. Then in the ninetieth minute a harmless cross ball came into our penalty area. I got into a bit of a fankle with goalie Graham Vearncombe, and the ball broke to the Rotherham centre who stroked the ball into the net. The whistle blew for full-time and other City players leapt in as Graham and I had a real verbal set-to. I felt it was his ball to clear and told him so in no uncertain terms. Graham obviously felt differently and also said his piece. By the time we got to the dressing room all was forgotten and we were pals again. Manager Trevor Morris saw it neither way and ripped into both of us! The pressure was really mounting on the boss. We really did want to do well for him but the harder we tried ...

Gerry Hitchens had suffered a lean spell until then, missing a couple of games through injury. He scored the first in our next match at home against the highly fancied, Derby County. We played our best match of the season, beat them 3-2, and my ankle held up fine. Onwards and forwards!

I walked into Ninian Park the following Monday for training feeling better than I had done in a while. On the way to the physiotherapy room, I passed a familiar looking guy in the corridor. He was wearing a sharp suit and nodded at me on the way past. I only realised who it was as I reached the physio's room. Last I knew, Welsh International centre-half Ray Daniel, had been a Sunderland player. Obviously things had changed. My heart sank to my feet. I swear to you I felt a searing twinge in my ankle as I pushed open the physio's door.

'Danny!' A voice called out from the end of the corridor. It was Trevor Morris. 'Can I have a word?'

Trevor called me into his office. I limped along the corridor and shut the door behind me.

'What's happening, boss?' I asked.

'You've just made the decision easy for me, son.' He pointed at my foot. 'I know you've been struggling with the ankle for a good while now. I want you to go and see a specialist and get it cleared up.'

I told Trevor I appreciated his concern, but that the ankle was fine and I could play on, no problem. He was forced to tell me he was leaving me out of the next match at Bristol Rovers. Ray Daniel would play at number five and that was the end of it.

I didn't travel with the team to Bristol that day, but by all accounts we did well, Gerry Hitchens notching both goals in a 2-0 win.

For the first time in ages I spent my Saturday afternoon at home with my feet up. I had gone to see the specialist the day before and he reckoned that all I had to do was rest the ankle for a few weeks. They'd taken a series of x-rays just in case, but the experts did not expect to unveil anything sinister.

Margaret had taken the opportunity to bail out to the shops for a break from our wee boy. Andrew was a happy kid all right, but he didn't sleep too well and many a time I'd have to kip down in the spare room to get some rest before a big game.

As luck would have it the little toe-rag conked out a few minutes after Margaret had left, and I spent the afternoon with an ear pressed against the radio trying to find out the scores. I was sitting back quite happily after I heard we'd won the match at Bristol when I suddenly remembered that there was the little matter of a cup final back home in Scotland – an Old Firm League Cup Final. I fiddled around with the knob of the radio until I picked up a crackly report on the match. Just for a moment I thought I'd heard the commentator mention Celtic had won by seven goals to one! Couldn't be! I shook my head, fiddled around again with the knob. As I turned the blasted thing around, the reception improved slightly. I leaned down, my ear resting against the small speaker: '... Willie Fernie grabbed the ball from hat trick hero Billy McPhail and slammed the penalty kick home to record a famous win by an incredible seven goals to one. Former Queens Park centre-half John Valentine had a shocker for Rangers, culpable for at least five of the goals ...'

I sank back in my chair, heaved a huge sigh. As I'd mentioned earlier, I was a big Gers fan and it really hurt when they lost, especially to their biggest rivals. 7-1. Not so much a loss. More a total annihilation!

I decided to take the wee guy for a short walk to the local park early on the Sunday morning. The ankle felt good. Whether it would have held up to the intense rigours of another football match, who knows? It looked increasingly unlikely that I was going to get the chance to test it, at least not for a few weeks. The specialist had estimated the length of absence in weeks rather than days. One thing was sure – I was going to have plenty of time to contemplate life. I guided the pram through the park gates and sat on a little wooden bench feeling decidedly sorry for myself. My mind began to drift away to my friends and family back in Scotland. I glanced at my watch. 8am. I wondered if my mother would be standing at her usual place in front of the stove, preparing to dish up breakfast to the multitude. It always amazed me how she managed to scrape up enough to feed everyone in the house. And feed them well at that! Mind you, my old man was well liked in the local community and we used to get all kinds of visitors bearing all kinds of gifts in return for a cup of hot, steaming tea and a piece of delicious, home made apple pie. Many a time the smell of gutted trout lying on plates on the draining board and 'curing' flesh from the carcasses of snared rabbits hanging upside down, swinging back and forth on door handles, would almost knock you off your feet!

I smiled as I recalled my mother standing by the sink, expertly gutting and disembowelling animals; a mother, like many others of that era, who would do anything for her family. I still miss her every day.

I suppose I was experiencing my first real bout of home sickness since our move from Scotland. I'd had a couple of pangs before then, but Margaret's positive attitude had helped me get through them. She was the type who could adapt to almost any situation. She was much stronger than I could ever be. And she'd made a couple of great friends along the way. Harry Kirtley and his wife Maureen had been a breath of fresh air for both of us. They had lived just a few doors away but their recent departure had left a bit of a social void in our lives. At least wee Johnny McSeveney and his family still lived nearby, Newport County taking over Cardiff City's lease on their house in Solva Avenue. Apparently, he'd only agreed to join City's near-neighbours as long as he was allowed to stay in the same house.

Margaret became very friendly with a local lass who lived in the very shadow of Ninian Park. Joan Richards was a fanatical City supporter who first met Margaret at the popular Victoria Park Club in Canton. The two of them were of a similar age, got talking, and liked each other's company. Not only that, Joan's parents Harold and Wyn were also smashing people who ended up taking a real shine to our son. Despite his mischievous habit of trying to flush Joan's high heeled shoes down the toilet, she happily agreed to be godmother to Andrew.

The wee boy also made quite an impression on the couple who lived next door to us in Solva Avenue. Joan and Alec Fraser had no children of their own. Joan was a primary teacher and Alec worked in a senior position as a tax inspector for the Inland Revenue. They were a lovely couple and became really good friends to both of us. Andrew must also have burrowed his way into the heart of the lady he would constantly refer to as 'Mrs Joan.' I well remember her floods of tears and smothering cuddles when it was time for us to move on. Joan and Alec had relatives in the north of Scotland, and for years afterwards they would appear from time to time on their way to visiting those relatives.

I was just getting ready to leave the house for the ground the following Monday morning when the phone rang. My heart raced when I heard a familiar voice. It was Willie Allison, chief sports writer with the *Daily Record* in Scotland. I'd met Willie a few times when I was with Dundee. He was one of the good guys.

'Danny, I'm glad I caught you,' he said, 'don't know if you saw the Rangers result at the weekend?' He sounded really pissed off. I knew Willie was a big Rangers fan and I drew in a sharp breath as I'd an idea where this was going.

'Aye. I heard. Bit of a disaster, eh?' I tried to sound calm.

'Disaster's an understatement! Heads are going to roll.'

'Scot Symon?' My heart sank a little as I knew Symon fancied me as a player. I'd heard from a reliable source that he'd enquired about me a couple of times when I was in Scotland. I figured if Symon had been sacked, I would have to wait until a new man with new ideas took over. But then, why the phone call?

'No. Symon's okay. For now at least. The league title win last season saved him. The players are carrying the can for this. The goalie, Billy Ritchie, is on his last legs. And do you know the big centre-half, John Valentine?'

Here we go!

'No. I've never heard of him.'

'They signed him from Queen's Park. That cup final was his first game, and last, by all accounts.'

'A bit unfair, isn't it?'

'That's the way it goes when you play for the Old Firm. Old man Lawrence has told Symon that Valentine never plays for the team again.'

John Lawrence was the businessman owner of the Ibrox club.

'That's too bad,' I said. I really did feel sorry for John Valentine, the man I'd never met. It was bad enough playing centre-half or goalkeeper with a provincial team. Play for a huge outfit such as Rangers and every single move you make is scrutinised and criticised. To lose seven goals is bad enough in any team, but when you play for Rangers it can be career threatening. Valentine was obviously going to pay the ultimate price. Billy Ritchie had survived by the skin of his teeth.

I always thought it unfair that, more often than not, these two positions should be held culpable in the loss of any goal. Heaven forbid the blame should land at the full-back skinned by a speed merchant of a winger. Picture the scenario: the winger hits the line, swings a perfect ball into the middle for a battering ram of a centre-forward; the centre nips into the area between the goalie and centre-half and bursts the net with a header. Who's to blame? Ninety nine times out of a hundred, it's the goalie and/or centre-half. 'Caught sleeping,' they'd say! What about the full-back? Didn't he get caught sleeping? Annoying!

'Anyway, I'll not keep you, Danny,' Willie continued, 'would you be interested in joining Glasgow Rangers?'

I walked into Ninian Park pain free that day, as if there had been a great weight lifted from my shoulders. Of course I'd told Willie Allison that I'd walk to Ibrox, if that's what it took. After all, Cardiff didn't want me anymore. At least that was the view I was forming in my mind. They'd bought another centre-half. Good luck to them. And, as I explained earlier, I was feeling homesick at that time.

On the way to the ground that day another thought thudded home. After our match at Old Trafford the previous season, I'd bumped into Walter Winterbottom, the England manager at the time. He was standing in the corridor outside the away dressing room talking to the United manager, Matt Busby. Mr Busby called me over to meet him and, as we made small talk, Mr Winterbottom asked me what in hell the Scotland selectors were playing at. As I stood, bemused, he went on to explain that if I had been English, he would have me in his team.

I muttered something about the centre-half berth for the national team always being occupied by players from the Old Firm before thanking him for his kind words.

I had turned his words over and over in my mind. It was true. I had played very well at times. I was used to getting good press, and had felt on many occasions that I had been unfairly overlooked. Yes, I had made the Scotland squads in past years, but since I'd moved to Cardiff, I'd been a perennial outsider when it came to international selection. If I was in the Rangers team, doing well, I was convinced I'd be a racing cert for Scotland. It was a no-brainer! I just had to go.

I walked right into Trevor Morris's office and gave it to him straight. I didn't see it as a great problem. I was certain that Cardiff would not stand in my way.

I tried to forget about it over the next few days and leave the clubs to come to an agreement. Willie Allison called daily to give me regular updates on the situation. Each time he said the talks were going along smoothly, and just to be patient. There was nothing else I could do anyway. I'd done my bit at the Cardiff end, stated my case firmly and succinctly. Trevor had been left in no doubt as to where I wanted to be.

Finally, on the Friday afternoon, Willie Allison called for the last time. He dropped the bombshell. He was really nice about it, but it was still a bombshell, nevertheless. He said the power brokers at Cardiff had been really sticky about the fee; that they'd paid £17,500 for me less than two years before; that they reckoned I was at my peak (I was twenty-six) and a highly sought after, prized asset; that, in their view, I was worth over thirty grand and if the Ibrox club really wanted me, that's what they would have to fork out!

They'd scared Rangers off. Willie went on to inform me that, earlier in the day, Rangers had made a simple phone call to St Mirren and pinched Willie Telfer for a fraction of the cost.

I was straight on the phone to Trevor Morris, blowing my top in the process. He explained that the decision on the fee had come directly from the moneymen. He apologised, said something about being glad I was still there, and that he wanted me back in the team as soon as possible. He said there'd always be a place for me in his team. I hung up on him, immediately feeling that I shouldn't have, and called back, apologising.

Everything was fine between us from that point on. Trevor asked me to cool my heels for a few weeks and take a well earned rest while I recuperated.

I actually met Willie Telfer a few months later on a visit to Scotland. He had known all about Rangers' interest in me and told me how sorry he was that it hadn't worked out. Then he went into some detail about how he was absolutely loving life at Ibrox! It wasn't meant to be said in a gloating sort of way, but at the same time, it wasn't exactly what I wanted to hear. At least Willie was a good guy, and I did feel pleased for him.

Over the next couple of weeks I received two other phone calls. The jungle drums were beating loud and clear to all and sundry that I was unhappy in South Wales.

Firstly, Davie Shaw, boss at Aberdeen FC, made a tentative enquiry about my availability. I hit that one on the head almost right away as I was not a big fan of the club. Maybe it was a Dundee thing, but I immediately felt I would be letting the Dens fans down by signing for their bitterest of rivals. It was a non-starter.

The second enquiry a week later did make my pulse quicken. Blackpool FC were a great side with fantastic players. They'd been pipped at the final hurdle by Manchester United the previous season and they were firmly back in the mix this campaign. Stanley Matthews had written favourably about me in his newspaper column, and I was already sold on a move. I went as far as running the idea past Margaret. She was also genuinely excited at the prospect of moving to the seaside. I told Blackpool I would be happy to talk to them. Both sides had a productive meeting and, once again, I sat back and allowed the clubs to, hopefully, settle on a fee.

This time I was careful not to build my hopes up too much. It was just as well as Cardiff again scuppered the move with their excessive demands. It looked as if I would be staying in Wales, at least for the time being.

On the pitch we managed to beat Lincoln at home by the odd goal in five. It was a decent performance, no more, and we would have to up our game if we were going to make an impression against the better teams. For me it was agony going to a match and not taking part. At least in the early days at Dundee I was playing games for the reserves. All I could do was make sure the manager was aware of me at training every day, make sure he could feel me itching to get back in action. My ankle was getting stronger, almost by the minute. I just had to wait for my chance to get back in. It would come. I had to be patient, again.

The next two games were away from home, against Notts County and Stoke City, two days later on the Monday. They were two potential banana skins and I felt that if we were to mount a serious challenge, we would have to take something from them. I decided not to travel with the team, and took the time off to spend with my family. Andrew was, by that time, nearly five months old and he was really beginning to become aware of his surroundings. I had been so used to playing on a Saturday that I'd forgotten there was life away from football. I don't think Margaret was too enamoured with having me around so much, though! She'd worked out her own routine and the last thing she wanted was to have some idiot moping around feeling sorry for himself.

I'd found out from a BBC sports report on the Saturday night that City had lost 5-2 at Notts County. It was only a very brief report (no Sky Sports in 1957) but I managed to catch enough to realise that we were fortunate to get away with losing only five. Brayley Reynolds and Johnny Nicholls scored our goals.

The lads stayed over in a Midlands hotel between matches before facing Stoke City on the Monday evening. A 3-0 reverse would make the journey back to Cardiff a depressing one.

The team was given the Tuesday off to recover and it was back to training first thing on the Wednesday morning. I had a quick word with Ray Daniel on the training pitch and it was clear to me that he was feeling a bit under pressure. Graham Vearncombe also seemed to be a little uptight. Little did he know he was heading for a spell on the sidelines, substitute keeper Ken Jones poised to take over for the foreseeable future. It was just as I'd said, 'Goalkeepers and centre halves.'

Trevor Morris called me into his office at the end of that session and told me he'd be bringing me back on the Saturday. At last! We were due to play one of our bogey teams at Ninian Park. Ipswich Town always seemed to cause City problems. And Sheffield United. This particular season was shaping up as if it would add a few more to the list.

The real bombshell came on the morning of the Ipswich match. The teamsheet was always pinned up on the wall just inside the dressing room, and I sauntered in and did a triple take, when I saw the line-up. Trevor Morris had kept his word. Oh, I was in the team all right. At inside-right!

Ray Daniel had expected to be dropped following a couple of poor results and everybody assumed that I would slot right back in at centre-half. Don't get me wrong, I've already made my feelings known about the position. I never liked it, and much preferred the wing-half role. I'd had two or three games at right-half the previous season, covering injuries, and I thought I'd done okay. And I'd played at centre-forward a few times for Dundee reserves. But this was different, a big step up in class. I wasn't prone to suffering greatly from nerves, but I must admit I felt a right few flutters in the run up to that match.

I recently heard the former Scottish defender, Gordon McQueen, being interviewed on the radio, and he described how badly he suffered with nerves before every single match he played. In fact the nerves were so bad Gordon would have to run to the toilet to throw up in the moments before taking the field. That day, before the Ipswich game, I certainly felt one or two rumbles.

Luckily for me, a big, burly inside-left by the name of Joe Bonson had only recently arrived at the club from Wolves, and he was to make his debut. A bit selfish on my part I know, but I hoped all eyes would be on the newbie to divert some of the pressure. I had played against Joe once when he was at Wolves and remembered him as a bit of a handful, so I was glad I was on his side.

Bonson had been bought to replace Johnny Nicholls who'd moved to Exeter after a disappointing stint at Ninian Park. Big Joe was a gem of a guy who was to later go on and form a formidable partnership with a certain Derek Tapscott. Admittedly, Joe and Tappy weren't the greatest players in the world, but they could do that most important thing during a game of football. Both could stick the ball in the net. I'll describe some of Tappy's exploits later on in the book.

In an all change line-up, injured centre Gerry Hitchens would make way for usual inside-right, Ron Hewitt. I can't recall the match in great detail, but I do remember the sense of apprehension in the stadium prior to kick off. My fitness levels were well down due to the recent lack of action and I felt the game kind of passing me by. We looked shaky at the back and were lucky to go in at the interval only one goal down.

Thankfully, Trevor Morris agreed with my personal analysis and decided to reshuffle the team for the second-half. I went to centre-half with Ray Daniel shifting to left-half. Derrick Sullivan, who had started the match at number six, slipped in easily at inside-right and, as a result, the team looked a lot more balanced. We should have won in the end, but still managed a creditable 1-1 draw, Joe Bonson scoring on his debut. Unfortunately, with about five minutes to go, I took a hefty kick on the ankle and hobbled off at the final whistle. Oh no!

An hour later I could hardly move my foot. Great! I was just back in the team. It didn't look good. I had a week to get myself fit again for the trip to Blackburn Rovers. It was going to be a race against time.

By the Thursday of that week my ankle was still sore and swollen and I knew that I was not going to make Saturday's game at Blackburn. The next target would be the following match, at home against Sheffield United. I had more than a whole week to recover and felt confident of turning out.

It was more family and recuperation time while waiting for the score from Blackburn to come over the BBC radio waves. A hefty 4-0 thumping would prove to be Ray Daniel's last outing for the club. He had played only six games. Not long afterwards he moved to his home town of Swansea.

My return to the team would be on the 23rd of November, 1957, and from then until the May of 1960, I was to miss just one more match.

I had a huge lump in my throat when the Cardiff fans gave me a tremendous reception before the Sheffield United match. I felt I played my best game of the season thus far, as we managed to keep a clean sheet for the first time in a while. Unfortunately, we couldn't score either, but at least we were back on the right track.

A creditable 1-1 draw against West Ham United at Upton Park followed, with Joe Bonson on the mark once again.

Our next match was at Ninian against the team that had put paid to our FA Cup aspirations the previous season, Barnsley. In front of our smallest crowd of the season to date, we gained no small measure of revenge, absolutely annihilating them 7-0. Inside-forward Cliff Nugent bagged a brilliant hat trick as we finally reproduced some of our first division form.

Gerry Hitchens was unwell and didn't play that day. We didn't know it at the time, but Hitch was being tracked by a host of clubs, including Aston Villa and, with Joe Bonson coming in and looking the part, the Cardiff hierarchy decided to ease some of their money troubles by listening to offers for the big centre. Our next match, at Fulham, was to be Gerry's last game for the club, Villa nabbing their man for a hefty fee of £22,500. He was a popular lad with everyone at the club and we were all sorry to see him go, but of course, wished him well.

I followed Gerry's career with interest after that, and wasn't surprised to see him hit the heights at Villa and later in Italy with high profile clubs such as Inter and Torino. The big striker also played a number of times with England, most notably at the World Cup in Chile in 1962. Tragically, Gerry was to pass away at the ridiculously young age of 48, during a charity football match in 1983.

Incidentally, a young player by the name of Johnny Haynes played inside-forward for Fulham that day, and capped a fine performance with a great goal as we were unfortunate in going down 2-0. Former BBC pundit Jimmy Hill also scored against us at Craven Cottage, and appeared in our dressing room as we were getting ready to take the train back home.

Jimmy had just become chairman of the PFA, and was in to try and get us to agree to a small deduction from our wages to help the organisation tackle some of the injustices in the game. The maximum wage of £20 per week was still in operation at that time, and Jimmy became a fervent campaigner to have this abolished. He finally succeeded in 1961, England International and Fulham teammate Haynes becoming the first footballer to earn £100 per week following the lifting of the ban.

Colin Hudson became an instant hero with Bluebirds' fans by scoring the only goal of the game at rivals Swansea in our next match on December 21st. 'Rock's' strike ensured a satisfying Christmas break for both fans and players, and it gave us a springboard for our next couple of games before the turn of the year. Two home games on December 26th and 28th, against Stoke City and league leaders Liverpool, respectively, yielded an incredible eleven goals. Hudson hit the opening goal in both games, with Joe Bonson (four), and Brayley Reynolds (three), among the scorers as we steamrollered the opposition 5-2 and 6-1.

The day of the Liverpool match, 28th December, had certainly been a memorable one for both Colin Hudson and Alan Harrington. As well as helping the team hit the 'Pool for six, Colin also had time before the match to get married in his home town of Newport. Not a lot of time as it transpired, when he and best man Alan Harrington only just managed to get to Ninian Park in time for kick off.

The Cardiff crowds were definitely improving along with our form, over 30,000 attending the Liverpool match. The racket the fans made was deafening, and we felt as if we could have beaten any team in the world that day.

Despite our poor form at the start of the campaign, we had recovered to claim a top half position in the table, and we really felt that we could kick on to challenge for the promotion places. Time would tell!

The next match on 4th January was the third-in-a-row instalment in the FA Cup, away against Leeds United, John Charles and all. Same round; same draw; same score with Alan Harrington and Cliff Nugent edging us into the fourth round with a fine 2-1 win. The pitch was an absolute nightmare that day and the match would definitely have been called off nowadays. We were made of hardier stuff back then, the Elland Road ground staff simply rolling the snowbound pitch flat. The only thing was the surface ended up like a skating rink as the temperature dropped. Scary stuff! Thankfully, everyone came through without serious injury.

People still ask me today about certain events which took place during City's game against Middlesborough, at Ayresome Park, on 11th January, 1958. Although the fine details of the game are a little sketchy after so many years, I do recall the sequence of events that led up to the major talking point that day.

Our team line up was almost identical to the one that had hammered Liverpool, Cliff Nugent coming in for the injured Brayley Reynolds. We began the match full of confidence and when Brian Walsh gave us an early lead, I felt we would go on and win comfortably.

It had been almost a year since the B international match between England and Scotland, but the 4-1 drubbing was still fresh in my mind, and I was well aware of the threat Brian Clough would pose in the 'Boro attack. He and I had exchanged a couple of friendly words prior to kick off and I soon settled in to the match deciding, in my own inimitable style, to let him and his strike partner, Alan Peacock, know that they were in a match. Nothing dirty, hard but fair! It was, and still is, part and parcel of the game. The wind-ups, the off-the-ball stuff, the verbals – all good fun!

Two or three tackles later, and the moans began. Another couple of hefty challenges, and the moans changed to sly kicks and off-the-ball flicks. It was fine by me. As I've mentioned, I could serve it up, so was prepared to take some in return.

Just before we scored the opening goal, Alan Harrington and I were breaking up a 'Boro attack and I went to clear the ball up the pitch, when I got a shout from Alan. Clough went flying in to try and block my clearance, studs up, and I followed through, catching my shin on the sole of his boot. Luckily, I'd held back a bit after getting the shout from Alan and, after a little treatment, was as good as new. I could have broken a leg though, and told Clough in no uncertain terms that he'd crossed the line. I also went on to describe exactly what would happen to him the next time he came near me – out of earshot of the referee, of course! Clough's face turned chalk white and he shuffled off out my way.

I detested sly players, the ones who would put you out of the game without batting an eyelid. The rough and tumble types didn't bother me. At least you knew what you were getting with them.

Alan Peacock was given similar advice to that delivered to his strike partner, and suddenly it was game on! The insults were flying thick and fast, but as long as we were winning, I had the bragging rights. At least that was how I viewed the situation. It was a big mistake. I had somehow made it personal, and when one of our defenders got caught in possession, Peacock went on to rob him and slide the ball past goalkeeper Ken Jones. I don't really know why, but I went absolutely ballistic. The red mist descended like a thick army blanket, and when we lined up to restart the game, I heard Clough shout across to Peacock: 'We'll score a right few goals against this lot.'

That was it! I had to be physically restrained by a couple of the lads as the pair of them laughed. I was furious, but more at myself for getting sucked in. In hindsight, it was stupid and completely unprofessional.

Minutes later, I asked the bench how long there was to go until half-time. I received a few choice words from Trevor Morris before he told me. At least in a few minutes I would get back to the dressing room, take some deep breaths and calm myself down, before going back out to face the second-half in a healthier state of mind.

Peacock hadn't said a peep since he'd scored, but Clough was still mouthing off at every opportunity and when our goalkeeper cleared the ball up the other end, he turned to face me as I jogged out of the penalty box. Everybody on the pitch had followed the natural flight of the ball heading up the other end, and I felt this awful urge course through my body when I saw Clough edge towards me. I clenched my fist tightly as he leaned in to say something. He didn't even manage to utter a word as I swung a right hook, catching him flush on the point of his chin. Down he went like a ton of bricks.

A huge roar went up around the ground as I turned and carried on walking up the park. Unbelievably, none of the officials had seen it! The referee came up to me, told me that he knew what had happened, but as he couldn't prove it, he could do nothing. He went on to say that he would be keeping an eye on me for the rest of the match ... I shrugged and strolled back to get in position.

Meanwhile, the whistle sounds for half-time as Clough is eventually brought round by smelling salts. The crowd boo me for all they're worth as I trudge off, flanked by two burly policemen. In the corner of an eye I see some people try and jump the barrier, presumably to come and get me. Pandemonium!

If the game had been played these days, as well as receiving a hefty fine and a lengthy ban using television evidence, I would have been subbed for my own safety. No substitutes in those days, however, and I had no other choice than go out for the second-half. Peacock and Clough never uttered another word for the rest of the match, but it was scant consolation. They did their talking on the park when they hammered us 4-1. At least I managed to stop Clough from scoring. In fact I was to play out of my skin against him on every other occasion we met after that. I made a point of it.

After the game I heard a familiar voice at the dressing room door, asking for me. It was my old Fifer pal, Willie Fernie, an inside-forward who had just joined 'Boro from Celtic. He had come in from the home dressing room with a huge smile on his face. Apparently, Brian Clough was not well liked by most of his own team-mates either, and Willie told me the 'Boro lads were struggling to keep a straight face at what had happened. 'I've never seen anything like it, Danny,' Willie said, 'Somebody's got him by the throat nearly every day at training.' I could believe it!

My wife had close relatives in nearby Thornaby who, ironically, just so happened to be big 'Boro fans. Worse, we were geared up for staying with them that night, planning to travel back to Cardiff by train the following day. Margaret's Uncle Jock was a tough, hard-bitten Scot whom I liked very much. You may recall I mentioned Jock and his wife Mary coming to see me play at Sunderland in only my third or fourth game for City.

As it turned out I needn't have worried about the incident because Jock was not such a big fan of Brian Clough anyway. Jock fashioned a strong fist, shaking it in front of me, before telling me I should've 'brought the other hand round as well.'

I managed a sickly sort of smile in response. I knew I had let everyone down as I'd gone on to play an extremely subdued second-half, which more or less handed the match to Middlesborough. Not my finest hour!

Next morning I apologised to everyone at training for my aberration. The general consensus among the players was that I hadn't punched Clough hard enough. Derrick Sullivan went as far as calling me 'Rocky' for a few days. There were even rueful smiles among the coaching and management staff. I think they felt that, because I was put under such intense provocation, nine out of ten players would have reacted in exactly the same way. It still did not make me feel that much better. Thankfully, everything seemed to blow over within a few days. I could get back to concentrating on the football.

As for Brian Clough, it was impossible to ignore the subsequent impact he made on English football. Some of it was good, some bad. As I said before, he was a very good player, unlucky to have had a promising career cut dreadfully short by injury. I suppose the natural progression for a confident and abrasive man such as Clough was to go into management and, along with his assistant, ex-goalkeeper Peter Taylor, he was to become one of the country's top bosses. Success at Derby and Nottingham Forest should have led to what is widely considered to be the ultimate job for an Englishman. 'England team manager' should have been displayed proudly at the head of Brian Clough's curriculum vitae. No doubt about it. A big ego and an even bigger mouth probably put paid to any chance of that ever happening. Speaking of big ego, I refer to Clough's sensational, forty-odd day tenure at Leeds United following Don Revie's acceptance of the England job.

It was no secret Revie and Clough hated the sight of each other and, the way I saw it, Clough really only took on the Leeds job to try and put one over on his arch-enemy. The previous history between Clough and Leeds from his Derby days had been so intensely hate-filled, there was no way the players (Revie's players) were going to accept him. Especially after that famous first day training session when he allegedly told them that, as far as he was concerned, they had won their trophies and medals by cheating, and that they might as well throw them away and start afresh, playing *his* type of football.

As you can imagine this didn't go down too well, and a group of the players, most notably Billy Bremner, Norman Hunter, Johnny Giles and Paul Madeley, made it their mission to get him out as quickly as they could. Forty-four days later, Brian Clough was walking out of Elland Road for the last time.

It was interesting to hear a recent radio interview featuring ex-Leeds and Scotland centre-half, Gordon McQueen. McQueen was a promising young player at Leeds in the early seventies, and was present at that first training session. He said his first contact with the manager was just before the session began, when Clough came up to him as he was getting changed and sat down shoulder to shoulder, staring across the room.

'They tell me you're the best young centre-half in the country at the moment,' Clough said. Then he came away with ... 'You'd better be, or I'll go out and buy whoever is!'

Without another word, Clough stood up and strode away to the training pitch, preparing to deliver that famous first day speech.

McQueen believed the more experienced players got the wind up as soon as they heard the story about Brian Clough taking over. At that time footballers were paid well enough, but nowhere near the riches that they take home nowadays. Win bonuses and testimonials were crucial to supplement incomes, and Gordon mentioned most players would have 'kicked their grannies' to earn an extra thirty quid or so. Players like Bremner, Giles, Madeley and Hunter were long service men, all coming up to testimonial territory, and McQueen reckoned they were convinced Brian Clough was going to sweep through the club like a chronic case of diarrhoea and get rid of all of them before their benefit games could take place. Don't get me wrong, I didn't like Clough, but I think he was on a hiding to nothing at Leeds United.

I had a wee chuckle to myself when I recently read Roy Keane's biography. Keane was a young player in Clough's Nottingham Forest side, and he recounted an incident which took place during one of his early matches. Keane had been having a nightmare and when he trudged into the dressing room at half-time, Clough was waiting for him. Apparently, Clough swung a punch, catching the Irishman flush on the nose and knocking him off his feet. Wonder where he learned to do that?

I also recall another televised incident at the end of a Nottingham Forest match where Clough, manager at the time, lost his temper at some of the crowd who had come on the pitch. I watched on in amazement as he waded in, swinging punches and throwing people to the turf.

Some people think Brian Clough was a misunderstood genius, always justified in his actions. I just think the man was an egotistical, arrogant idiot.

Leyton Orient were our next opponents at home the following week, Ron Hewitt scoring in an undistinguished 1-1 draw. The press releases after the game outshone any of the on-field action as a Scottish centre-forward by the name of Tommy 'G-Man' (G for goals!) Johnston went to town in the papers, spouting all kinds of stuff about how he was going to 'score five goals in his next match,' and how his team would 'demolish the opposition' in their forthcoming, fourth round FA Cup tie. Their opponents? That's right, Cardiff City!

The lead up to the second instalment of the double header was spent playing verbal volleyball with the Orient players, in particular Johnston, who waded in with a few personal attacks on yours truly! I was fine with it. Like I said before, it was part and parcel of the game. And I was confident I could do my talking on the park. The off-field shenanigans certainly fuelled interest among the City fans as almost 36,000 filed in to Ninian Park, as opposed to only around 13,000 for the league encounter the previous week.

The game itself: 'G-Man' Johnston's boasts evaporated into the atmosphere as Joe Bonson scored twice in a 4-1 rout. To be quite frank, it could have, probably should have, been eight or nine. I'd never had an easier match and my performance that day prompted manager Trevor Morris to declare publicly on my constant omission from international squads: 'if Scotland has a better centre-half than Danny Malloy, he must be outstanding.'

The 36,000 fans became only 1,500 at Ninian Park, as the prestigious FA Cup gave way to the Welsh Cup the following Wednesday. The match against Southern League team Hereford United would surely be a walkover into the next round. Well I don't know if it was the lack of atmosphere, or a reaction after our great win against Orient, but we had a nightmare that night, tamely going down 2-0 and handing Hereford the greatest result in their history, at least up until that point.

After a mercifully short shaky spell at the start of the season, I felt I was hitting top form again. I was definitely fit and raring to go in every game. Yes, we were in a lower division, but the standard was still excellent and there were a lot of great players plying their trade in the second tier. Some games, we were so full of confidence, we felt we could do almost anything. The Cardiff fans used to love it when I took the ball for a mazy run up the park and try to play in one of our forwards. I was always comfortable enough with the ball at my feet and it wasn't unusual for me to try to dribble sixty or seventy yards deep into the opposition half. Admittedly, if I did find myself there it could often be a different story, the typical defender with a nosebleed loitering in unfamiliar territory syndrome.

I do remember a special match at Cardiff on the last day of the previous season against Manchester United of all teams, when I somehow managed to take the ball for a seventy yard sortie deep into United territory, before threading a through ball for Gerry Hitchens to score. The reception I got from the fans as I jogged back into position made me feel ten feet tall.

The beginning of February saw us travel to London to take on Charlton, the team who had finished below us in the First Division the season before. We had revenge in mind as they had beaten us easily at our place back in September. But we were playing so much better and chock full of confidence that we couldn't possibly lose. Or could we? We could, and did, 3-1. Deserved? No excuses.

On the morning of Thursday, 6th February, 1958, the world woke up to the horrific events that had taken place in the early hours at a snowbound Munich-Riem Airport.

League champions Manchester United and an entourage of supporters and press people were returning from a European Cup tie in Belgrade, when they were forced to stop at Munich for re-fuelling. The press reports stated that the pilot aborted takeoff twice in horrific conditions, deciding to make one more attempt rather than fall behind schedule by choosing an overnight stay. Unfortunately, more snow had fallen by the time they were ready to make that third attempt, and a thick layer of slush at the end of the runway prevented the plane from taking off.

The aircraft crashed through a fence before hitting a nearby house. From the forty four on board, twenty three died instantly, with another three subsequently losing their fight for life.

Among the dead were eight journalists, including former England and Manchester City goalkeeper Frank Swift, three members of the coaching staff and a total of eight players: Geoff Bent, Roger Byrne, Eddie Colman, Mark Jones, David Pegg, Tommy Taylor, Liam

Whelan and Duncan Edwards.

Duncan was to survive for close on fifteen days following the accident. He was even able to ask if he would be fit to play in a forthcoming FA Cup tie against Wolves. Sadly, his injuries were so serious he would never have been able to play football again, even if he'd survived. The world had lost a fantastic talent who would possibly have gone on to become the greatest player of all-time.

I recall many years later, watching a documentary about the tragedy. Duncan Edwards's mother featured in the programme, and even though the incident had taken place a long time before, the poor lady was beside herself with grief as she struggled to get the words out. Yes, football mourned the loss of a great player, but much more importantly, a mother had lost her loving son.

Among the survivors of the tragedy were three members of the press and team manager Matt Busby, whose injuries were so severe he was given the last rites three times. Mr Busby remained in hospital for many weeks afterwards, happily going on to make a good recovery.

Two players – Johnny Berry and Jackie Blanchflower (brother of Spurs' Danny) – survived the crash, but were unable to play again. A further seven resumed their careers after the tragedy with varying degrees of success: Bobby Charlton, Bill Foulkes, Harry Gregg, Kenny Morgans, Albert Scanlan, Dennis Viollet and Ray Wood. The heart and soul had been ripped from this great club. It would take many years for the scars to heal.

I can still feel the eerie minute's silence within Ninian Park before our next game against Doncaster Rovers, a couple of days after the Munich tragedy. You could have heard a pin drop as the occasion was impeccably observed by every single person in the ground.

Strangely, the atmosphere in the dressing room the hour before we stepped on to the park was also subdued. The practical jokers, the comedians of the team, like Derrick Sullivan and Brian Walsh, were like the rest of us. Nobody seemed to know what to say. We just sat in silence, everyone going through their pre-match routines as normal. But in silence.

As I sat waiting to go out, my mind drifted back to the last time we played United. It was at home on the last day of last season – the day we were officially relegated. As I mentioned earlier, I had somehow succeeded in taking the ball on a mazy, seventy yard run before sending a defence-splitting pass through for Gerry Hitchens to run in and slip the ball under goalkeeper Harry Gregg. As we celebrated the goal United captain Roger Byrne, one of the players who lost his life in the tragedy, patted me on the back, congratulated me on 'a fantastic piece of play.' That was the measure of the man. I had only met Roger a couple of times prior to that game and liked him very much. It was a tragic waste of a young life.

Tommy Taylor was another victim, and a great player. His goal scoring record for his first club, Barnsley, then Manchester United and England, was incredible, and his aerial prowess was unrivalled, except maybe by Nat Lofthouse and John Charles. I'd heard Matt Busby had turned down a world record offer of £65,000 from Inter Milan for Tommy Taylor, the year before the tragedy. I wasn't surprised. He was that good and would be a real contender for the centre-forward position in one of my all-time great teams. I'll cover this later in the book. Lofthouse or Taylor? Wait and see!

The match against Doncaster seemed unimportant given the circumstances. I remember making another seventy yard run to release inside-forward Cliff Nugent. Cliff's cross to the back post was headed home by Brian Walsh. We won the match 3-1, the other goals coming from Nugent and Hewitt.

Ninian Park was jumping for the visit of Blackburn Rovers in the fifth round of the FA Cup. Our biggest crowd of the season – nearly 46,000 – packed the ground to the rafters, with the crowd in the Bob Bank really making their presence felt. Cup fever had hit the town, and there was a fantastic buzz of anticipation as we took the field against top-of-the-table Rovers. I hadn't played in the league game at Blackburn three months before, but I'd heard from some of the lads they were a good side with some very good players.

Billy Eckersley was a long serving left-back who had been good enough to play seventeen times for England. Our right-winger, Brian Walsh, would have his work cut out to get past this fine player.

Right-half Ronnie Clayton was another England international and long serving Blackburn man who had caught the eye in the league game between the clubs. Ronnie was to go on and represent his country at the World Cup in Sweden that year.

Inside-forward Peter Dobing had made his debut for Blackburn at just seventeen. Three years on and he was an accomplished player with an incredible goal scoring record for his position. He was to go on and score twenty that season, greatly contributing to Rovers' promotion to the top division. A highly rated footballer,

Dobing was snapped up by Manchester City three years later as a replacement for Torino bound Scottish icon, Denis Law.

Centre-forward Roy 'Taffy' Vernon was to be my direct opponent that day. Taffy was another youngster who had made his debut at just eighteen. Already, he had broken into the Welsh national team and was to play at the World Cup the following summer. Taffy was lean, skinny, ten stone at most. By all accounts, he had a terrific left foot and a fair degree of skill. I expected a tough time from the Welshman. Vernon was to join Everton in the early sixties where he went on to score many goals, a large percentage coming from the penalty spot. Sadly, I later read that chain-smoker Taffy had died at only fifty-six, a victim of cancer.

Bryan Douglas was another long serving Blackburn player who had just made the England team. He was a quick and tricky right-winger who had terrorised City's Scottish left-back Alec Milne in the league game. Manager Trevor Morris decided to switch big Alec to right-back, with Ron Stitfall moving into the firing line. I can still hear the blood curdling screams coming from the dressing room when the line up was announced. Only kidding! Seriously though, Stitfall was not pleased about the switch, and not looking forward to the match. Not one bit.

Alec Milne, in his new right-back role, maybe wouldn't face Bryan Douglas, but I felt it right he should know something about the left-winger he was to come up against that afternoon; definitely a case of 'out of the frying pan' as I gave Alec the lowdown on Scottish wide man, Ally McLeod.

The former Scotland team boss was probably best remembered for the national team's ill-fated, World Cup campaign in Argentina, in 1978. Now I'm certain that every Scot who is old enough to remember that tournament reflects on it with a smile. Okay, we crashed out at the group stage, as usual, but I really think the squad we had then was as good, if not better, than Willie Ormond's in Germany, four years earlier. And that squad was good. Ally being Ally had the Scottish public whipped into a frenzy in 1978. He had most people really believing we were going to bring home the World Cup. I recall chuckling when I saw a televised press conference around a week prior to the squad leaving for South America. A reporter asked Ally what his plans were after the tournament was over. 'To retain the trophy,' he replied, an engaging smile on his face. What started off as an innocent, off-the-cuff remark suddenly sparked a rollercoaster ride of pure emotion.

Ally McLeod was as likeable a man as you could ever hope to meet and, although it was always going to be a long shot that Scotland would actually win the trophy, everyone, without exception, would almost have given their right arm to see it come true. Now you might think I'm absolutely bonkers, but I'm also convinced if we'd had a couple of slices of luck at the right times, we could have gone very close to actually winning the World Cup. Let's look at the facts; Ally McLeod was an accomplished coach. He hadn't just been installed as national manager because we had a dearth of suitable candidates. Ally had served his time, firstly at Ayr United, where he performed miracles with hardly any money or resources, then at Aberdeen, where he was instrumental in paving the way for the start of Alex Ferguson's incredible success story.

Ally was both smart and tactically astute, and he knew how to handle players. The squad itself boasted a host of superb players, some of whom I'm sure would have walked into any of the other teams in the tournament; players such as Sandy Jardine, Derek Johnstone, Martin Buchan, Kenny Dalglish, Graeme Souness, Joe Jordan and Gordon McQueen. In addition, we had others who were to make their names in the years to come; Kenny Burns and John Robertson were young players set to taste European glory with Nottingham Forest.

The tournament saw us in the same group as Peru, Iran and Holland. Peru were considered one of the weakest of the South American teams on show. They had an ageing squad, including defender Hector Chumpitaz and talismanic striker, Teofilo Cubillas. Cubillas had enjoyed a glittering career, but was thought incapable of cutting it any more at that level.

I remember watching the match with a couple of pals. I think it was a Saturday night, and as we watched with a beer or two in hand, Joe Jordan put Scotland in front early on. We were playing well and I settled back, expecting us to kick on from there. Peru obviously hadn't read the script and hit back to easily win 3-1. Cubillas netted two, one of them a fantastic free kick that goalie Alan Rough couldn't get near.

The nation was stunned. And worse was to follow; the former Rangers winger, Willie Johnston, was one of the players randomly picked by Fifa's drug testing team to provide a urine sample following the match. Johnston was found guilty of taking a banned substance and sent home in disgrace. If the result was bad, the aftermath was a million times worse. The press wanted answers. The knives were being sharpened.

The unforgettable images of Ally McLeod sitting in an open dug-out, head in hands, squirming at the unfolding horror of the 1-1 draw against minnows Iran, will never leave me. If the Scottish media had been cruel after Peru and after the Willie Johnston episode, they were about to turn positively sadistic.

We woke up the next morning to the predictable public outcry. It was all about 'this one should have been playing' and 'that one was hopeless' and 'he should never have been there in the first place.' Okay, granted Ally McLeod made mistakes. He was too loyal to players who weren't doing it for him. He was unwilling to change his system when, clearly, it wasn't happening. In a way, he made a rod for his own back with his outrageous predictions, although, in fairness to Ally, the statements he actually made were so obviously 'pumped up' by the press to sell newspapers.

I imagine the three or four days between the Iran game and the final group match against Holland, must have been the longest and most stressful days of Ally McLeod's life. It was bad enough we had lost against has-beens and only drawn against, arguably, the poorest team in the tournament; bad enough the squad itself was polluted by jealousy and in-fighting; bad enough we were thousands of miles away from home with the English, who incidentally hadn't qualified for the finals, again, absolutely knotting themselves at the Scots' latest predicament.

As if that lot wasn't bad enough, in the next game we had to go out and play one of the favourites to lift the trophy. Holland had played brilliant football all the way to the final in Munich four years before, only losing by 2-1, the winning strike typically fired home by a certain German striker called Gerd Muller. This time the Dutch were being hotly tipped to go one better. Lucky white heather? Not exactly.

Incredibly, other results in the section meant that Scotland could still qualify for the next phase. It would be a tall order, but it was possible.

Peru were looking a certainty to finish top of the section, with their last match to come against Iran. They were not expected to slip up in the same way as the Scots had and, all going well, they would finish top with any kind of a win, irrespective of the Holland

– Scotland result. Scotland's task was simple. Win by three clear goals! Any other result would send Holland through to the next round.

I later watched a televised interview with a much more relaxed Ally McLeod two or three months after that World Cup. Ally was no longer team boss and, I must admit, looked ten times healthier for it. He had that sparkle in his eye, a cheeky grin on his face when he was asked to describe that period between the Iran and Holland encounters. He mentioned he had been asked by the SFA to invite the scribes to an impromptu press conference, by way of defusing any potential unpleasantness in the run up to that final group game.

The press conference was held at a little beach front bar near the team's headquarters. Everyone had just sat down when Ally started things off by calling over a little stray dog that had wandered into the bar.

'See what it's come down to!' he quipped, patting the wee dog on the head. Bizarrely, the dog lifted its paw to shake hands with him before rolling on to its back, legs in the air, for a tummy tickle. 'At least I've still got a pal!' he added.

It was the perfect ice breaker. Ally went on to describe how he'd walked in on the kit man who was on his knees pulling a suitcase out from under his bed. 'Send one up for me as well,' he said. 'I need all the help I can get here.' The place echoed with the sound of laughter. The hacks laughed along and everybody began to relax. Well, after all, we were never going to win the World Cup anyway, were we? Thoughts turned to Holland. If only. I wondered? Surely not! But then ...?

When Rob Rensenbrink stuck away a penalty kick in the thirty-fourth minute to put the Dutch into the lead, we thought, 'ah well, that's it.' Up until that point we'd played, by far, our best football and were extremely unlucky to go behind. Even when Kenny Dalglish lashed home a fantastic equaliser just before half-time, we all thought, 'Nah! If we can hang on for a draw. Now that would be some result.'

In typical Scottish fashion the team came roaring out of the traps in the second-half, diminutive midfielder Archie Gemmill converting a forty-seventh minute penalty. We had the bit between our teeth and were playing some of the most exciting football of anyone at that World Cup. The Dutch seemed to run scared, retreat into their shell. They must have wondered what had hit them as wave after wave of attacks rained down on their goal.

I remember looking at my watch when Dalglish picked up the ball just outside the Holland penalty box, on the right hand side. I'm thinking, 'if we can nick one here, one more'll put us through!'

On 68 minutes Dalglish expertly shielded the ball, drew three Dutch players to him, and laid it off to Gemmill. The rest is etched into Scottish football history as wee Archie twisted and turned his way past four defenders, before expertly chipping the ball over the diving keeper, Jongbleud.

We had invited some friends over for the match and my son, who was just about to turn twenty-one, had asked if he could bring a couple of pals over as well. I think every beer bottle and glass in the Malloy household was upended in the aftermath as we all realised that maybe, just maybe, we were going to do it! It was 3-1. One more goal and the Dutch would be going home. We'd be in the next round.

Holland centred the ball. The cameras moved in for close-ups of some of their players before sweeping the bench. I'd seen the looks before many times. I'd been in their position. I knew exactly what was going through their minds. They were shell shocked. Just at that moment, we had them. I was sure of it. They were a defeated side. We were going to send them home. I remember turning to a friend to utter the immortal line, 'If we can just keep it tight for a few minutes ...'

As everyone knows the moments immediately following the scoring of a goal can often prove costly for the scorers; something to do with taking the foot off the gas, before re-grouping for that final assault. I remember screaming at the Scottish midfield to 'Mark up! Don't let him run with the ball!'

Too late! Our guys just switched off at the vital second as the Dutch centre-forward, Johnny Rep, carried the ball from a deep position. Mind you, he was well over thirty yards from goal, and still had an awful lot to do. Rep took a final touch before unleashing a ridiculous drive into the top corner, leaving Alan Rough clawing mid-air.

It was like a dagger to the heart and although Scotland did their best to try and recover from it, everyone knew we were going home early once again.

The match finished 3-2 and the team was cheered from the pitch like heroes. Whoever said twenty four hours was a long time in football had got it spot on!

We had restored some pride. The Dutch said some nice things about us and the squad was able to fly into Glasgow airport to a decent reception instead of a lynch mob, and that was good. I was happy in the end for Ally McLeod. He was one of the good guys.

Ally had started his career at the now defunct Glasgow team Third Lanark and I played against him a few times when I was with Dundee. Ally wasn't quite as quick as Bryan Douglas on the other side of the Blackburn attack, but I recall the Dundee right-back, Gerry Follon, getting a bit of a chasing from him on one occasion. And that didn't happen very often to Gerry. Of course I didn't want to give City full-back Alec Milne the full story as to what to expect on the day of the cup-tie. The last thing I wanted to do was have him tighten up with nerves. Just enough to make him aware – I was sure that was the way to go.

Cardiff's earlier 4-0 league defeat to Blackburn Rovers turned out to be significant. It had been Ray Daniel's sixth and last game for the club, and I went into the match determined not to carry the can for another heavy defeat. The big crowd at Ninian Park for the cup tie was in full voice as we pinned Blackburn down from the very start. Firstly, Joe Bonson and then Colin Hudson had terrific efforts on goal, both striking the woodwork. As we pressed home our territorial advantage, the same duo then missed incredible chances – open goals – to put us ahead before half-time. The two lads trudged off at the break looking absolutely sick. That's the way it goes sometimes and the rest of the team did their best to lift them for the second-half. We went on to absolutely pummel the Rovers' defence in that second period, but just could not turn our advantage into a goal. We had limited their forwards to very few chances, successfully stifling the supply line from the back.

The team received an incredible ovation from the crowd as we trooped off at the end. It was typical of the Bluebirds fans. They loved their players to give 100 percent; they would demand no less. The fans knew exactly how much we had put into the match. It felt to many of us as if we were the unluckiest side in the world, but we were still in the cup. No doubt we deserved to win, but at least we had a replay to look forward to. Could we get through? More of the same would be required.

The match was to be played the following Thursday at Ewood Park. I knew Blackburn would have to play better than they had done at our place to get through. If they did we'd have to be on top form to get a result.

As in the first game we raced out of the blocks and really should have gone in front early on. Rotten luck and poor finishing was again to be our Achilles heel. As I predicted, Rovers would come into the game in front of their own fans and they carved out a number of chances both sides of the break. As it transpired, two quick goals in the early part of the second-half would prove too much for us to overcome. We gave them a real fright, however, as firstly, Ron Hewitt cut the deficit to 2-1 near the end, and then Joe Bonson cruelly struck the woodwork for the umpteenth time over the two ties, in the final moments of the game.

I thought Blackburn were excellent that night and probably deserved to go through to the next round. Over the two matches, though, I'd say we were very unlucky to go out.

I enjoyed a very pleasant dinner with Ally McLeod after the game as we took the opportunity to catch up on news from back home. He'd heard all about the business with me and Rangers. Ally actually thought I'd had a lucky escape and went on to tell me why. He reckoned a Malloy in a Rangers shirt would have had to possess the touch of God to succeed. Hadn't thought of it that way.

Our form was up and down over the next few games. We lost, as per usual, to our perennial bogey team, Sheffield United. A good 2-0 home win against a more than useful Notts County side was followed by a couple of defeats, against Ipswich, by 3-1, and then near neighbours, Bristol Rovers.

At centre-forward for Notts County that day was a young lad, seventeen or so. He was tall, dark haired and aggressive in the air, a real handful. Many years later I recognised similar attributes in a former Coventry, Milan and Monaco player, then at Rangers. England international Mark Hateley was a better player than his father Tony, and much more competent with the ball at his feet. Nevertheless, Tony did well enough for himself, attracting attention from big teams like Villa, Chelsea and Liverpool. He tended not to last too long at each club, however, as he was a kind of one trick pony – an out and out target man – and the teams I mentioned all liked to get the ball down and pass it around. I laughed when I read a comment from Tommy Docherty, the Chelsea manager at the time. The Doc quipped that a pass from Tony Hateley ought to be labelled, 'to whom it may concern.' When it was pointed out that

Hateley's main asset was that he was so good in the air, Tommy came right back with, 'aye, so was Douglas Bader, but did you ever see *him* kick a ball?'

The Bristol match at Ninian Park was significant for a couple of reasons. If you discounted Welsh Cup ties, I played in front of the smallest crowd of my professional career; 5,867 brave souls turned up to see us crash 2-0. There definitely was a link between lack of atmosphere and poor form! We were pathetic that day against a very ordinary Rovers team. Normally we would have taken care of them, no trouble. Manager Trevor Morris must have been feeling the pressure in the lead up to that game as he went absolutely mental at our goalkeeper, Ken Jones, before kick off.

Ken had done all right after making his debut in my comeback match, a goalless draw against Sheffield United in November. Graham Vearncombe, our number one until then, had been given a rest after a loss of form, and couldn't get back in due to Jones' continuing good form.

On the day of the Rovers match, Ken had settled down to watch a televised FA Cup semi-final between Fulham and a post-Munich, Manchester United team. He had become so engrossed in the game that he completely forgot the time, arriving at the ground moments before the team sheets were to be handed in. Trevor's face was like thunder when the big, laid-back goalkeeper sauntered into the dressing room, wondering what all the fuss was about. He soon found out all about the fuss when a 2-0 defeat proved to be the straw that broke the camel's back. Ken found himself out of the team for the next game against familiar opposition.

The last game of March saw us once more come up against our cup conquerors, high flying Blackburn Rovers, in a thrilling encounter. Just over 10,000 Ninian Park fans watched Ron Hewitt fire a tremendous hat trick, and Joe Bonson finally break his Blackburn duck by grabbing the fourth in a brilliant 4-3 win. Unfortunately, Graham Vearncombe, who had been drafted in to replace Ken Jones for the match, also incurred Trevor Morris's wrath by conceding three goals, and found himself back out the team for the next game. Fun and games!

By the beginning of April it was abundantly clear we were not about to be challenging for any honours sometime soon. Thankfully, we were not in relegation trouble either, but although we tried not to, the remaining matches saw us stutter and stumble towards the end of the season.

A 16,000 crowd at home against a useful Bristol City team saw us unluckily edged out by the odd goal in five, Ron Hewitt grabbing both goals. Then in a rare Dr. Jekyll moment, we beat Derby County by two goals to nil at their place without too much trouble. The Mr Hyde in us was just around the corner as we headed the other way across the Severn to Bristol, only to return with our tails between our legs and a 2-0 defeat.

Eventual champions West Ham were obviously more up for the next match at Ninian Park than we were, and it showed when we went down tamely 3-0.

A draw at Barnsley was followed by another disappointing defeat at Rotherham, before we got the train back on the tracks for the last home match of the campaign, against Fulham.

The team played its best game of the season as we absolutely thumped a very talented Fulham team by three goals to nil. Unlikely scorers, Colin Baker and Derrick Sullivan (two), gave us a deserved victory and I felt as though I had played one of my best games in a Bluebirds' shirt. And there was a little added spice that afternoon as I again crossed swords with Fulham's legendary inside-forward, Johnny Haynes. Now it was not a secret among the lads that I did not exactly care for the Haynes who, as I mentioned earlier, went on to make history as the first £100 a week player. However, there was no denying the fact Haynes was a fantastic player who would go on to captain his country on numerous occasions.

Another of Fulham's young lads played at right-back that day. George Cohen looked every inch a future international and later became one of the select few to pick up a World Cup winners medal, forming a formidable partnership in the England team with another fine full-back, Ray Wilson of Huddersfield Town.

Our last match of the season was away to Lincoln, the clash attracting almost 20,000 spectators, many of whom were hoping that their team could secure victory to preserve their second division status. To be fair to them, they must have sensed an end of the season feel from us and simply dug in to record a famous victory. We finished a very disappointing fifteenth in the table. Not good enough. Not by a long shot.

*****

Often during pre-season at Cardiff, as well as the friendly games, players were asked to participate in charity fund raising events, community projects and the like. A lot of the boys were cynical of the club's blatant PR. In truth, they really couldn't be bothered with such exercises as they usually entailed a trip out to some small town in the valleys. Personally, I loved attending these nights as it gave me the chance to chew the fat with the people that mattered – the fans.

As a result of my willingness to take part, I ended up in all sorts of places. I remember a very enjoyable evening in the company of Welsh boxing legend, and the world's first flyweight champion, Jimmy Wilde. Jimmy and I were part of a four man, sportsman's panel set up in a small village hall, near Merthyr, I think it was. The place was absolutely packed to the rafters and the format for the evening was a question and answer session in which the public were encouraged to ask the panel members about anything and everything, not only sport related. This made for some memorable exchanges, especially with a couple of drinks thrown into the mix.

The funniest part of the night came when our attention was drawn to a wee newspaper vendor who had come into the club to sell a few editions of the local rag. After a couple of minutes his huge cloth bag was dumped at his feet as he stared up at us on the makeshift stage.

'You don't remember me, do you?' The wee man directed the question at Jimmy in a thick Welsh brogue. Jimmy took a good look, eventually shaking his head. 'I fought against you,' the man continued. 'Even knocked you out!'

Cardiff City had a real connection with Welsh professional boxers. I recall British heavyweight champion Joe Erskine trained with us on a number of occasions prior to a fight. Joe was a smashing bloke with a great sense of humour and we all used to look forward to watching him go through his paces. The club had a couple of punch balls installed for him and when you watched him use them you could sense the awesome speed and power he could generate through his flying fists.

Joe was actually small for a heavyweight, but he made up for it with sheer courage and determination, often defeating much heavier opponents. Indeed, legendary trainer Angelo Dundee, after watching Joe outbox his title contender, Willie Pastrano, on the way to a classy points win, was so impressed by his skill and technique, he was quoted as saying, 'If only Erskine was a bit bigger, I'm convinced he'd be a world beater'. Around the same time, Joe would go on to beat the great Henry Cooper on two occasions.

Joe was a big City fan and would regularly come and watch us play. Of course the lads and I were only too happy to return the favour. I remember watching a couple of cracking fights. A British title tilt at fellow Welshman Johnny Williams, at Maindy Stadium in Cardiff, was terrific and saw Joe edge the fifteen rounder on points.

As well as the bout with American Willie Pastrano, Joe was to go on and fight other world class boxers such as Ingemar Johansson, Brian London, Karl Mildenberger, Jack Bodell and Billy Walker. His big fight in Canada came against the brutal George Chuvalo. Chuvalo had been earmarked for a world title fight against the champion of the time, Floyd Patterson, but first would have to get past Joe Erskine. The Canadian eventually lost the bout in the fifth round through disqualification for persistent head butting. It was reported Joe was viciously butted a total of eight times.

That night in the small village hall near Merthyr was the first time I had met Jimmy Wilde. He was a real character and we got on like a house on fire. I reckoned he must have been at least in his mid-sixties, but what a fit looking man he was and an absolute gentleman.

Jimmy was a typical flyweight – absolutely tiny – with the heart of a lion, and we had a right good chin wag at the end of the night. He told me a little about his early career and how he got started in the business. Nicknamed The Mighty Atom, Jimmy first fought at sixteen in brutal, fairground boxing booths, regularly knocking out much heavier opponents. Rated by many to be the greatest flyweight of all-time, Jimmy racked up more than 152 fights, winning 137 with an incredible 100 bouts decided by knockout.

I was appalled to later learn that Jimmy Wilde had been the victim of a vicious assault at a train station in Cardiff in the mid-sixties. Apparently, he never really recovered from this cowardly attack and sadly died four years later, aged seventy-six.

Season 1958-59

City president Sir Herbert Merrett kept an earlier promise to have a cover constructed over his favourite Bob Bank enclosure before the start of the new season. The ground really looked the part; Ninian Park was covered on all four sides, with a capacity to accommodate 62,000 spectators.

Also, during pre-season, under pressure boss Trevor Morris accepted an offer to manage our bitter rivals, Swansea Town. It was a no-win situation! We didn't want to see the Swans do well, but Trevor was such a nice man that everyone at City just had to wish him all the best ... within reason. Coach Bill Jones took over as acting manager. He'd had limited experience in non-league football and there were a few murmurings of discontent when the announcement was made. The general consensus was that the board had shown a complete lack of ambition and gone for the cheap option. Time would tell if their choice was to be a success.

On the playing side goalkeeper Graham Vearncombe was off to do his National Service. And inside-forward George Kelly had already signed from Stoke City before Jones's promotion. Kelly was tall and showed up well in training. The only problem I could see for him was that he hadn't been the present manager's choice.

An ambitious Bill Jones wanted the job permanently. It was no secret that he and I hadn't exactly seen eye to eye since he'd joined the club, and I believed there would be few chances flying around for anybody Bill didn't like. Derrick Sullivan also aired his views in private on the appointment. He didn't much care for Bill Jones either, and was of a similar mindset to myself. Players who weren't doing it for him from the get-go would be shipped out and moved on, pronto. We were sure of that.

Just before the start of the season, another well respected old-timer left the Cardiff family to join Exeter City. Full-back Charlie Rutter had joined the club in 1949. He was a fine player, an England B cap, whose long spells of injury limited his appearances to only 118. Charlie always had a nice way about him and his dressing room banter was sorely missed.

An earlier match against Doncaster had seen us score a very fortunate goal when the ball ricocheted into the net off the Rovers' centre-half. Now the stopper was a black man called Charlie Williams (yes, that's right, it was indeed the Golden Shot guy) and someone joked, using snooker terminology, that it was 'in off the brown – should have been four away.' Charlie Rutter, quick as a flash, piped up with, 'don't you mean seven away for in off the black?'

After his playing days were over, Charlie owned a very successful tropical bird business slap bang in the middle of Cardiff's central market. A market trader with the gift of the gab, that was Charlie

Rutter.

An early casualty of the Bill Jones' regime was his namesake, goalkeeper Ken Jones. We'd had a disastrous start to the league campaign, losing 1-0 at home against Barnsley before going down 3-0 at Bill Shankly's Huddersfield. The start would cost Ken his place in the team to new signing Ron Nicholls from Bristol Rovers and his appearances after that were limited to injury cover and the Welsh Cup.

Misery ensued as we went down 1-0 in our next match away to Rotherham United. Three games, three defeats, no goals scored. The pressure was already mounting on the new manager. To his credit Jones didn't panic. I thought he reacted well in adversity, tweaked a few things and we came roaring back with two home victories and six goals against Huddersfield again and Sheffield United. It certainly was a good way to say sorry to the fans for a bad start.

Getting back to the first Huddersfield match I have to say it was a terrific performance by the home team that day and it gave me a first look at the sensation that was Denis Law. What a player! He gave us all a hard time in more ways than one. Law was a great player, there was no doubt about that, but despite his appearance, he was also as hard as nails. I recalled Bill Shankly describing Law as skinny and frail looking. Well let me tell you this, he may have appeared to have been both of those things, but he could look after himself.

As I mentioned earlier we didn't have long to wait for our revenge, Colin Baker, Brian Walsh and Cliff Nugent scoring for us in a tight 3-2 victory. The game provided a bit of light relief, courtesy of a couple of incidents between Denis Law and me. We'd had a right few ding-dongs during the match; nothing really bad; a few flying arms, shirt tugs, sly nudges and wee fly kicks.

Law was another who accepted the rough stuff as part and parcel of the game. I'd had my fill of the prima donnas; the players who'd put the boot right into you without hesitation, but would squeal like a stuck pig when it came right back at them. You kicked Denis and he didn't make a big thing about it. He'd either kick you back there and then, or slyly bide his time, whisper some choice words in your ear while you were lining up for the next corner. 'Don't f****** turn your back on me, Malloy!' was a particular favourite of his.

Not long into the match the ball was rolling for the touchline and I was ushering it out of play for a goal kick. Law was right at my back, and as I shielded the ball out of play, he was yanking at my shirt, kicking my ankles and raking his studs down the back of my legs.

'For f***'s sake!' I shouted, bending to pick up the ball. 'Calm down! I bloody carried you about twenty yards there!'

'F*** off!' Denis retorted and we traded verbals as we walked up the park. Nothing serious ... or so I thought!

Next thing the referee was in between us, notebook in hand. He turned to face Law. 'Name?' he said.

'Naw, it's all right,' I said. 'Nothing happened. We're fine.'

'I'm taking *your* name as well,' the ref replied, licking his pencil. I couldn't believe it!

A full couple of minutes spent trying to convince Hitler didn't get us anywhere and we both ended up getting booked for bugger all. Then, just before half-time, Law and I were tussling for the ball when it broke away from us and was trundling out of play around the halfway line. He lunged in to try and catch the ball before it crossed the line, but I was determined he wasn't about to get anywhere near it. I saw my chance and gave him a little nudge just before he reached the ball. Denis flew through the air and across the track before vaulting the little barrier wall right in among the Cardiff fans in the front row. There were legs and arms, pies and cups of tea flying everywhere as the place erupted in gales of laughter. Luckily, Denis saw the funny side and we had a right old chuckle about it in the players' lounge at the end of the match. I had actually forgotten all about these incidents and it wasn't until many years later that a chance phone call from a City fan who had been at the game reignited memories of it.

Near neighbours Bristol Rovers were our next opponents away and the grim 2-0 defeat marked a long spell on the sidelines for inside-right, George Kelly. Two goals in six games would seem like a fair return to most people at City, but manager Jones obviously had different ideas.

Kelly's replacement was a player I had noticed at training on my first day at the club nearly three years previously. Graham Moore had been a raw fifteen-year-old at that time but, even then he was big and strong with a powerful shot. I remember thinking it was only a matter of time before the lad hit the big time. Graham made his debut on 13th September away to Brighton and Hove Albion and I was chuffed to bits for him when he cracked in a late equaliser to earn us a battling point.

The next match was four days later and our topsy-turvy season continued with another poor display against Bristol Rovers in the home return. The one bright spot that afternoon was another classic Moore goal. A 4-2 reverse, however, would see us languishing near the bottom of the division and the pressure was really beginning to tell on the manager. Personally, I felt I had actually started the season quite well and Bill Jones had obviously agreed as I went on to play in every game including the League, FA Cup and Welsh Cup. Fellow Scot Alec Milne must have been doing something right as well as he was also an ever present.

The day after the Rovers defeat, Bill Jones made arguably one of the most influential signings in the club's history. Former Welsh international forward Derek Tapscott had been languishing in Arsenal's reserves with injury problems and Jones somehow managed to coax our directors to part with £10,000 for his services. It proved to be a master-stroke and it went on to cement Jones' position as team manager as well as give him a chance to freshen up the side. Jones knew Tappy well from their time together at Barry Town. He knew he was a proven goalscorer and exactly the tonic we needed at the time. We'd lost the goals of Gerry Hitchens and, whilst Joe Bonson had done well since his move from Wolves, he had picked up an injury and missed a few games at the start of the season. And, it was taking the big man a wee while to settle back in since his return.

As I'd said, Bill Jones had made up his mind that George Kelly was not the answer. Added to that, Cliff Nugent was also soon to leave and Brayley Reynolds, though a very good player, was not a prolific scorer. The scene was set for mercurial Welshman Tapscott to take centre stage. The next match was at home to Grimsby and Tappy was ready to make his debut.

Jones decided to give Graham Moore a spell back on the sidelines following a successful start to his Cardiff career. Two goals from two games for the quiet, unassuming kid was a fantastic return and I was almost as disappointed as Graham was when I was told he was losing his number eight shirt to Tappy. I was convinced Graham's time would come. I was not wrong.

As well as the return of flying winger Brian Walsh after a couple of games on the sidelines, another of the young brigade was to make his debut that day. Wing-half Steve Gammon was only seventeen, but he was another fine prospect. Calm and assured, Steve would definitely have gone on to become one of the club's greats had his career not been cut short due to a couple of horrendous injuries. Bizarrely, I believe Bill Jones had to shoulder a lot of the blame for the youngster's unfortunate first leg break, when up against a certain Denis Law. I'll explain my way of thinking a little later in the book.

Although Tapscott didn't score on his debut that day, he had a good game and gave us an extra dimension as we hammered Grimsby 4-1. Ron Hewitt waded in with a couple of goals and Joe Bonson notched one to get off the mark for the season. I have to say the partnership of Bonson and Tapscott looked very promising. As I mentioned in an earlier section of the book, neither of them could be described as technically gifted, but they certainly could do the business as far as knocking the ball into the net.

Anfield was the next port of call and over 40,000 fans saw Liverpool take an early lead before Bonson and Hewitt struck to give us another deserved victory. We were moving up the table!

On the 4th of October, Middlesborough, Clough et al, visited Ninian Park. Over 20,000 fans attended that day, our biggest crowd since the opening match. I hoped against hope they hadn't turned up expecting to witness Malloy v Clough – round two! I was determined I was going to keep my cool this time. It was up to Mr Clough.

As it turned out he didn't utter a peep to anyone before, during or after the game. We ran out 3-2 winners, but really it should have been much more comfortable.

Although Tappy went on to score his first goal for City in our next match at home against Ipswich Town, true to type, we managed to concede two at the other end. The encouraging thing for me about that period though, was that we were beginning to hit some decent form. We were definitely playing better and the introduction of Tapscott, along with the knock on effect for other players such as Bonson, Walsh and Hewitt would stand the team in good stead for the forthcoming fixtures.

Bill Jones was confirmed as permanent team boss on 23rd October, 1958 and would celebrate in some style two days later as we defeated a very useful Stoke City side by 2-1. Early on in the match the Cardiff fans were treated to an event which was even rarer than hen's teeth – or a Danny Malloy goal. Or so I thought! The stadium erupted when long serving full-back Ron Stitfall expertly stuck one away. Now I thought that goal was the only one Ron had scored in all his years at Cardiff. It was the only time I can remember him getting anywhere near the opposition goal in my time at the club. Wrong! Apparently, Ron played a handful of games at centre-forward in season 1949-50, scoring six goals! What do I know?

The goal celebrations in those days were nothing like some of the shenanigans you see nowadays, but even back then, the regular scorers used to have their little routines personal to them after scoring a goal. From a simple fist pump to a nod and a wave to the crowd, the prolific goalscorers just did what came naturally. To a quiet individual like Ron Stitfall, one word would spring to mind when he found himself the centre of attention ... uncomfortable!

As well as manager Jones signing on as permanent boss at the end of October, he continued to endear himself to the Cardiff faithful when he brought back popular ex-forward Wilf Grant in a trainer/coach role. Wilf had been manager at Llanelli and even got them promoted to the top division of non-league football. However, it was no secret that he yearned for a more hands-on role and when Jones offered to team him up with our existing backroom staff of Bob John and Ernie Curtis, he jumped at the chance.

Englishman Wilf was not a big man but he had the heart of a lion. By all accounts quick and no mean goalscorer, Wilf had left Cardiff for Ipswich Town the year before I'd joined. He'd enjoyed a useful career to date, been a team-mate of Alf Ramsey at Southampton, and won an England B cap in 1952. Unfortunately, England's opponents France B rattled in seven goals that day and the drubbing would prove to be the one and only time Wilf would represent his country at any level.

Wilf *was* a genuinely nice man who would do anything to help anybody out, but he could also be a hard taskmaster, demanding 100 percent all of the time, at training and during games. Understandably, Wilf's personal focus was on speed training and he had no small measure of success on that front, sharpening up a few of the slowcoaches at the club. I hasten to add Danny Malloy had no need for such instruction.

Bob John was born in Barry and had spent a little time with Barry Town and Caerphilly before playing out the rest of his career at Arsenal. He must have been some player as he won an FA Cup and three First Division titles with the Gunners. He also played in the

1927 FA Cup Final, losing out to, of all teams, Cardiff City.

He'd been a coach at Cardiff between 1949 and 1950 before leaving to manage Torquay United. During my time at City, Bob worked as a scout for the club. He was a great character, a true gentleman and one of my favourite people of all-time. Nobody but nobody had a bad word to say about him. That's how much Bob John was liked by everyone at the club.

Ernie Curtis was another hugely likeable man. Cardiff born, Ernie had been only nineteen when he won the FA Cup with City in 1927. He had, of course, lined up against his old pal, Bob John, in that final. A left-winger, Ernie also enjoyed spells at Birmingham and Coventry during his career, winning three Welsh caps in the process. After retiring from playing, Ernie devoted most of his time to the Bluebirds in various roles within the club.

We kicked off November pretty well with a brilliant 3-1 victory at much fancied Derby County, makeshift number nine Brayley Reynolds getting his name on the score sheet. Brayley was a better player than he was given credit for and really unlucky with injuries. Later, he was to go on and enjoy more success and play a whole lot more games at Swansea. Brayley was such a nice lad that, even though he did well for the Swans, everybody at City was pleased for him.

Lincoln City were our next visitors at Ninian Park and we again hit fine form, running out easy 3-0 winners.

Our home form over the next couple of months was very good, defeating the likes of Leyton Orient, Bristol City, Rotherham United and Brighton, and coming from 2-0 down to battle to a 2-2 draw against Sheffield Wednesday. Our away form during the same period was also not too bad with great wins against Sunderland and Bristol City, and narrow defeats to the likes of Scunthorpe United and Barnsley.

Our presence in the FA Cup that season was again fairly brief. We were drawn away to Plymouth Argyle in round three and managed to turn them over fairly easily by 3-0, Hewitt, Reynolds and Bonson on the mark.

The next round saw us drawn away again, this time at Norwich City. The Canaries had knocked out Manchester United in the previous round and were confident coming into the match.

We were desperately unlucky to go down 3-2 in front of a bumper crowd of 38,000. Ron Hewitt and Joe Bonson repeated their scoring feats from the previous round, but big Joe really should have scored four or five that day. It certainly wasn't like the big man. One thing he was normally good at was sticking the ball in the net. We came within three minutes of getting Norwich back to Ninian Park for a replay when their free scoring striker, Bly, crashed in an unstoppable shot from a ridiculous angle to put them into the next round. That's how it goes sometimes.

Bill Jones had been manager of Southern League side Worcester during a previous life and he decided to take a gamble on their prolific scorer, Harry Knowles. Harry had been scoring goals for fun in the lower league and Jones was confident that he could make the step up to the Football League. Eight games and no goals in two seasons answered that question! To be fair Harry did score against the likes of Rhyl and Wrexham in The Welsh Cup and in his second season, he managed to find the net against Swansea during a 2-1 win in the same competition. It was a feat that made him an instant hero among the City fans and I was pleased for Harry as he was a decent man. He would have been the first to admit he had stepped a little out of his class at Cardiff.

Our excellent home form continued into the next match on St Valentine's Day against Liverpool. Derek Tapscott was on fire that day and he capped off a fine display with two of the goals in a 3-0 win, Brayley Reynolds hitting the other.

As expected, I got a hot reception from the Middlesbrough fans on my first visit to Ayresome Park since 'that match'. The game was a drab affair and finished 1-1 with Brian Walsh scoring for us. That's right, you-know-who failed to hit the net again!

We'd had a good run up to the end of February and there was some idle talk flying about the place. We were in fourth position in the table and that dreaded word promotion was again rearing its ugly head. But in true Cardiff City style, we pressed the self destruct button again and again over the next few games – nine games, five points, promotion chance over.

A solitary 1-0 win at Stoke and consecutive draws against Derby, Ipswich and Charlton were to cost us dear. Defeats at Lincoln and Sheffield Wednesday and inauspicious home losses to Charlton and Fulham drove us further down the division. Also, in that run of nine games was another depressing statistic which I knew nothing about until after the match. Our 1-0 defeat to bitter rivals Swansea at the beginning of March was our first ever loss to them at Ninian

Park in a league game.

Centre-half Mel Nurse scored the winner for the Swans that day and, while our team was sick about losing that record, at least it had gone to a decent man. Big Mel was a gem of a lad who always had a smile on his face. I had a lot of time for him as I had for most of the Swansea boys. As I'd said, when the whistle went it was every man for himself in these games.

Speaking of Mel Nurse, I received a telephone call about him from *The South Wales Echo's* sports reporter, Mervyn Thomas, a couple of years later. Mel had been chosen to play at centre-half for Wales against an England side which included Brian Clough, who was gaining his first full cap. The match was to take place the following midweek at Ninian Park and Mervyn called to ask a favour of me. He wanted to know if I could pass on any tips to Mel in dealing with Clough's goal threat. The last match between Middlesborough and Swansea had ended in a 6-2 victory for 'Boro, Clough bagging a hat trick against Mel in the process.

Mervyn knew that, apart from my very first match against Clough – the B international tie between Scotland and England where he bagged a goal – I hadn't given him a sniff in umpteen matches since. Considering myself an adopted Welshman, I told Mervyn that I'd be glad to help, but also that it would be up to Welsh manager Jimmy Murphy, and whether or not he thought it would be worth me having a chat with Mel. An hour later the phone rang again. I spoke with Jimmy first and then Mel Nurse came on the line. A quick five or ten minute conversation ensued where I was able to give Mel a few pointers, some things I had noticed during my games against Clough.

I made a point of going along to watch the match a few days later and was absolutely delighted for Mel when he showed up really well during a creditable 1-1 draw. The England scorer? Jimmy Greaves! I was also well chuffed for young Graham Moore who made his debut for Wales that day, especially when he headed a last minute equaliser.

Our next game after the Sheffield Wednesday defeat was another away match. Again we made the short journey to the Vetch Field to enjoy another tussle with Swansea. We came away with a surprisingly easy 3-1 victory with Mel Nurse this time hitting an o.g. Remember he'd scored the winner at Ninian Park only four weeks previously.

We had four games to go, two at home and two away. Defeats to Scunthorpe and Orient, a creditable 1-1 draw at Sheffield United and a 2-1 win against Sunderland helped us to an improved ninth place finish. Better than last term, but still not good enough. I wondered what next season would bring.

Three days after the Sheffield match we travelled to Newport for the Welsh Cup Final against lowly Lovell's Athletic. They were a confectionery factory side from Newport, a team full of honest, hard working battlers, but we were confident. We had enjoyed a fairly comfortable run to the final beating Gloucester (3-0), Rhyl (3-1) and Wrexham (6-0) on the way.

We lifted the cup after a hard fought match ended 2-0, with goals from Bonson and Hudson.

I was knackered. As I said earlier, I'd played in every game.

5

Back in the Big Time

Season 1959-60

I was both delighted and proud to be named Cardiff City FC club captain at the start of the campaign. And I was determined I was going to play a major part in getting the Bluebirds back into the top flight where they belonged. Margaret and I celebrated by buying a new car. We'd managed to save enough to buy a spanking new, powder blue Ford Cortina, complete with column gear change and heater (yes, heaters were extra in those days).

I was beginning to think somebody had sneaked onto our drive overnight and painted a big bullseye on the side of the car as, when we set off on our first outing, some unusual things began to happen.

A quiet relaxing drive to town turned into a fight for survival as I had to swerve and brake like a madman in order to preserve my paintwork. In those days traffic was much lighter than it is now and 'health and safety' were words mostly used separately. Instead of safely locked into a car seat in the back, Andrew was sitting on his mother's knee when yet another idiot cut out in front of me, I had to brake so sharply he went flying at the windscreen. The sickening thump of head on glass, the resultant screams, and the instant swelling all combined to turn me into a raging maniac as I tore off in pursuit of the perpetrator. The guy must have been terrified as I stuck to his tail like super-glue all over town, swerving in and out of traffic and down side streets.

Margaret and Andrew clung on for dear life as I took some corners on two wheels, eventually tailing the poor man into a petrol station where he screeched to a halt. I leapt out of the car just as he stepped out to face the music. Rage quickly turned to laughter as he closed his eyes and prepared to lose some teeth. Why laughter? The man was about the same height as Danny de Vito. I just couldn't have.

If you were that man and you're still with us, and you were wondering who the idiot was who terrorised you all those years ago ... sorry!

*****

During the close season Brayley Reynolds was allowed to leave the club for Swansea. I was sorry to see him go as he was a popular lad in the dressing room and I couldn't help feeling at the time that we'd let him go a bit too soon. As I'd said Brayley was a very good footballer and I wasn't surprised to later find out that he'd gone on to play more than 150 games for Swansea, scoring over fifty goals.

Possibly a more surprising departure at the time was Ron Hewitt's move to Wrexham for what was to me a meagre fee of £5,000. Ron had been our top scorer for the past two seasons and I felt that we should have tried to hang on to him for at least another season.

Bill Jones' decisions were perhaps vindicated when he pulled off a major coup, securing the signature of experienced winger Johnny Watkins from Bristol City for a bargain £2,500. Johnny would make a significant impact that season, featuring in every single league match bar one, in the outside-left position.

A week before the season began Graham Moore, who had already made his debut in the September of the previous campaign, lined up in a public trial match to get some game time and ended up cracking in four superb goals. The feat was to earn Graham a start in our first game at home against Liverpool.

Our forward line as part of the common 2-3-5 formation of the time was formidable that day, with Brian Walsh, Derek Tapscott, Graham Moore, Steve Mokone and Johnny Watkins looking the business.

South African Mokone had just signed from Dutch club Heracles and was to go on and play only five games for Cardiff. However, he didn't take long to make his mark in his debut, firing home from close range after only five minutes.

That year was the club's fiftieth anniversary and we were looking to get off to a flyer. Everyone was raring to go that day against Liverpool and we looked set to kick on after taking such an early lead. Typical! By half-time we were behind. Worse, two own goals tipped the balance in Liverpool's favour, Worse still, guess who was credited with the two own goals? That's right.

In my defence, and as I'd mentioned earlier in the book, shots from outside the area and deflected in off a player would always be credited to the defender, more often than not, the pivot. When you're throwing everything at the ball, these things are going to happen. Enough said! But we were not to be denied that day and Graham Moore rattled in a beauty to level things early on in the second-half – and save my bacon.

The scene was set for a hero and, as Liverpool melted away in the sweltering heat, debutant Johnny Watkins rifled a tremendous shot, swerving the ball in off the goalie's far post. A great goal and one fit to win any match. We were off and running.

The next game was in midweek, at home against Middlesborough who also had high hopes for the coming season, especially with the prolific Brian Clough in their ranks. It finished 2-0 for the Bluebirds, Moore and Watkins again with the crucial strikes. I let Clough out of my pocket at the end of the match. All joking aside, it was just too easy.

Next up was Charlton away, and although young Graham Moore scored again, we lost narrowly, by 2-1. I really felt that, despite the defeat, we were playing some of the best football since I'd joined the club. There was a confidence flowing through the team and this was borne out by the next five results.

Big Joe Bonson came back into the team at inside-left for the return game at Middlesborough, Johnny Watkins firing home once again in a tight 1-1 draw.

Home games against Bristol City and Derby County resulted in comfortable 4-2 and 2-0 wins respectively. Someone had the bright idea of me handing over the captaincy to Johnny Watkins for the one game against Bristol City. Apparently, it was to do with a bit of superstitious mumbo-jumbo or something. Johnny had only just left City under a bit of a cloud, and although he wasn't keen on being acting skipper for the match, he eventually agreed. He was truly immense that day and it was fair to say I'd have let him take on the captain's role for good if it would have guaranteed a similar outcome at the end of every match.

Away games sandwiched in-between the victories over Bristol and Derby saw us run out 2-1 winners both times, once more at home against Derby, and Scunthorpe United.

After eight games we were top of the pile, and looking good.

Young Steve Gammon had come back into the team at right-half and really looked the part. Goalkeeper Graham Vearncombe was another who was playing out of his skin. Having just returned from National Service, Graham had displaced Ron Nicholls and was to go on and play every game in the league that season, except one.

On 19th September we were at home to Rotherham United and really raring to go, fancying our chances more and more by the minute. A Man called Ironside had other ideas! No, not the San Franciscan police chief, but a goalkeeper called Roy Ironside who hit an incredible vein of form that day as we relentlessly pounded the Rotherham goal, throwing everything *and* the kitchen sink at him. By the time Derrick Sullivan managed to finally steer a shot past the keeper, we were already heading for a heavy defeat. 4-1 was most definitely not a true reflection on proceedings and the only comparable occasion I can think of came many years later, in late 1973, during an England World Cup qualifying match at Wembley against Poland. The Poles' goalkeeper, Jan Tomaszewski, had an unbelievable game that night, performing a string of breathtaking saves as shots rained in on him from everywhere on the pitch.

I must admit I had a little chuckle to myself when I heard my old 'pal', Brian Clough, on the TV panel at the end of the match, describe Tomaszewski as a 'clown' who had put his country through to the finals in Germany by sheer good fortune rather than any great skill. For me, this comment certainly smacked of a hefty helping of sour grapes. Northern Irishman Derek Dougan, also on the panel that day, must have agreed with me and took offence to Clough's comments as he shifted uncomfortably in his chair. Derek glared at Clough as if he wanted to rip out his throat. I knew the feeling!

In hindsight, I could maybe see where Clough was coming from as the goalie sported an unfortunate shock of curly, black hair which kind of gave him a look more akin to a Marx brother than an international footballer.

Jan would have the last laugh, proving a point by helping the Poles to a very creditable third place in the competition. Not bad for a clown!

The Rotherham result proved to be a minor blip as we launched into an eleven game, unbeaten run, scoring a right few goals in the process. Three at Lincoln, five against Orient and four in a thrilling four all draw with Stoke City were the highlights of that period. A 2-1 win at home against rivals Swansea was another satisfying result, Derrick Sullivan again on the score-sheet with one of eight goals for the club that season. As I said before, if only Sully had been regularly fit. No point in going over old ground, I suppose. I'll just say that he could have played anywhere in the team. In fact I think he did play in every position at one time or another.

I recall an incident that took place later that season involving Derek. We were playing at Wrexham in a Welsh Cup match when I heard a familiar voice asking for me at the dressing room door. It was Reuben Bennett, my old trainer at Dundee, and the irrepressible Bill Shankly. Shanks had just taken over at Liverpool and had already set up the famous Boot Room, alongside Reuben and other Merseyside legends, Bob Paisley and Joe Fagan.

Interestingly, the Boot Room was exactly that, a room for storing players' boots that doubled as a meeting room for the coaches. The story went that they would pick the team and plot the downfall of the opposition, as well as make time for an odd glass of whisky or three. Whatever they did in there it certainly worked as the club entered the most successful period in its history with world class players passing through the ranks on their way to countless domestic and European honours.

Another interesting fact about the Boot Room was that Reuben Bennett would be the only one of the four not to actually manage the club, but he would remain at Anfield the longest. I remembered Reuben well from my Dundee days. He was an Aberdonian – a straight talker – who would let you know in no uncertain terms what he wanted. Of course, I had met Bill Shankly on previous occasions and had formed a similar opinion of him.

This opinion was cemented when the pair of them brushed past a startled City manager Bill Jones, plonked themselves down next to me on the bench, and proceeded to ask me about Derrick Sullivan. They were blatantly tapping Jones' player right in front of him. You should have seen the look on his face. Priceless!

I hardly knew what to say. Of course, Bill Jones and I didn't really get along, but there was no way I could condone the actions of the Liverpool pair. It was well out of order. On the other hand Derrick was a great friend and I wanted to let them know just how good a player he was. In the end I agreed to speak to Reuben on the phone the next day to give him my thoughts on Derrick Sullivan. Problem solved.

Any chance of a move kind of fizzled out in any case as Liverpool decided not to follow up their interest.

The 1-0 victory over Huddersfield on 17th October was one of Bill Shankly's last games in charge before his legendary move to Liverpool. The match was notable for a couple of reasons: firstly, a penalty miss by Denis Law, secondly, just how well we played, despite having the likes of Alan Harrington, Derrick Sullivan and Graham Moore away on international duty with Wales.

Our impressive unbeaten run came to an end in Birmingham on 12th December, against one of the other front runners, Aston Villa. Unbelievably, 54,000 spectators turned up to watch a cracker of a match which was eventually settled by two late goals as a blanket of thick fog descended. It was nice to see my old pal and Villa centre Gerry Hitchens once again, although it was mighty inhospitable of him to open the scoring.

The next match could have gone either way. A new manager either instigates the lifting of a performance, as in, 'I need to impress the boss so that he keeps picking me,' or, the talent to do well is not there in the first place. Liverpool had been languishing in the lower reaches of the division for the past few seasons. We always seemed to do very well against them, usually scoring a fair few goals in the process. This time, however, Bill Shankly was in charge. Of course we know how much of an absolute legend he became, changing the face of English football forever. Was the revolution about to begin at Anfield that day?

The answer was a resounding *NO!* as we delivered an awesome performance, full of skill, pace and power. In fact, we were so dominant and impressive that Shankly himself had to admit it nearly took his breath away. Tappy with two, Bonson and Watkins ensured an easy 4-0 win which really could have been eight or nine. We all agreed that the hard bitten Scotsman would have a real job on his hand to turn that team around. Well, what did we know?

We went straight into a Christmas double header against Sheffield United, and when Bonson and Tapscott netted during a comfortable victory at Ninian Park, confidence was high for the return match two days later. As I've already mentioned, Sheffield United had always been a kind of bogey team for the club and the jinx was to strike once again as we tumbled to a 2-1 defeat. Tappy fired in our goal – one of twenty he scored in the league that season.

The shock of that defeat seemed to unleash the fire in our bellies as we launched into a terrific ten game unbeaten run, scoring an incredible thirty two goals – six at home against Lincoln, five at

Charlton, four against both Scunthorpe and Orient, and three against Bristol City and Hull City were the main highlights of the run.

Promotion was now well within our grasp, and after our thrilling 4-3 victory at Leyton Orient on 27th February, we moved three points clear at the top. We had gone two down in the Orient match, but showed grit and drive to level early in the second-half through, guess who? That's right, Tappy and Bonson!

The fans of both sides must've thought it was Christmas revisited as the match swung from end to end, goalmouth incidents and last ditch tackles in abundance. As the game wore on our superior strength and power began to tell, and in the seventieth minute, we scored one of the finest goals I've ever seen. Brian Walsh sent Derek Tapscott clear down the right. I thought the pass looked a little heavy, but Tappy was renowned for his speed and just managed to get to the ball before it crossed the by-line. He fired in a fantastic cross, chest high, perfect for big Joe Bonson. Fifteen yards from goal, Joe still had plenty of work to do and launched himself at the ball. It thudded off his forehead, exploding into the net past the goalie's despairing drive. What a goal!

Joe Bonson was a big favourite with the City fans who, as I've already said, loved one hundred percenters, but that goal alone was to cement his place in City folklore. Tappy then made the game safe at 4-2 before Orient grabbed a late consolation goal. 4-3, a great game!

The next match saw us go behind early on against Huddersfield before Graham Moore and Johnny Watkins struck back to give us the victory. There must have been an extra ingredient in Johnny's porridge that morning as he almost burst the net with a rocket shot from that left peg of his.

It's a funny thing, but I always thought left footed players were set up to strike the ball harder than right sided ones. I don't know why this should be, but I can think of a few examples to back up this theory. As I've said, Johnny Watkins at Cardiff couldn't half strike a ball. Roberto Carlos, former Brazil and Real Madrid full-back, was another with a thunderous left foot. Ex-Celtic and Scotland player Tommy Gemmell was also renowned for having a powerful left peg, scoring a tremendous goal in Celtic's 2-1 defeat of Inter Milan in the 1967 European Cup Final.

Across the city in Glasgow, I recall three predominantly left footed players at Rangers a few years back; Davie Cooper was so left-sided, in the mould of the legendary Jim Baxter, that they used to say his right leg was the 'swinger,' or, merely 'for standing on.' At Cooper's testimonial dinner, former team-mate Ally McCoist presented the winger with a mystery package; something he was 'in dire need of.' Davie tore open the gift to reveal a dummy right leg!

I remember chuckling into my cornflakes one morning at a newspaper article following a Scottish Cup Final match between Rangers and Aberdeen in the mid 1980s. Rangers had eventually won a tight match 3-2, Davie Cooper firing in an absolutely unstoppable free kick from the edge of the box past the despairing dive of former Scotland goalie, Jim Leighton. Not long after that game the pair were on international duty for Scotland and Davie listened intently as Jim told some of the other lads in the squad of how he managed to get fingertips to the afore-mentioned free kick. 'Aye, on the way back out, maybe!' Davie quipped, sparking uproar.

Giovanni van Bronckhorst and Jorg Albertz both played in the same Rangers team in the late 1990s/early 2000s. Dutchman van Bronckhorst had more of a cultured left peg, but could also let rip when the situation demanded. I recall him unleashing a tremendous effort into the roof of the net in an away Champions' League tie – at Borussia Dortmund, I believe.

For sheer power and ferocity I don't think there has been another who can even come close to matching *The Hammer*, better known as Rangers' former German midfielder, Jorg Albertz. Some of his goals could only be described as 'awesome.' One in particular, was a free kick from around 30 yards and it came against big rivals, Celtic. I swear the ball never rose more than a foot from the ground as it zipped into the net, just inside the post. I don't think the Celtic goalkeeper even had the time to dive before big Jorg was wheeling away to take the adoration of the Rangers' fans.

Incidentally, I happened to mention my left footed player theory to my son, Andrew. He thought about it for a few minutes and came back to me with a couple of names designed to ridicule my idea, one still playing, the other retired a while back: Alex of Chelsea and Brazil, and former Leeds and Scotland right-winger, Peter Lorimer. Aye, all right then.

Ourselves and Aston Villa had opened up an eight point gap on the chasing pack with nine games to go. It was just as well we were in such good shape as we went on to take only two points from our next four games. A 1-1 draw at Ipswich was followed by a dire 4-1 defeat at home against Portsmouth, a team that was to escape relegation by the skin of its teeth. Unbelievable!

We got ourselves back on track early on, away at Swansea with Bonson, Moore and Walsh putting us three up before half-time. In typical Cardiff end-of-season style, we proceeded to concede three goals in the second-half, hanging on grimly for a point in a game that really should have been in the bag.

Incredibly, our next home match against another lowly side, Brighton, saw us crash 4-1, as we had against Pompey, Derek Tapscott also scoring our consolation goal in the process. I took a whack on the calf near the end of the Brighton match and ended up limping off. The knock didn't feel so bad the following day, which was a relief, but I still had the feeling it would be touch and go for the next match at Stoke City. As the week wore on the opinion among the physio and trainers was that the game would come too soon for me. Reserve centre-half Bob Peck readied himself for only his second game of the season (the first had come in the Welsh Cup away at Swansea).

Promotion had begun to look less of a stick on in the lead up to the Stoke match, but in the end, there was no need to worry as Bob Peck played out of his skin with Johnny Watkins hitting the only goal.

We felt the pressure ease right off after that win. It gave us a spring in our step and left us in a very favourable position with only four games remaining. The diagnosis was simple: one win would guarantee promotion back to the top flight. But it wouldn't be Cardiff City if we didn't have to do things the hard way, and I must admit to experiencing a right good few nerves in the run up to our next match against fellow title contenders, Aston Villa.

Maybe it was fate or destiny lending a hand, but as well as having the opportunity to clinch promotion on that date, the 16th of April, 1960, we also celebrated fifty years as a professional club on the exact same day. Ironically, our first opponents way back in 1910 were ... you guessed it, Aston Villa! The anticipation of success could be felt all around the city in the week before the Villa game, so much so that manager Jones took the decision to ban all talk of the 'P' word. I remember thinking at the time it was a shrewd move.

Now I know that I have been critical of the manager in some sections of the book, but I have to admit Bill Jones got all the important decisions spot on that season. He had moulded together a fine team with a good blend of youth and experience and the signings of Tapscott and Watkins along with the continuing development of young players such as Moore and Gammon had worked like a dream. All we had to do was get ourselves over the finishing line. Easier said than done.

On the eve of the match we had just wrapped up some light training when one of the girls in the office passed a message to me that my wife had been trying to get in touch with me. I called Margaret from the ground and immediately knew by the tone of her voice that something was wrong.

'Andrew's gone. He's disappeared. He was out in the garden and now he's gone,' she sobbed.

I couldn't get my head round it. 'He's only three,' I said. 'How far can he get?'

By the time I'd rushed round to the house, the wee toe-rag was sitting in our lounge watching television, unaware of the fuss he'd caused. One of the neighbours had found him playing away in some builder's sand which had been dumped at the end of the road. Disaster averted!

A massive crowd of 52,364 packed out Ninian Park on that April afternoon. The welcome we got from the fans as we walked out on to the pitch is something that has always remained with me. It was absolute bedlam and the sheer tension generated seemed to get to us early on, both sets of players conspiring to make the opening exchanges nervy and tense.

After twelve minutes Brian Walsh rode a tackle on the halfway line before sending the ball down the Canton end towards the corner flag on our right, and Colin Hudson. 'Rock' had come in at inside-left as a late replacement for the injured Joe Bonson, and he slipped as he prepared to cross the ball. Luckily, the unintentional pass sat up perfectly for Graham Moore and he hardly needed to break stride before slamming an unstoppable right foot shot into the roof of the net. What a goal!

There wasn't much good football played during the rest of the game in what was a dour and stuffy affair, but when the whistle went at the end, the feeling of pure relief we felt was only matched in its intensity by the reaction of the Cardiff fans. In seconds every square inch of the pitch was taken up by supporters as they chanted every player's name in turn. I ended up being escorted off the pitch by two burly policemen and, along with the rest of the team, Bill Jones and Ron Becher, was encouraged to say a few words. It's not every day that you're asked to speak in front of over 50,000 people so with the pure excitement and enormity of the occasion, I have to admit to being unable to recall any of what was said that night. The main thing for us all was that when the dust settled, we were back in the big time.

At the time of writing, it was to be the last time a Cardiff City team gained promotion to the top division.

The victory over Villa put us top of the table and, with only three games left, we were looking good to finish champions as well. Our run-in didn't look too difficult on paper. But then, as someone used to famously quip, 'the game isn't played on paper,' and we finished off taking only two points from a possible six which effectively handed the title to Aston Villa.

A disappointing 1-0 defeat at home to lowly Plymouth Argyle was followed by a couple of languid draws: 1-1 at Sunderland and 2-2 at Ninian Park against near neighbours, Bristol Rovers.

On a personal note, I conspired to miss a penalty against Plymouth. It was the first spot kick I had missed in my career and I decided to refrain from taking any more after that. Selfishly, I was glad that wee Brian Walsh also missed a penalty in the same match. Two spot kicks in one game, I hear you exclaim. No, Cardiff City were not in the habit of being awarded penalties. Those two were the only ones we were given all season!

I don't know if it was the pressure of trying to do well in the league, but our FA Cup run stalled at the first time of asking, Port Vale of the lowest division knocking us out at home by 2-0. And that in the middle of a real purple patch in the league when we'd scored twelve goals in three games.

We fared better in the Welsh Cup, going all the way to the final. It had been a long hard season by the time we lined up against Wrexham on 2nd May, and we could only manage a 1-1 draw, going down 1-0 in the replay. The competition had started very well for us that year as we hammered Lovells Athletic by 5-0. The next round saw us drawn away against Swansea with the tie scheduled to be played on Thursday, 25th February. The only problem was that we had a massive match in the league at Orient two days later, which could have put us top of the table and we felt that the Swansea game would ruin our preparations. As soon as the problem was identified the Cardiff City chairman applied for the date to be changed to the following Wednesday. The early rounds of the Welsh Cup tended to be played on a monthly basis so we couldn't see a problem and expected our request to be granted. Imagine our consternation when the Welsh FA point-blankly refused.

Bill Jones was seething and, quite correctly in my view, reacted by sending out what used to be called our Football Combination team. Nowadays, the term is simply, Reserve Side. That decision caused major unrest, not only at FA HQ, but also in our opponents' ranks. The Swans considered our choice of team to be disrespectful to both them and the competition and they countered by fielding their strongest eleven, the intention, no doubt, to humble their big headed opponents.

The tie turned out to be one of the most bitter and controversial ever played in the history of the competition. The Cardiff first team squad had enjoyed a light training session on the morning of the game and had all decided to travel with the lads to Swansea to give them a little support. It had been raining for most of the day and the match kicked off in very heavy conditions. The circumstances surrounding the game had obviously nurtured some bitterness within the Swansea ranks and I felt some of their players were out of order, dirty tackles flying in all over the place.

A shot from Steve Mokone was deflected into the Swansea net and when Harry Knowles hit our second fifteen minutes from time, it seemed to galvanise our opponents. Goalkeeper Ron Nicholls had been absolutely brilliant that night, but when former Cardiff inside-forward Brayley Reynolds finally beat him to pull a goal back near the end, Swansea laid siege in their efforts to level the tie.

Colin Hudson was sent off for a particularly nasty foul before, right at the death, Mokone and Swansea's Harry Griffiths clashed near the touchline and wrestled each other to the ground. As they got to their feet the pair of them began to hurl lumps of mud at one another, giving the referee no option but to order them from the field as well.

I remember thinking it was maybe a good job I hadn't been playing as I'd have been a prime contender for an early bath. Not that I was in the habit of being sent off. Despite the hard man tag, I was only ever dismissed once in my career. It had come when I was at Dundee, in a reserve league game at Brechin. In my defence, I felt that the referee had been conned by some outrageous play acting by the Brechin forward. I genuinely hadn't touched the guy and felt so strongly about the injustice that I stormed into the Brechin dressing room at full-time vowing to really sort him out if our paths ever crossed again. Thankfully, the Brechin manager didn't make a big thing of it and I got off with a stern talking to. I must've made some kind of impression on somebody at Dundee though, as I was selected to make my debut the following week. Sometimes it pays to take the initiative!

*****

Socially, 1959 in Cardiff was notable for at least one thing. The docklands area that had witnessed the birth of singer Shirley Bassey would be the main setting for a movie starring one of Britain's most famous actors, John Mills. *Tiger Bay* also starred Mills' youngest daughter and child actress, Hayley, along with the then unknown German actor, Horst Buchholz.

Buchholz had just signed on the dotted line to appear in a big budget, Hollywood western based on *The Seven Samurai*, a Japanese film. *The Magnificent Seven* is considered by most to be the finest western ever made. As a self-confessed western nut (especially those featuring John Wayne), I would disagree. I think there are several better: *The Searchers, Winchester '73, The Naked Spur, She Wore a Yellow Ribbon, The Big Country* and *How the West was Won* are all superior as far as I'm concerned, but there is no doubt *The Magnificent Seven* is a fine movie – and what a musical score!

Bet you can't name all seven actors without looking it up?

Tiger Bay premiered in a theatre in the centre of Cardiff and the players and their wives were invited to the exclusive showing and also the lavish party that followed.

It just so happened that John Mills (Chelsea) and Horst Buchholz (Hertha Berlin) were big football fans and I was lucky enough to enjoy a little chit-chat with them about the game during the party. Hayley Mills was probably around twelve or thirteen at the time and was allowed to attend up to a certain time. She was a really sweet girl, very well mannered and it was easy to see why she would later become the 'Darling of the Disney movies'.

The following year – 1960 – also saw the release of the scariest film ever made. Or it certainly seemed so at that time! Margaret and I, along with another couple of City players and their wives, were invited to see an exclusive screening of the latest Alfred Hitchcock film, *Psycho*.

In today's terms, *Psycho* would probably be regarded as 'tame', but when it hit the screens back then, it was the real deal. I saw the evidence with my own eyes. A young man sitting about four rows in front of us went out like a light during the famous shower scene.

Season 1960-61

Now that City were back in the big time, the decision was taken to install floodlighting at Ninian Park. We were among the last clubs to introduce the facility, but at least the wait had been worth it for the system ranked with the best in the world at that time.

The team christened the lights in a pre-season glamour friendly against Grasshoppers of Switzerland. We were going into the last minute 2-1 down when I picked up the ball just inside my own half. The Swiss defence parted like the Red Sea as I went on a mazy run, waltzing past a couple of defenders, and made to lay the ball off before lashing an unstoppable shot into the net to give us a deserved 2-2 draw. Eat your heart out, Mr Messi!

Manager Jones made a few changes in personnel during the close season with Scunthorpe's free scoring forward Peter Donnelly taking the step up to the first division. I remembered playing against Peter on a couple of occasions during the past two seasons. He'd proved to be a handful both times and I was pretty confident he'd do well in amongst the big boys.

Unfortunately, the player going the other way was big Joe Bonson. Joe had missed a few games at the start of the season, but still managed to score nineteen goals. I felt he linked up well at inside-forward with Derek Tapscott and Graham Moore and also felt we'd definitely miss Joe's aerial presence. I heard later that northerner Joe had requested a return to his roots and that Scunthorpe United were going to pay him more money for the privilege. Good enough!

Welsh international full-back Trevor Edwards arrived from Charlton along with goalkeeper Maurice Swan, signed from the Irish League club, Drumcondra.

Shrewsbury Town's inside-forward Brian Edgeley arrived for a £10,000 fee at the same time as Harry Knowles returned to Worcester City in exchange for young winger, Peter King.

We kicked off our season back in the top flight against Fulham at Craven Cottage on 20th August, 1960. Racing into a commanding 2-0 lead by half-time with goals from Brian Walsh and Graham Moore, the team looked to be full of confidence and packed to the brim with talent. In fact, had Tappy had his shooting boots on that day, we would surely have been on easy street at the interval.

In typical Cardiff fashion we went on to concede two goals in the second-half, Johnny Haynes hitting the equaliser seconds from the final whistle. I recall thinking at the time it was going to be a long, hard season. The difference in players we were going to face every week threatened to be significant if they were anywhere close to the quality of Haynes. He was the best passer of a ball I'd ever seen and would surely have been a stick on to lead the England international team to glory at the World Cup in 1966, had he not suffered a serious cruciate ligament injury following a bike crash in Blackpool of all places. Surgical procedures for dealing with these type of injuries were much more primitive at that time and, nine times out of ten, players were either forced to retire, or came back a pale shadow of their former selves. With Johnny Haynes the latter was true and the injury signalled the end of his international career.

Haynes was generally not well liked by some of his team-mates and I remember former Fulham, Newcastle, Arsenal and England centre-forward Malcolm McDonald launching a scathing attack on him through a book he had written. I tend to agree with McDonald's analysis.

Nearly 32,000 spectators packed into Ninian Park for our first home league game the following midweek. Sheffield Wednesday were the visitors and the match gave us a chance to test the effectiveness of the new floodlights.

I felt I had one of the best games of my career that night as some rotten luck, great goalkeeping and unusually poor finishing – especially by Graham Moore and Derek Tapscott – saw us narrowly defeated by 1-0. Admittedly, the goalie we'd faced just happened to be England international Ron Springett and Wednesday *were* a top side at that time, but I can remember trudging off at the end thinking we should at least have got a draw. Still, our main aim now that we'd got back into the top division was to make sure we stayed there. If we played as well for the rest of the season as we had that day we would have nothing to worry about, of that I was certain.

Talented guys like Moore and Tapscott would soon rediscover their touch and began to get themselves regularly on the scoresheet. And, we wouldn't be facing goalkeepers like Ron Springett every day either! Springett would go on to make the squad for the 1966 World Cup, losing his place to one of the best goalkeepers in the world at that time, the fantastic Gordon Banks of Leicester City. I was to witness Gordon's technique up close and personal later on that season as we were due to play Leicester in late October.

It was straight into another mouth watering game, also at home, against Preston North End. It was a case of mixed emotions for me that day as I learned that the great Tom Finney had been forced to retire at the end of the previous season due to a persistent groin injury; sadness that I would never again be able to pit my wits against the player I considered to be 'the best in the business'; relief that I would definitely be in for an easier game – and that was no disrespect to Finney's replacement. As far as I was concerned, any other centre-forward in the world would have been easier to play against.

I have often been asked what was so special about Tom Finney. Well, let me think ... he had a rocket shot in either foot; he could very comfortably play in all five forward positions (Finney had starred on both wings and as centre-forward for England); he had very quick feet à la Messi, tremendous balance, with a God-given talent that allowed him to pass the ball like a dream; and, for a relatively short man, he possessed tremendous heading ability. Apart from these attributes, Tom Finney was an average player.

Some years later, I remember laughing out loud when I heard a radio interviewer speak to Bill Shankly about Finney. Shanks was asked to compare a top player of that time to the Preston legend. 'Aye, he's as good as Tommy all right – but then, Tommy's nearly sixty, you know!'

Both Colin Baker and new signing Peter Donnelly had hobbled off at Fulham the previous week resulting in them missing the midweek match against Wednesday. They had been receiving intensive treatment three times a day since Craven Cottage and it was going to be touch and go for either to make the game against Preston. Bill Jones left his decision right to the wire, announcing the side to include both an hour before kick-off. It was an anxious time for Colin and Peter as they didn't want to let the team down by declaring themselves fit only to break down early into the match. There was also a fair bit of pressure on the manager as he would ultimately carry the can if the plan backfired. In the end there was no need to worry as we raced into a two-goal lead within sixteen minutes, Derek Tapscott once again sparking into life to fire in a couple of unstoppable strikes. A superb header after only three minutes was only eclipsed by a scorching right foot shot which nearly burst the net. Terrific!

I was very happy for Derek to get his name back on the scoresheet as he had, uncharacteristically, scorned quite a few chances in the first two games and Bill Jones, never one to shy away from making a decision, must've surely been on the verge of dropping him. Tappy should probably have bagged a hat trick that day, but he unselfishly squared the ball to Peter Donnelly who was in a much better position to score. Unfortunately, Peter side footed the ball wide. It was his only mistake in the entire match. Later, he explained he'd missed due to the effects of a pain-killing injection taken earlier in his right foot beginning to wear off.

We were absolutely in command that day and probably should have scored six or seven. If it hadn't been for goalkeeper Fred Else, the woodwork and desperate goal-line clearances from defenders, Dunn and Fullam, we would have scored a right few. The defence also played very well. I think we limited Preston to just one chance in the entire match, Graham Vearncombe easily smothering a close range shot from inside-left, Davie Sneddon. All in all, it was a good day at the office.

It was off to Hillsborough the following midweek and our Sheffield hoodoo continued with a 2-0 reverse against Wednesday. We just didn't perform that day. The same team which should have thrashed Preston went down tamely. No excuses.

We were away again on 3rd September, this time at previous season's champions, Burnley. I was expecting a really tough match, but in all honesty, we'd hardly had an easier time. Burnley had lost their previous home game and were under a bit of pressure to turn things around quickly, especially against one of the promoted teams from the previous season.

We hit the road running and indeed, could have been six up by the time we did open the scoring. Tappy and Donnelly ran amok that day hitting the post twice and having point blank shots blocked by Burnley keeper, Blacklaw. The goal, when it came, was hotly disputed by the Burnley players. Johnny Watkins crossed from the left and Tappy nodded home before turning to celebrate. We cursed our luck when we saw the linesman's flag had gone up for offside. But in those days referees really were in charge and he confidently overruled his assistant by pointing to the centre spot. Inexplicably, we took our foot off the gas after that and allowed Burnley an equaliser through Jimmy Robson. Then we avoided a deserved rollicking from Bill Jones when Johnny Watkins danced through the Burnley defence to score a great goal in the very last minute. Two wins, two defeats and a draw, thus far. Not a bad start.

Our next four games only yielded one point, at home against the team that came up with us, Aston Villa, as a combination of injuries, bad luck and dodgy form hit hard. Nottingham Forest, Villa away and Manchester City were too good for us as we went into freefall.

A big crowd welcomed Arsenal to Ninian Park on 24th September. Understandably, the team was feeling decidedly fragile due to recent results and the growing injury list, and any little slice of luck would be gratefully accepted. To say that we experienced the rub of the green that day would be grossly understating things.

The game itself was nothing special until a few mad moments towards the end really set the cat among the pigeons. Derek Tapscott had been languishing in Arsenal's reserves until he'd received the call from Bill Jones to join up at City. The Gunners' manager at the time was ex-goalkeeper and hard-bitten Yorkshireman George Swindin and it was no secret that he and Tappy had not exactly been bosom buddies during their time together. I should have realised something was in the air as early as an hour before kick off. Tappy was charging about like a man possessed, making sure that everyone was getting themselves up for the game. There was no doubt – he wanted to stick it right up Arsenal, or rather, right up their manager.

With the game poised at 0-0 going into the final quarter, stand-in winger Rock Hudson fired the ball across the Arsenal goal. Tappy arrived like a train at the far post and threw himself at the ball. He hadn't a hope of getting to it – at least not legally – and reached out his hand to punch the ball into the net. The referee was standing not far from me when the ball went in and I could hardly believe my eyes when he turned to point to the centre spot. The officials must have been the only people in the ground who hadn't seen the hand ball.

I know the game took place a long time ago, but I can actually recall the referee that day. Now I couldn't tell you his name or anything like that, but I do remember the type of man he was. I don't know about officials these days, but at that time most of them could be split into two different groups: friendly and approachable or downright snooty and condescending, like an over-zealous head teacher. The ref that day definitely fitted into the latter category and when he signalled for a goal there was no way in this world that the protestations of the Arsenal players, coaches and manager were going to make the slightest bit of difference. He had made up his mind and that was it.

To compound matters, mere seconds from the end, the Gunners' centre-forward just beat me to the ball from a corner kick and bulleted a header towards goal. It was flying in under the bar until one of our players standing on the line jumped to blatantly punch it over. Worse, the man on the line just happened to be Tappy! Worse still, instead of pointing to the spot, the ref signalled for a goal kick. Chaos ensued as the referee was again surrounded by the opposition. I can still see George Swindin's pop-eyed, crimson face as he bellowed at the feckless officials. Once again, same outcome.

Seconds later, the whistle went amid bedlam as the players surrounded the referee who was eventually escorted off the field by a couple of policemen.

To add insult to injury, Tappy got himself bathed and dressed in double quick time and thought he would nip next door to say hello to some of his old pals. Understandably, Swindin went ballistic at the sight of the Welshman at the door and a right old barney took place with the pair of them throwing off their jackets, ready for fisticuffs.

Towards the end of the following season, Cardiff felt it necessary to appoint a new manager. Yes, that's right! George Swindin was coming to boss Cardiff ... and Tappy.

Again injuries took a stranglehold and we went down heavily by 5-0 at Newcastle in our next match on 1st October. Worse, Graham Moore suffered a broken leg in a freak accident. Thankfully, the injury was not as bad as we had first thought, although no one could believe their eyes when young Graham trotted out to face Preston on New Year's Eve. Talk about a quick recovery!

Interestingly, our two heaviest defeats that season came against teams destined to finish second and third bottom of the league. As well as Newcastle hitting five, Blackpool hammered us 6-1. Full-back Trevor Edwards carried the can for the drubbing, with Ron Stitfall reinstated for the next game at home against Everton.

In between the Newcastle and Blackpool defeats we managed

a fine 2-2 draw away against much fancied Wolves, Rock Hudson and, centre for the day, Trevor Edwards, netting.

The next match, at home to Bolton, saw me in direct opposition to my big pal, Nat Lofthouse. I always enjoyed my tussles with Nat. He was my kind of footballer – big and strong with the heart of a lion. A great player, Nat Lofthouse was also a top man with an encouraging word for every young footballer, even an opposing one.

We were unlucky to lose by a single goal against Wanderers but managed to bounce back with a fine win at home to Leicester City, Peter Donnelly hitting the first and new signing Derek Hogg also scoring on his debut.

A left-winger, Teesider Derek had only just signed from West Brom for £10,000 two days earlier. The signing had actually taken place on a live television sports show so he was already a bit of a celebrity before we even got to meet up at training the day before the Leicester game. The thing that struck me about Derek was how frail looking he was in the flesh. About seven stone dripping wet was how I'd have described him. But he could play all right, and he was a lot tougher than he looked.

Some might say our first goal against Leicester was controversial. Now whilst I think goalkeepers nowadays are afforded far too much protection, at that time they used to come in for some really rough treatment from over eager forwards. Probably the most famous 'shoulder charge' of all-time was the one perpetrated by Nat Lofthouse in the 1958 FA Cup Final, when he sent Manchester United goalkeeper Harry Gregg and the ball into the back of the net on the way to a 2-0 triumph. In my book that has to be a free kick every day of the week, but back then it was deemed part of the game. The reason I brought the subject up was because our first goal against Leicester was the result of a very similar challenge by Peter Donnelly on their goalie. The incident took place at the famous Canton end of our ground which was often regarded by many as a 'graveyard' for goalkeepers of a nervous disposition. The experience didn't seem to do Gordon Banks any harm in the long run as he went on to become a World Cup winner. I remember having my Scottish heart broken by Banks on many occasions during the annual cross-border battle with the Auld Enemy.

The match before the loss to Blackpool was at the beginning of November at the home of champions elect, Tottenham Hotspur.

Spurs had been sweeping every team aside all season with their brand of attacking football. A couple of Scots played in key positions for the White Hart Lane outfit, one of whom I knew very well from my time at Dundee. Scotland goalkeeper Bill Brown had become established in the team at Dens just before I left for Cardiff at the end of 1955. Bill was from Arbroath – the same town as my Cardiff team-mate, Alec Milne – and, as we were around the same age, we had become good friends. In fact, I was delighted when Bill and Bert Henderson took the time to travel down to Bonnybridge for my wedding to Margaret on 25th March, 1955.

The other Scot in the Spurs team was a guy called Dave Mackay. I'd played against Dave in Scotland where he starred for the team he grew up supporting, Hearts. I liked him but he was a right wind-up merchant and a huge pain in the arse to play against. Just ask Graham Moore. I'll explain later. Dave was also described by his great rival of the sixties, George Best, as the hardest man he had ever faced ... and the bravest.

Nearly 50,000 supporters packed White Hart Lane to the rafters and the small Cardiff contingent was not disappointed as we went toe-to-toe with Tottenham. We went two down early on, but a couple of goals by in-form Peter Donnelly were enough to draw us level at 2-2, not long from the final whistle. Then a minute from time their winger skipped past our full-back, Trevor Edwards, inside the box. There was absolutely no contact whatsoever, but the Spurs player took his chance and went down like a wet lettuce. Incredibly, the referee pointed to the spot. Now Trevor was one of those quiet types who just liked to get on with the game, but he became like a man possessed at the sheer injustice of the situation. The veins were almost bursting out of his neck as he confronted both cheat and referee, but his frustration would matter not a jot as we went down by the odd goal in the most sickening fashion.

From the middle of November, when we faced Everton at home, until well into January, we managed to string together a right few decent results. The injury situation was definitely easing and the team was really beginning to gel with Derek Tapscott hitting top form at the right time. Tappy weighed in with eight goals during the period as we won five, drew four and lost only one game – at West Ham. Colin Baker, at left-half, also pitched in with three in four games as we began to climb the table.

Johnny Watkins scored our goal in the 1-1 draw at home to

Everton before we travelled to Blackburn the next week to fight out another thrilling draw, this time 2-2.

Manchester United were next up at Ninian Park and we ran out comfortable winners 3-0. Mind you, they had to play most of the match with only ten men after Dennis Viollet limped off. Derek Hogg had a terrific match, scoring a cracking double, but somehow the victory felt a little hollow and meaningless when you considered the pre-Munich team. United were still rebuilding, yes, but I felt they would never be able to reach anywhere near the heights Duncan Edwards, Tommy Taylor, Roger Byrne and the rest scaled. It was a crying shame.

Following our defeat at West Ham we hit a real purple patch with three brilliant home victories against Chelsea, Fulham and West Brom, scoring seven goals in the process. Tappy hit four of them and we only leaked two in the three matches.

A couple of cracking 1-1 draws away at West Brom and Preston ensured a top ten league position going into the New Year.

Goalie Graham Vearncombe was feeling more than a little apprehensive going into the home match against Chelsea on 10th December. And with good reason; the Stamford Bridge outfit had unleashed this fresh faced kid on Division One defences up and down the country. Not only that, he was terrorising goalkeepers in particular and he had already forged a reputation as a lethal goalscorer, especially in a one-on-one situation. I recall Graham pleading with Stitfall, Gammon, Baker, Harrington and myself not to afford Jimmy Greaves the luxury of running through on goal unchallenged. He'd obviously heard all kinds of horror stories from the goalies' union of how Greaves would have guys slithering back and forth across the penalty box like performing seals, while he rolled the ball into an empty net. Many years later I recall watching a television programme about probably the greatest one-on-one finisher of all-time, George Best.

In 1970 Fourth Division Northampton Town reached the fifth round of the FA Cup. They had drawn the mighty Manchester United at home and Town's scout had spent the couple of weeks since the draw checking out their illustrious opponents. Northampton had been in decent form in the run up to the match and even began to fancy their chances of actually picking up their fifteen quid win bonus. Unfortunately, the Northampton scout had been unaware of one very important fact while on his visits: George Best had been suspended during the four weeks leading up to the game for kicking the ball out of a referee's hand and he was reportedly itching to take his frustration out on someone.

Goalkeeper Kim Book just happened to be that someone as George went on the rampage, hitting six goals in an astonishing 8-2 victory. In fairness I've seen the film footage of the goals and have to say that the goalie was left hopelessly exposed in the lead up to almost every one of them. Kim Book was supposed to have asked Best that famous question as George stroked the last of his goals into the net: 'haven't you had enough yet?'

Northampton defender Ray Fairfax also saw the funny side of things when he joked that the closest he got to Best all day was when he shook hands with him at the end!

The funniest part of the show was Kim Book strongly denying the story that did the rounds in the days and weeks following the debacle; George and he were walking in opposite directions along a Manchester street when George nodded across the road as they passed each other. Kim threw himself on to the road, right under a double-decker bus.

I hope Kim Book didn't feel too badly about his experience as, usually when legends like George Best are involved, things like that can happen to the best of them. I recall watching a match in which the great Gordon Banks was left on his backside looking like a prize chump, while George stroked the ball into an empty net.

Our defence didn't make the same mistake as the Northampton rearguard had against Best and allow Jimmy Greaves to run through on Graham Vearncombe. We ran out surprisingly easy 2-1 winners, Walsh and Baker hitting the net. Greaves was quieter than I expected that day. Well, maybe playing wise, at least. As you would expect, he certainly had a lot to say for himself.

Chelsea had a young forward line at that time. They were known as Drake's Ducklings after manager Ted Drake and their right-winger was an absolute flying machine – an unknown quantity who scared the hell out of our left-back, Ron Stitfall. To make matters worse, Ron was also knocking on a bit, though to be honest, a cheetah would have had trouble trying to catch this kid.

One of the main roles of the old fashioned centre-half or pivot, in the days well before twin centre-backs and all that stuff, was to tuck in behind the full-backs; to double up on a tricky winger. At least that was the plan ... along with a good, old fashioned crunching tackle or two in the first few minutes. 'Now mind, Danny. Make your presence felt early on.' The wise words of my old Dundee coach Reggie Smith would come to the fore from time to time. All right, I admit I was slightly late on the little right-winger. Well, maybe a bit more than slightly to be fair, the wee guy flying twenty yards through the air to land in a heap among some photographers. Anyway, I was trying my best to explain my innocence – I did a lot of that – to the referee as he brandished his book, when Greaves strolled up to add his tuppence worth. I can't exactly remember what I said in response, suffice to say Jimmy didn't dare come near me for the rest of the match.

Jimmy Greaves was a rare breed in the game; a natural finisher who was to go on and score an incredible forty-one goals that season. I also think he was one of the world's unluckiest players, thanks to one man: Sir Alf Ramsay. Greaves could score goals for fun against any team in the world. That would make him a shoe-in for Ramsay's World Cup eleven of 1966, right? Wrong! A leg injury sustained against France opened the door for Greaves' replacement, Geoff Hurst, to show what he could do. And, as the old cliché goes, the rest is history.

Ramsay was heavily criticised in the press for not giving Greaves a starting slot when he became fit again, preferring to stick with the young West Ham player. Of course, Ramsay's decision was completely vindicated for reasons I don't need to explain.

Later, Jimmy Greaves' half-hearted celebrations and subsequent behaviour during the post World Cup Final party indicated exactly how he felt about the snub. As the celebrations continued into the next day, Greaves and his wife were conspicuous by their absence, a few days on the Costa del Sol their preferred choice.

We played the previous season's champions, Burnley, at home in front of 26,000 supporters and ran out comfortable 2-1 winners, the scoreline definitely flattering them as our team hit some fine form. On a personal note, I felt I was playing some of the best football of my career, but once again, it would not be enough for the Scottish selectors to consider me for international duty. I would be voted best centre-half in Britain by the sportswriters at the end of that season, but even that was to make no difference to the selectors' way of thinking.

Nottingham Forest had beaten us at Cardiff in the early part of the season and completed the double against us in our next match, a 2-1 defeat which well and truly burst our good form bubble.

The next match saw us up against a useful Manchester City team, complete with my old pal Denis Law, who had signed from Huddersfield.

You may recall my reference in an earlier chapter to the young City right-half, Steve Gammon. Steve had done exceptionally well since his step up to the big team the previous season and was now one of Bill Jones' first names on the team sheet. He was also fast earning a reputation for shackling inside-forwards and was confident of doing well against Law. The rigid 2-3-5 formations of the time had the wing-halves and inside-forwards lock horns for the majority of a game and it made for some real edge-of-the-seat scraps.

I have to say I was uncomfortable about the way Bill Jones was handling the pre-match preparations. He was strutting around the dressing room telling everyone who would listen he had the answer to the problem that was Denis Law. 'Young Steve here is the boy for him. He'll show Law, mark my words,' he said, patting the young lad on the shoulder.

Worse, Steve was beginning to believe his press. He'd never lined up against Law before, had no idea what to expect, but he was bouncing in that dressing room. Jones had him wound up like a corkscrew. I knew exactly what Denis Law was all about and I knew fine well he could look after himself. I still had the scars from our last meeting.

Just before we took the field I pulled Steve to the side. 'Just watch yourself,' I said, 'I know this guy doesn't look like much but he can handle himself. Believe me.'

Steve nodded and patted me on the back, told me not to worry.

A few minutes into the match I heard the crack of Steve Gammon's leg breaking from my position in the middle of the pitch as he and Law clashed near the tunnel. I still feel sick to this day when I think about it. When the dust settled it was discovered the lad had suffered a compound fracture of his right leg.

Now I couldn't be sure, but I'd like to think Denis Law never meant to inflict such an injury on a fellow professional. I believe that probably a little bit of youthful exuberance mixed with steely determination contributed to the accident.

I know I had built up a reputation over the years as a hard man and I suppose this tag was probably well deserved. I can honestly say that no opposition player caused me any sleepless nights before a game and I played against some real rough and tumble sorts throughout my career. You got to know the different types of centre-forwards, from the gentleman sort such as Lawrie Reilly or Tom Finney who didn't have a bad bone in their bodies, to the hard but fair men like Nat Lofthouse or John Charles who could dish out the rough stuff but never ever moaned when it came right back at them. Then there was a third category of player: the one you had to be wary of; the one likely to leave his boot in or go over the ball. I'm not about to name any names or anything like that, but I would encounter this type of forward from time to time. Not nice.

One thing I can say with my hand on my heart is that I never deliberately went out of my way to injure another player ... well, unless you discount the right hook I planted on Brian Clough!

Steve Gammon went on to break the same leg on two further occasions over the next three years while trying to battle back to fitness. He'd been knocking on the door of the full international Welsh side before that first break, but eventually came back a shadow of himself before moving on to non-league club Kettering Town, and obscurity. On a happier note, I later found out from Cardiff City historian Richard Shepherd that Steve had done very well for himself in the garden centre business after hanging up his boots. There is a God!

In the match against Manchester City we were 3-1 up at one point but eventually drew 3-3 as the game degenerated into a bad tempered affair.

Welsh international forward Dai Ward joined the club from Bristol Rovers after the City match, Johnny Watkins and £11,000 going the other way in exchange. Dai had fallen out with Rovers' manager Bert Tann, threatening to quit football altogether if he was not allowed to leave the club.

It was a bit of a shock to see Johnny leave as he was a regular in the side and had weighed in with important goals at vital times. And he had one of the hardest shots in football. Although he would do much better during subsequent campaigns, Dai Ward would go on to play only four games during the remainder of that season, scoring one goal, against Everton, but also ending up on the losing side each time he turned out.

Derek Tapscott was given a hot reception on his return to Highbury after the shenanigans of the first match against Arsenal at

Ninian Park. You will recall Tappy punching the ball in at one end before keeping it out of his own net in similar style. As if that wasn't bad enough, he'd then decided to pay his old mates a visit before they left for London, manager George Swindin going absolutely mental when he saw the Welshman at his door.

Some 35,000 fans saw us hit some real form at Highbury, winning by 3-2. At least Tappy didn't score. I think that would really have rubbed it in. Moore, Walsh and Donnelly struck to give us a real boost going into our next two home matches.

Newcastle were next up at home and we were determined to avenge a 5-0 mauling at St James's Park earlier in the season. We came flying out of the traps, Graham Moore sending us into a two goal lead early on. Then, our Irish goalie, Maurice Swan, suffered an unfortunate broken collar bone after an accidental clash with a Newcastle player. In the days before substitutes, Derek Tapscott donned the gloves and we prepared for the worst.

To compound matters, we even went down to nine men at one stage, Barrie Hole hobbling off with a bad foot injury. Barrie had just come into the team following Steve Gammon's injury and he had done well. Fortunately, he was able to return later, although still feeling the effects of the injury.

The hero of the hour was undoubtedly Tappy as we hung on grimly to register a 3-2 victory, Newcastle throwing the kitchen sink at us in the final minutes.

Walsh, Donnelly and Tapscott gave us yet another tremendous 3-2 victory at home against high flying Wolves in the next match as a renewed confidence flowed right through the team. We felt as if we could beat anyone on our game and lowly Bolton away in the next match held no fear for us. We moved up into sixth place in the league following the Wolves victory, our highest position in the top flight for many years. Indeed, the club has never come anywhere near that achievement since that day more than fifty years ago.

Fate tempted once again, we went right off the boil at Bolton, going down deservedly by 3-0.

Our next match, at home against double chasing Spurs on 11th March, was to go down as one of the club's greatest ever nights. Personally, I felt I played my best game for Cardiff against one of the finest teams in English football history.

The scene was perfect. The match was to be played at night due to the Welsh rugby team playing an international game at The Arms

Park earlier that afternoon. In those days many of the Cardiff fans also followed the rugby and it was not uncommon for them to enjoy one or two sherbets during and after the oval ball game.

By the time it came close to kick off in the early evening, many of the supporters were pretty merry to say the least. And with our fantastic floodlight system now fully functional, the scene was set for a cracker.

Nearly 50,000 fans shoehorned into Ninian Park that night to witness a game that is still talked about fondly by all and sundry at Cardiff. The roar we heard when we walked out on to the pitch reminded me so much of the reception we received walking out to play Villa in our promotion clincher at the end of the previous season. Only this time we were facing a team full of Spurs legends: Bill Brown, my old mate from Dundee in goal; right-back, Peter Baker; the classy Ron Henry at left-back; the incomparable Northern Irishman, Danny Blanchflower; commanding pivot, Maurice Norman; another old 'mucker' of mine and chipped out of granite, Dave Mackay; quicksilver Welshman, Cliff Jones; Scotsman, John White, tragically killed three years later by lightning while out on the golf course; big, bustling centre-forward, Bobby Smith; vastly underrated inside-forward, Les Allen and tiny winger, Terry Dyson. And the team that night was so good it had no place for another old pal of mine, Welshman Terry Medwin.

Three minutes into the match and we found ourselves one down, Dyson firing home from close range. After only ten minutes I witnessed one of the finest goals I have ever seen. Now I knew that left-winger and recent signing Derek Hogg was a good player. What I didn't realise until that point was just how good a player he was. Derek picked up the ball in the centre circle and danced his way around five or six Spurs defenders before unleashing a tremendous shot into the top corner. Our crowd nearly took the roof off the main stand when the ball hit the net.

I was genuinely pleased for Derek as he took the acclaim. He was a top man, had had a couple of niggling injuries during his short time with the club. He was to miss a few games after that night before finishing strongly with a glorious double at Old Trafford on the final day of the season.

Just as we were preparing to go in level at half-time, Spurs inside-left Les Allen's deflected shot slipped past Ron Nicholls just inside his near post. The whistle sounded as we centred the ball.

Even though we were losing, we still trooped off at the interval to tremendous applause. It was typical of the Cardiff crowd. They knew we had given our all against the best team in the country. It made us all the more determined to win the game for them in the second-half.

Three minutes into that second-half and we were level, Brian Walsh stabbing home from close range in a packed goalmouth. We were all over Tottenham at that point and the crowd went into raptures when fans' favourite Derek Tapscott swept home a low cross at the near post to put us in front for the first time in the match.

Credit to Spurs, they wanted the points. They had a championship to win and they weren't about to lie down. They battled and scrapped for everything as the game wore on.

I recalled from the times we had faced each other back in Scotland that wind-up merchant Dave Mackay used to try every trick in the book to unsettle the opposition. That night Dave latched on to young Graham Moore who was playing directly against him at inside-right. Graham was a quiet lad who just liked to get on with his game, but Mackay just wouldn't leave him alone. He was merciless, taking every chance he got to noise up the youngster, put him off his game. Unfortunately, his tricks were starting to work and Graham was getting angrier by the minute. He was a big lad who could undoubtedly handle himself and it would have been a crying shame for him to get sent off when we were doing so well.

Eventually, the taunting became so intense I felt I had to intervene and I got the chance to have a word with Dave when the game was stopped for a player to receive treatment. 'Davey, for f***'s sake, leave the lad alone! He's only a youngster trying to play his game,' I said, red-faced, in the heat of the moment (I think that might have been the sanitised version!)

'Aw, you know me, Danny! That's what I'm like. It's nothing personal,' Mackay replied.

Thankfully, he agreed to tone it down a bit.

In a nice touch at the end of the match, Mackay took time out to congratulate young Moore on having played a great game and explain that his antics were part of his make up. Fair enough!

Now Davey might have agreed to go easier on Graham Moore following my intervention, but I think it may have shifted his focus which spelled one or two painful incidents for goalie, Ron Nicholls. As the match was drawing to a close and Spurs became more and more desperate for an equaliser, they started throwing in high balls with Mackay and muscle bound, England international centre-forward Bobby Smith, taking it in turns to try and barge big Ron into the net as he came out to gather the ball.

The big goalie had played only a bit part that season but he did very well to give nothing away. I was always good in the air and managed to step in a couple of times to give Ron a bit of protection.

The final whistle sounded and Ninian Park erupted. We had beaten the double winners, and deservedly. It couldn't get any sweeter.

We were sitting seventh in the league, much better than anybody could've hoped for at the start of the campaign, and the feeling around the place was that we could push on from there, maybe even grab a top four slot. Aye right! The Cardiff self-destruct button was pushed and we proceeded to lose six out of the next seven, a solitary point at home against Blackburn scant consolation.

We managed to rally a little for our final two games, a home point gained against West Ham, before finally closing out the season at Old Trafford with a thrilling 3-3 draw.

We had slipped to a disappointing fifteenth in the table. Don't get me wrong, we would have bitten your hand off for that at the start of the season, especially given the injury situation, but on reflection, we should really have finished so much higher. Never mind, we were still in the top flight and looking forward to the next campaign. Unfortunately, for me things were to take a turn for the worse.

*****

Our FA Cup involvement stalled at the first hurdle, although it took three games against Manchester City to settle the issue, the final match played at neutral Highbury. Denis Law scored the first in their 2-0 win in London and the Scotsman would go on to score an incredible six goals in the next round against Luton Town ... before the match was abandoned. Denis would score again in the replayed game ... in a 3-1 defeat.

We had a decent run in the Welsh Cup, thrashing non-league Knighton Town 16-0 in the first round at Ninian Park. Tappy scored a club record six goals and Graham Moore four that night. Even yours truly got himself on the scoresheet. We were already ten up when I gathered the ball in my own half and decided to go on a run. The Knighton players backed off and backed off until I found myself just outside the box. I could hear Tappy and Moore shouting for a through ball, but as we were winning so easily, I thought, why not have a go? I kept my head down and fizzed in a daisycutter that went in off a post.

The next round gave us a home draw against Newport County, Derek Hogg and Graham Moore earning us a 2-1 win.

The semi-final was played at Newport, arch-rivals Swansea providing the opposition. A 1-1 draw prompted a replay at Llanelli where we eventually went down 2-1.

Season 1960-61 also saw the launch of the Football League Cup, a competition which kicked off early season at the beginning of October. Our first match was away to Middlesborough, and a final crossing of swords with my arch enemy, Brian Clough. A crowd of almost 16,000 saw us overcome the second division side 4-3, Walsh, Donnelly, Hudson and a Trevor Edwards penalty firing us into the next round where we would face Burnley. And, before you ask, no, he didn't score.

We had beaten Burnley home and away in the league that season, but on a rain sodden, Ninian Park pitch they took their revenge, making sure that our involvement in the competition was short lived. In fairness manager Jones decided to give a few of the fringe players a game and I reckon the decision backfired with too many changes made at once. It wasn't the first time I had disagreed with one of Bill Jones' decisions. And just before the start of the new season, the manager and I would disagree for the final time.

If you recall I'd earlier referred to Fulham winger Jimmy Hill, head of the Players' Union, who had visited our dressing room following a game at Craven Cottage a few seasons back. Jimmy explained to our players that he was actively campaigning for the abolition of the maximum wage and that it was only a matter of time before this bill would be passed. Well, at last the time had come!

All of the football league clubs' powerbrokers braced themselves for the inevitable backlash, with players free to negotiate better pay scales.

Now I'd heard all about Johnny Haynes at Fulham and the jungle drums were sounding out around the footballing world. The wages had pretty much stayed at the same level since I'd joined the club and, with our reaching the top division and staying there, I felt we deserved some kind of rise. Any kind of concession would have been perfect.

The Cardiff City board needn't have worried too much as Bill Jones quickly managed to secure everyone on the same wages as the previous season ... except one player. Guess who? That's right. I recall the one-to-one meeting pretty well, even though it did take place fifty years ago. Jones kicked it off by thanking me for my efforts over the season. He said he was delighted that we'd stayed in the top flight and reckoned that I had played an important part in the achievement. Fair enough. I was one of the last to meet him and, through a couple of players I was close to at the club, I managed to find out just how he was going to handle the small matter of the abolition of the maximum wage. At the meeting Jones went on to explain that, as with most of the clubs in the division at that time, Cardiff City were not in a great financial position. If he were to sanction wage rises willy-nilly, it could put the club in a precarious position.

'Okay,' I said, 'I appreciate what you're saying, but I've been on the same wages here for years and I'm the club captain. Surely that should count for something?'

Jones shook his head as if nothing I had said mattered. 'We're looking at the same pay rates as last term, but we'll look again at the position at the end of the season. If we stay up, I think it'd be hard for the club to refuse any reasonable request for more money.'

Jones sat back in his chair, looking pleased with himself. He had made his pitch and assumed the persona of a man about to close the deal.

The next few minutes were to prove the most crucial of my career.

I was on the verge of agreeing the same terms, but just before I said as much, a few thoughts flashed through my mind. Had I outstayed my welcome? I had been at City since December 1955, away from family and friends in Scotland. I'd already suffered from bouts of homesickness, though the longer I'd been in Wales, the less severe they'd become. I was nearly thirty-two. I'd always been a good trainer, but it was getting tougher to stay fit the older I became. And I'd been lucky to be blessed with an almost injury-free career, though it was becoming more and more difficult to shrug off knocks. Players at that time were definitely not as fit as they are today and it was generally thought that if you managed to compete at the top level into your mid-thirties, you were doing well. The phenomenon that was Sir Stanley Matthews was the notable exception in those days, the mercurial winger incredibly playing top level football into his fifties.

In modern times a couple of players who stood out for me were both centre-halves – Richard Gough, and more recently, Davie Weir. Ex-Rangers captains, the pair played into their forties. Indeed, Weir was still playing for the Gers at forty two.

As I'd stressed to Bill Jones at our meeting, I was captain of the football club. In all walks of life, managers and supervisors are paid more for their services. Surely the added responsibility was worth a few extra quid? Even though I say it myself, I'd done well most of the time. I was a consistent performer, had faith in my own ability. I'd even been voted best centre-half in Britain by the sportswriters. Remember, this was 1961. I wasn't sitting beside agents and lawyers, quibbling about a £30,000 win bonus, an Aston Martin or a weekly salary of £200,000. Ten quid a week extra! The figure just popped into my head. If I got my way I would be on a staggering thirty pounds per week! Somehow, I knew what the answer would be. It would not be a surprise.

Bill Jones was to get back to me the next day. No need. I knew my request would be refused. I began to consider options. For the first time in years I worried about not having a job. Should I go back, accept Cardiff's offer, eat humble pie? After all, Margaret and I had loved our time in Wales. My son was born there. I loved the club and the people. We'd even considered staying in Cardiff after I'd stopped playing. I was torn this way and that.

The phone rang around 7.30 that evening. It was a reporter asking me if the rumours were true that I was refusing to sign new terms with Cardiff City. What struck me right away was that the man didn't have a Welsh accent. He was definitely not a local newspaperman. More like North of England, I guessed. When he mentioned he was actually calling from Doncaster, I lost interest straight away. Doncaster Rovers were in the fourth division and I felt that I had too much to offer to drop down as far as the bottom tier of English football. I told him I was going back to City in the morning to finalise my terms, and left it at that. I'd spoken with Margaret and we'd decided I'd accept the current deal and stay on in Cardiff.

Just before I left the house, the phone rang again. It was the Doncaster reporter. He had been asked again to speak to me by Rovers, sound me out about a move. I told him I didn't particularly want to go and play in the fourth division and, even if I did, how could they possibly pay me first division wages?

He said they weren't just looking for a player. They wanted a manager as well. He said they had big ambitions, were looking for a young, forward-thinking player-manager. And they were willing to pay for it.

I began to think, what harm would talking to them do?

I went from the briefest of meetings at Ninian Park, where the powers there threw out my application for an extra ten quid a week, to a hotel room in the centre of Cardiff where a keen-as-mustard deputation from Doncaster wanted to speak to me about their all important vacancy. And they wanted to give me more money than I was asking for at Cardiff.

I was destined to make the biggest mistake of my footballing life!

6

Doncaster Rovers – a Big Mistake

I returned from my first day in the job, slung my bag into the corner of the room and slumped down on the chair. Leaving Cardiff had been a massive wrench for the entire family. We hated having to say goodbye to all of the great friends we had made in the city. From the lads at the club such as Derrick Sullivan, Ron Stitfall, Graham Vearncombe, Alan Harrington, Colin Baker and the rest, to fantastic neighbours, Alec and Joan Fraser and true friends, Harold, Wyn and Joan Richards. Not only that, but we had to leave my kid brother Ian, along with his lovely young wife, Margaret and their beautiful baby daughter, Angela.

Now we were sitting in our new home in Doncaster, surrounded by cardboard boxes full of memories. I smiled as I watched Andrew playing happily with some little cars. My mood changed when Margaret walked in the room.

'Don't bother emptying the boxes. We won't be here long,' I said, somehow ashamed of myself for bringing us to Yorkshire.

In a matter of weeks, I had gone from the prospect of another season in the top flight of English football, lining up against the likes of Spurs, Manchester United and Chelsea, to visiting places such as Workington, Rochdale and Mansfield. One thing I was not was a quitter and pure determination would drive me to do my best. As well as my heart, my head was also not in the right place. But, who knows? Maybe I could turn it around.

I decided to get stuck in, starting at training the following morning. To be fair to them, the people at Rovers had gone out of their way to make me feel welcome. One of the directors was an elderly gentleman with a little too much time on his hands. Unfortunately, he spent a lot of that time sticking his nose in team affairs. I think he meant well, but it was another problem I could have done without.

And, watching the lads at pre-season training, things just felt wrong. There certainly was plenty of effort and enthusiasm. They seemed keen as mustard and desperate to do well for me. Maybe with a little guidance ...

I recall watching a television interview some years later with the former Rangers and England striker, Mark Hateley. After his playing career came to an end, Hateley took over as manager at the then League Two club, Hull City. Both during training and actual games, he remarked on how he was delighted with the physical effort, attitude and work rate of his players. He said he couldn't have asked for any more. But Hull hardly won a match during Hateley's tenure and it was only towards the end of his time that he finally realised why. He'd expected too much of them. The players just weren't capable of performing in the way he'd set them up to do. Instead of making sure the defence stayed tight, did the simple things, Hateley reckoned he gave the players too much rein. Elementary mistakes cost them dear and Hull eventually failed to make an impact.

In the past few seasons I had played with and against some of the game's greatest players and it was clear to me after watching a handful of training sessions that I was going to have big trouble trying to adjust to the country's lowest tier. As usual, consistency would be the key.

An inauspicious start saw Rovers second bottom after six games. Three draws, three defeats – three points. Then, we went on a six game winning run, reaching the giddy heights of fifth place. We were actually playing some decent football and I was happy with the way things were going. The same team then went on a six game losing streak, dropping to eighteenth. Consistency!

I decided to grab the bull by the horns and request a meeting with the directors of the club, at which I would tender my resignation. I wasn't enjoying the game anymore and just wanted to be elsewhere. There had been a couple of enquiries from back home in Scotland and I asked for permission to speak to the teams involved: Clyde and Partick Thistle.

Although the board of directors was supportive, understandably, they didn't want to be left high and dry and we came to a compromise. I would stay until the end of the season and then move on.

I couldn't believe it when I read not so long ago that recent manager, Dean Saunders, had been Rovers' twenty seventh manager since 1922. Looking down the list there had been a number of high profile characters in charge, most of them sticking around for a year or two before moving on; men like Billy Bremner, Dave Mackay, Ralph Brand, Lawrie McMenemy and Stan Anderson had given it a go in Doncaster. I guess the job must have been much more challenging than I'd first thought.

The one bright spot during the whole Doncaster episode came at Millwall. We'd been short of players through injury and I had to slot in at inside-right. Millwall were a good side, physically strong. And, they could put the boot in. I would have expected no less from one of Reggie Smith's sides. The ex-Dundee coach was back home at the place where it all started for him and we had a cup of tea and a wee blether at the end of the game. I think the game finished drawn and Reggie was full of praise for my performance at inside-right. This was a man from whom any sort of accolade had to be earned so I was pleased to say the least.

Exeter City were also in the bottom division that season and I was thrilled to come up against my old team-mate Derrick Sullivan who had left Cardiff around the same time. Sully brought his wife along to the game and we had a couple of beers afterwards before heading back up the road to Yorkshire. The talented Welshman was a terrific bloke and I had a lot of time for him. As I'd said, I always felt Derrick could have gone on to become one of the game's greats given the right circumstances.

Near the end of my time at Doncaster, I received an invitation to play in a testimonial match. For the life of me I can't remember anything about the match or even who it was for but I can certainly recall one of my team-mates that day. The recently retired Tom Finney would be playing at centre-forward for my team! If anyone can fill in some of the details? I think the game took place around 1962 and ended up as a high scoring affair – five or six goals to two seems to ring a bell.

Doncaster Rovers eventually finished third bottom in 1962. By then, Margaret and I couldn't wait to pack up and leave for Scotland ... and Clyde.

7

Back Home with the Bully Wee

After the traumatic last few months spent at Doncaster, I was delighted to be home at long last. During the close season of 1962-63, Margaret, Andrew and I moved back to Denny in Stirlingshire, Central Scotland. It's a small town around a mile from where I was born and I've been there ever since.

Towards the end of my nightmare in Yorkshire, I received a number of phone calls from clubs up and down the country. Decent contracts were on the table and at least some people felt I still had something to offer. However, the pull of returning home was so strong that it knocked out every offer, except one – Clyde Football Club.

Ex-Scotland trainer Dawson Walker was one of the part-time coaches at Clyde. Dawson had been alerted by my situation at Doncaster and persuaded Clyde manager Johnny Haddow to give me a call to sound me out about a move. Johnny told me I'd been a player he'd admired for some time and reckoned I could do a job for him.

'Fair enough. Where do I sign?' I'd made up my mind almost right away.

I knew a little about Clyde, had played against them during my time at Dundee. Based at Shawfield Stadium, very close to illustrious neighbours Celtic, Clyde actually had a decent set-up and some good players. Their recent history boasted a famous Scottish Cup Final win over Celtic, ex-winger Tommy Ring scoring a fantastic winning goal.

I knew Tommy pretty well, having played against him during his brief spell down south, at Everton. I also roomed with him while on Scotland squad training sessions. Tommy was one of the good guys, very unassuming and down to earth. In these days of MP3 players and iPads, matching team tracksuits and multi million pound shirt deals, Tommy Ring would definitely have been branded a dinosaur. Hair Brylcreemed to death, shirt buttoned to the neck and boots wrapped in brown paper and string, Tommy didn't look anything like a footballer. A footballer he certainly was and a good one at that.

Pre-season training at Clyde went ok I suppose and I was sort of looking forward to a new challenge. I know! Not exactly inspiring stuff, is it? Getting the feeling that my heart wasn't in it? That would be right, but I did try. I really did. In fact, I even turned up for extra training sessions on a few occasions as I battled to get fit after my Doncaster nightmare.

A couple of others would sometimes also turn out for extra sessions: namely Jim McLean and his younger brother, sixteen-year-old Tommy. Of course, Jim gets the name of being a miserable so-and-so, courtesy of his dealings with the media, staff, fans, officials, players – everyone – while he was boss at Dundee United. Did I find him mean and moody? Well, no. Not really. Don't get me wrong, Jim would never tickle your ribs with one-liners or tell you what a smashing guy he thought you were. He was a quiet man who preferred to hold his counsel, unless you pissed him off! Young Tommy certainly qualified with flying colours on that count.

There was poison in the air one particular morning at training. Jim, Tommy and I were the only ones out on the park and we were getting ready to wrap it up when all hell broke loose between them. I can't remember what kicked it off, but I just remember the murderous look on Jim's face as he lunged at Tommy and wrapped his hands around the wee fellow's throat. I dread to think what might have happened had I not been there. Although it wasn't funny at the time, I afford myself a smile or two when I think back to the incident. I struggled to prise the two of them apart. Tommy aiming jabby little kicks at Jim's shins and Jim roaring like a bear as he swung punches in retaliation. I'd witnessed the famous McLean temper, up close and a bit too personal.

At that time, Clyde were cruelly branded a yo-yo club, bouncing from Division One to Two, back to One and then Two again, all within a few years. The club was back in the top flight that season and I was looking forward to playing against the country's best sides. At least that was the plan. The reality was to be a little different as I only managed fourteen games in half a season before calling it a day at the age of thirty-two.

At least I managed to play against some of the big boys one last time; champions Rangers were a completely different side from the one I faced in 1955. As with Dundee, most of the Gers ageing players had retired, paving the way for a younger, fitter outfit. John Greig and Ronnie McKinnon were beginning to form an effective partnership in their defence, and the regular forward line in 1962 was made up of Willie Henderson, Ralph Brand, Jimmy Millar, Davie Wilson and George McLean. Although both Brand and Millar had just broken into the 1955 side, Henderson, Wilson and McLean were new faces to me. Oh, and I nearly forgot – there was another newcomer in the Ibrox side at left-half; a tall, dark haired Fifer by the name of Jim Baxter. Apart from his nickname – Slim Jim – one other word could perfectly describe him – 'genius'. Not only that, Jim was actually a nice guy.

Later, Jim Baxter would go on and torment England during a couple of notable Wembley encounters. In one game he lay down on the pitch beside stricken Rangers team-mate Eric Caldow, who had suffered a bad leg break during early exchanges. An obviously upset Baxter comforted left-back and normal penalty kick taker Caldow as he received treatment. Jim later scored from the spot as a battling ten-man Scotland side triumphed 2-1.

And I'll never forget watching the big Fifer famously toying with the English, cheekily playing keepy-uppy during the 1967 game. World Cup winners such as Alan Ball and Geoff Hurst raged as the gifted Scotsman ripped out their very souls with an unforgettable performance during as one-sided a 3-2 victory as you're ever likely to see. Baxter didn't just anger the Auld Enemy that day. He also annoyed a particularly patriotic Denis Law, who would have much rather pressed home the Scots' obvious advantage with a more resounding win. Denis was, no doubt, still smarting from England's unexpected World Cup Final win over West Germany the previous year. Legend has it that Denis Law had the golf course to himself the day of the final, his heart sinking to the soles of his feet when he witnessed the early throes of rampant celebrations through the clubhouse window, on his lonely trudge up the eighteenth! Years later, Denis would turn down an invitation to a dinner to honour those who helped lift the World Cup for England. 'Why would I want to meet a Russian linesman I don't even know?' he is reported to have said!

Celtic were very much in the shadow of Rangers in the fifties and early part of the sixties. In fact Jim Baxter later revealed that he wound up on the losing side only once in an Old Firm game. In typical Baxter fashion he went on to claim 'if we beat them again we get to take them home and put them on the mantelpiece!'

Nobody knew what was around the corner. Really, who could have known that five short years later, Celtic would overcome Italian giants Inter Milan to become the first British club to win the European Cup? In 1962, some of the players who won that cup in Lisbon had been signed, but had still to break into the team; men such as Tommy Gemmell and Bobby Lennox. Some were to sign for the club later – Ronnie Simpson, Jim Craig, Willie Wallace, and Bertie Auld. The rest – Bobby Murdoch, Billy McNeill, John Clark, Stevie Chalmers and Jimmy Johnstone had already played for the first team.

I had played against goalie Ronnie Simpson while at Cardiff as he had spent nine years with Newcastle United. Ronnie's strengths were sure handling of the ball and shot stopping. He was unable to command his area due to a lack of height and I likened him to former Rangers keeper, Andy Goram – with one significant difference; in my opinion Goram was better. In fact, so good he just had to appear in a later section of the book. Read on to find out.

I'm thrilled to tell you that a couple of my fourteen games at Clyde just happened to be against Dundee at Dens and at Celtic Park and, as well as visiting old friends back home, it gave me the chance to have one last crack at the Hoops. I'd a decent record against them with Dundee, winning three, drawing one and losing two. I'd even scored a couple of goals against them, including one that turned out to be the winner during a League Cup tie in Glasgow.

Walking back through the front door of Dens Park, I had the good fortune of meeting a couple of gentlemen, one I knew and the other I would get to know very well some years later. The man I already knew was the then current Dundee manager, Bob Shankly, brother of Bill. Bob brought a league championship to Tayside that season and I was delighted for him. He was a real gent and it's fair to say I preferred Bob Shankly's company to that of his more famous sibling. As with John and Mel Charles, they were also ... well, just different.

The other man I got to know really well when I went to work for his construction firm in the late sixties. Duncan Ogilvie was also a popular man in Scotland's central belt, and his company, based in Stirling, still build quality homes. In fact the Ogilvie Group is doing so well that Duncan junior made it into the recent *Sunday Times* rich list with a personal fortune of £35 million! I don't personally know the lad but by all accounts, he is also a nice guy, just like his old man. I suppose it shows you don't have to be a single-minded shark to be good at what you do!

My Clyde team earned a creditable 1-1 draw at Celtic Park and although Murdoch, McNeill, Clark and Chalmers looked as if they were very good players, that day one man stood head and shoulders above the others. Not many players gave Clyde left-back Harry Haddock a chasing at any time during a long career at Shawfield, but Harry certainly got a hounding from flame haired winger, Jimmy Johnstone. I really don't need to tell you how good Jinky was. Everyone knows the little man was a special player.

Former Rangers left-back Davie Provan was unlucky enough to play at the same time as, and in direct opposition to, Jimmy Johnstone, and often ended up cross-eyed trying to catch the little genius. I know big Davie pretty well as he hails from nearby Bonnybridge. The mere mention of Jimmy Johnstone's name still sends shivers down his spine! Seriously, the big man was a fan of Jinky's and felt privileged to be on the same pitch, but he just can't bear to watch archive footage of one particular Old Firm game when Johnstone famously dribbled rings around Davie, then went back to do him again ... and again! 'Why the f*** do they have to show that game?' Davie would squeal in anguish.

Henderson v Johnstone

Willie Henderson was another very good player who later became best friends with the man who was his main rival for the Scotland number seven shirt, Jimmy Johnstone.

A Rangers legend, Willie hailed from Caldercruix, near Airdrie. Like Jimmy Johnstone, Willie was lucky enough to play for his boyhood heroes.

The pair were quite different in style; Willie was quicker and more direct with a great shot in either foot, while Jimmy was simply the finest dribbler of the ball I've ever seen ... well maybe Lionel Messi could have given him a run!

In the games I played against the Old Firm, Clyde left-back Harry Haddock did a bit better against Henderson than Johnstone. Harry was also quick and could therefore match Willie for speed but Jimmy on his game could tie the best full-backs in the world up in knots. Leeds United full-back Terry Cooper described Johnstone as 'my nightmare,' after their famous European Cup semi-final ties in 1970.

Willie tended to be more consistent while Jimmy scored more goals in his career. Both played a similar number of games, Willie turning out for Scotland on six more occasions. And I'm sure both could have made a fortune doing stand-up routines on the comedy circuit.

I remember Jinky speaking about his experiences with Celtic in the European Cup, the tiffs with manager Jock Stein, the fear of flying (I can relate to that one), the famous 'death threat' story where Jimmy was told he'd be shot if he played in a certain game ... or rather, he deliberately wasn't told of the danger by the Celtic management and proceeded to run out and play one of the finest matches of his life. Jimmy's description of how he felt when the news was eventually broken to him was hilarious.

Then there was the famous incident prior to the World Cup of 1974 when Jimmy and Rangers' Sandy Jardine were caught messing about with a rowing boat near Largs. Jimmy ended up alone in the boat, drifting into a busy shipping lane, helpless, as there were no oars on board. Reports said drink was involved.

Probably the funniest Jimmy Johnstone story recounted the events in the tunnel before that famous 1967 European Cup Final with Inter Milan in Lisbon.

'There they were: Facchetti, Domenghini, Mazzola, Cappellini; aw six-footers wi' Ambre Solaire suntans, Colgate smiles and sleek-backed hair. Each and every wan o' them looked like yon film star, Cesar Romero. They even smelt beautiful. And there's us lot: midgets. Ah've got nae teeth, Bobby Lennox hasnae any, and old Ronnie Simpson's got the full monty – nae teeth top an' bottom. The Italians are staring doon at us an' we're grinnin' back up at them wi' our great gumsy grins. We must have looked like something out o' the circus.'

I've already mentioned the fact that Willie Henderson and Jimmy Johnstone became great mates through football. In those days Old Firm players did become friendly off the field, despite the intense rivalry on it. I remember Jim Baxter and Paddy Crerand becoming very close. The same could be said about Willie Henderson and big Tommy Gemmell.

Left-back Gemmell could never be likened to a shrinking violet during his playing days. In fact, as I've already said, nearly all the 'back kicks' in those days looked as if they could punt you over the stand. I'm sure some of the full-backs in many of the sides at that time must have been able to make grown men cry.

The Gemmell – Henderson tussle was always an interesting one, mind you. Willie was a very durable wee character with huge thighs and he wouldn't be slow in kicking you back.

Most Rangers and Celtic fans didn't want to know or hear anything about friendships between Old Firm players, especially the dyed-in-the-wool supporter, the fanatic who would scream blue (or green) murder if his team lost the toss. It was the only game that mattered as far as he was concerned. It's them and us. War!

I remember standing in the Rangers end at Parkhead during a game in the mid-sixties. Willie Henderson was really in the mood that day, and as a result, he and Tommy Gemmell were seeing a lot of the ball. Adrenalin was pumping hard and some of the tackles between the pair should have carried an X-rating. The crowd was really getting wrapped up in the excitement of it all, and when a couple of particularly nasty exchanges ended up with big Tam grabbing Willie by the scruff of the neck, almost lifting the wee man off his feet, the atmosphere of sheer hate and venom felt around the ground was incredible. Fans of both sides bayed for blood as the players broke apart, their faces screwed up in fury, fingers pointing accusingly ... or were they?

Many years later, I read a newspaper piece featuring Willie Henderson and in it he spoke about that game. I sat open mouthed as he explained ...

'It was great! People thought we wur huvin' a real go at each other – ready tae go fur the throat! Naw! Nuthin' o' the sort! Ah wiz tellin' big Tam that he wiz oan the bell when we goat tae the pub and he wiz sayin,' you're a fox, wee man, it's your turn tae get the drinks in.'

Not many people knew that Willie Henderson was as blind as the proverbial bat and legend has it that, during one Old Firm match, he turned to the Celtic bench to ask Jock Stein how long there was to go.

'Ask your own effin' manager,' Stein replied.

Henderson or Johnstone? Johnstone ... but only just!

*****

Halfway through that season at Clyde, I decided to call it a day. There was one main reason for my decision, apart from my not really enjoying the football anymore. Johnny Haddow parted company with Clyde only about three months into the season after a run of poor results. There were a few names bandied about in the days following Johnny's departure and I eventually found out the favourite to take over through an unlikely source.

We were away to Third Lanark at Cathkin Park, and after the match, ex-Rangers and Clyde player Sammy Baird, who played a season at Thirds, came into the away dressing room to see me. Sammy was a Denny man, around the same age, and we had played together many times at youth and juvenile level. Sammy asked if I was going straight home after the match and I said I was. He suggested we meet up for a quick pint in the Last Chance pub in Muirhead. As the watering hole was, literally, two minutes off the main drag on the way home, I agreed. Sammy said he'd something important to tell me. I hadn't seen him for some time anyway, so I thought it would be nice to catch up.

'Danny, I've got some bad news for you,' Sammy said as we sat down with our beers. 'I've heard John Prentice is taking over as boss at Clyde.'

Silence. Long gulp of beer.

'You're f****** joking!' Another long gulp. 'Ah well, that'll be that then!' I sat back, a look of abject resignation on my face.

John Prentice was an ex-team-mate of Sammy's at Rangers. Prentice and I had locked horns when I was at Dundee, one particularly bad tempered affair at Ibrox standing out in my memory. The match ended with the two of us kicking lumps out of each other, players separating us as we walked off the pitch at the final whistle. It was one of those things. It happens sometimes. We didn't like each other.

I think I know the real reason for it, but it will remain a secret.

A week later Prentice strolled in to Shawfield, and I walked out.

8

Pre-Season Experiences

As I mentioned earlier in the book, my first sniff of a possible pre-season tour of a foreign country was exactly that; a sniff.

I'd done my time as understudy to Doug Cowie at Dundee and was ready to take my chance in the big team. I'd been told by the manager I was going to South Africa for a once-in-a-lifetime tour, taking in matches against provincial teams such as Southern Transvaal, Orange Free State and Natal as well as the South African national team itself. One unfortunate ankle injury later and that dream went up in a puff of smoke.

Since the early twenties, Dundee teams had travelled regularly to foreign climes with successful trips to Spain, West Germany, Austria, Italy and, in the years prior to 1953, Denmark, Sweden, Belgium, Israel and Turkey. The South African trip was by far the lengthiest and most extravagant the club had ever taken part in and lasted more than two months when you included the travel time.

Yes, I'd gone and missed the trip of a lifetime, and with money problems set to bite deep into Dundee FC, the prospect of similar trips in the future didn't look too good. By the time the money woes were healed and the squad embarked on a tour of North America in 1959, I was gone.

At least I got to play in some other exotic places during my short stay at Dundee; in benefit games and testimonials at the likes of Brentford, Millwall, Reading and Sheffield. Marvellous!

I made up for the lack of pre-season activity at Dundee when I moved to Cardiff City, though nothing close to the scale of a South African trip. The Welsh club's directors had a bit of money about them at the time of my move. A couple of years earlier they had shelled out £30,000 for centre-forward Trevor Ford, and didn't hold back when it came to investing in a little down time after a long, hard season.

Most of the other clubs in England and Wales – apart from the big boys – tended to stay in the British Isles during close season, many making the trip across the sea to Ireland. The Emerald Isle was the choice of destination towards the end of my time at Cardiff. Shamrock Rovers (a 2-2 draw in which I scored a rare goal!) and Waterford (a 4-0 victory) provided the opposition on our whistle-stop, week long tour, but it was never the games I remembered about these trips. It was all about the camaraderie among everyone on the trip. And not just the players.

A bus tour of Dublin and the surrounding districts was memorable for me in that the countryside reminded me so much of Scotland. Also memorable was a visit to the General Post Office on O'Connell Street, the scene of a legendary shoot out between Republicans and British forces during the Easter uprising of 1916. The bullet marks along the front of the building are still there to this day.

On that particular trip the highlight for me was the ferry ride over there. We stayed at a city centre hotel in Cardiff on the eve of the tour, and by the time they stepped on the ferry gang plank the next day, most of the lads were a bit under the weather. I have to say drink may have been involved somewhere along the line.

It was an extremely choppy crossing that morning, and when Derrick Sullivan happened to describe in meticulous detail exactly how much he liked a fried breakfast (the greasier the better), Alec Milne bolted for the exit door. Everybody fell about the place at the sight of big, green Alec hanging over the side of the boat.

Graham Vearncombe and Alec Milne used to room together on the trips. They became quite friendly and when Alec ran outside, Graham followed to see if there was anything he could do. Graham must have been feeling queasy as well and when he took a closer look at big Milne's plight, the next thing we knew he was right up there beside him, chucking up into the Irish Sea!

The pre-season jaunt to Amsterdam in 1960 started off shakily and descended into chaos. The general rule was that we left from an agreed location at an agreed time and when Derrick Sullivan was posted missing, the bus driver was instructed to go straight to Sully's house to pick him up. As I explained earlier, manager Bill Jones and Sullivan were not exactly bosom buddies, and incidents like this didn't do their relationship any good at all.

When Derrick answered the door at his house looking as if he was suffering the hangover from hell, I looked across at Bill. His face was getting redder by the second and when Sully stepped out minutes later carrying an old bag stuffed with clothes for the trip and a neck-tie for a belt, I thought Jones was going to blow a gasket.

And Sullivan wasn't finished there. A couple of days into the tour we'd finished a light training session, the manager giving us the rest of the day off. It was a beautifully sunny day in Amsterdam and half a dozen players, including myself and Sully, decided to take a walk around the city. As we strolled around taking in the sights, I was aware that Derrick seemed to be lagging behind the rest of us. By the time I realised what he was up to it was too late.

Amsterdam was, and probably still is, the bicycle capital of the world. Bikes were the prized possessions of the lowlanders, and they tended to look after them in much the same way as a new car. Ninety nine percent of the bikes were oiled, cleaned, greased and polished ... and chained up when not in use. Of course, Sully found the one percent that hadn't been chained and when he tucked his trousers into his socks, jumped aboard and tore off up the street, we knew he was going to be in deep doodoo!

It wasn't long before Derrick was picked up by the police and they were all for jailing him for a week before an impassioned plea from a club representative managed to keep him the right side of a cell door.

Amsterdam was also the last place I'd have expected to witness a full scale riot at a football match. It was the last day of the tour and somebody had heard tell of an amateur game due to take place at a stadium on the outskirts of the city. Apparently, the two sides hated each other with a passion, and every time they met there were fireworks. We could hardly believe our eyes as the players started kicking lumps out of each other before turning on the referee and linesmen. The fans then took part in running battles on the pitch. Throw in dogs, horses and riot cops along with a stadium full of broken seats and shattered windows and you might have some idea of what went down that day. There's an old story that does the rounds in Scotland about the bitter rivalry between Ayrshire junior sides Auchinleck and Cumnock, but this was on a whole new level.

Amsterdam was a lovely city, but Copenhagen would take your breath away. Denmark was the destination for a memorable pre-season trip for Cardiff City towards the end of the 1950s and the obligatory day long, coach tour through the capital was the real highlight for me; the Christiansborg Palace which houses the Danish parliament, the magnificent Tivoli Park and the fantastic

Copenhagen harbour area with that famous Little Mermaid on a rock made it an unforgettable experience. I've seen the statue a few times since and, like most visitors to Copenhagen, I still can't believe just how tiny it is.

On the footballing side, we played a couple of games on Danish soil, beating Bronshoj Boldklub 3-1 and hammering Esbjerg 4-0. As usual, a few of the lads had overdone things a bit with the old strong beer and most of them were left feeling a bit queasy on the morning of our coach tour. I hasten to add I was firmly in the moderate drinker's corner. Derrick Sullivan, on the other hand ...

Then again I'd been sitting next to Sully on the coach and I can honestly say he was neither up nor down following the hefty drinking session. The same could not be said for some of his team-mates, however, as a combination of the heat and the constant shuddering of the coach threatened to have players bolting for the exit door.

'Keep walking, Danny. Don't turn around.' Derrick grabbed my arm and ushered me on when he heard chundering noises coming from directly behind us. I cringed when I heard vomit spattering on the pavement and resisted the urge to turn round. In fairness the player involved wasn't known as a drinker and had probably been led astray the previous night. That's the only reason he's not being named and shamed.

We later discovered that being caught vomiting in a public place was still punishable by death ... according to some ancient Danish law.

In the May of 1960, as a reward for gaining promotion to the top flight, the team was scheduled for a very special visit behind the famous Iron Curtain, to take in a couple of games against East German opposition. A well-publicised U2 spy-plane incident at the time resulted in the communists closing the border and we were re-routed to the most beautiful country I had ever seen, Switzerland. Not a bad substitute, I recall thinking. And we would be lining up against familiar faces as we were booked to take on Sunderland in Berne.

Now it could be said that Graham Vearncombe was your typical goalie – mad as a hatter. Graham was a good lad who was popular among the rest of the team. In fact he was well thought of by everyone at the club. Well maybe everyone except coach, Wilf Grant. Wilf seemed to be eternally on the wrong end of the Vearncombe practical joke and I can recall a couple that still make me laugh.

We were on a bus snaking our way up a mountainside heading for the Alps. The views from up there were quite breathtaking, but Vearncombe had other things on his mind. He'd tried the old 'burn the back of the hand with the teaspoon' prank with everyone in the team at one time or another. We'd all seen it coming a mile off when he flashed the spoon against your hand straight from the cup of hot tea, but Wilf got such a fright that he upended a table full of cups, saucers, cakes and buns, much to everyone's mirth.

As if that wasn't enough, next day Wilf and Graham were paired together on a chairlift heading up the side of a mountain. Joe Bonson and I were right behind them, and I have to say I was quite unnerved as I realised that we were swinging on a thin wire 1,000 feet in the air. Not as unnerved as Wilf Grant, mind you, and when Vearncombe began to lurch from side to side like a demented ape, I thought poor Wilf was going to have a heart attack. Suffice to say, the air turned as blue as the morning sky. Hmm … I hadn't thought Wilf capable of such language!

In 1956, not long after I'd joined Cardiff City, the club were invited to Jersey to help celebrate the Channel Islands' liberation from the Nazis. We played Bristol Rovers in St Helier and lost 1-0 in a tame match. Lovely place, though.

I suppose the PC brigade might look upon pre-season tours as invaluable 'vehicles' during which a football club can develop 'team bonding' and work out 'strategic manoeuvres' for the season ahead. Baloney! You went to unwind, have a bit of a laugh and a kickabout with your mates. Same thing, I suppose.

9

My Top Teams – Then and Now

I'm often asked about specific teams, games and even goals from my time in football. The old memory is not quite what it used to be and this makes it difficult to recall events with crystal clarity. However, I do remember the fantastic skills of some of the great players I played with and against, and I thought it might be interesting to list my best team from that era; my era. Then I'll give you my top eleven from the past twenty years or so.

I'm sure for those of you old enough to remember, the following players will get some of the juices flowing again:

Goalkeeper: Bert Trautmann of Manchester City

The big German was a former Luftwaffe paratrooper who fought in World War Two. He was awarded the Iron Cross for bravery, the highest honour the German people could bestow on one of its own. Trautmann was famous for playing the last seventeen minutes of an FA Cup Final with a broken neck!

A commanding and athletic goalkeeper, Bert Trautmann had everything.

Right-back: Alex Parker of Falkirk, Everton and Scotland

Alex wasn't the quickest of players, but his positioning and timing in the tackle was spot on. He'd good patter as well and used to entertain everybody with his quick wit. Alex was known as 'King of the Goal Line Clearances' and once described Falkirk and Liverpool stopper Bert Slater as 'the best goalkeeper I've played behind!'

Left-back: Alf Sherwood of Cardiff City and Wales

I've already mentioned earlier in the book just how good a player Alf was. Sir Stanley Matthews described him as 'the best left-back I ever faced.' Need I say more?

Right-half: Danny Blanchflower of Tottenham Hotspur and Northern Ireland

Double winning captain of Spurs, Danny was an incredibly influential player who knew how football should be played. And he wasn't afraid to air those views. A true gentleman, inspirational, and the ultimate winner, Danny would have been captain of my team all day, every day.

Centre-half: Doug Cowie of Dundee and Scotland

Big Doug would have been a multi-millionaire had he been playing today. No question. And he hated the position with a passion!

Left-half: Duncan Edwards of Manchester United and England

Rangers and Scotland legend Jim Baxter would have been a stick on for left wing-half if not for the genius that was Duncan Edwards. The world was robbed of a superstar by the tragic events in Munich. The kid was a sensational player who could do anything with a football.

Outside-right: Stanley Matthews of Blackpool and England

One of the greatest players of all-time, Matthews would have walked into any team in the world.

Inside-right: Johnny Haynes of Fulham and England

Haynes wasn't exactly a friend of mine, but his ability was never in question. A brilliant passer of a ball and a great reader of the game.

Centre-forward: Nat Lofthouse of Bolton Wanderers and England

One of a long line of battering-ram England centre-forwards, big Lofthouse was also the best, in my opinion. Manchester United's tragic centre, Tommy Taylor, was close, very close, but I think Nat just edges it. He was a big, bruising forward who terrorised opposition defences. Lofthouse would be among the first names on my team sheet. Well, maybe after Finney.

Inside-left: Billy Steel of Dundee and Scotland

I've run out of superlatives to describe the wee man.

Outside-left: Tom Finney of Preston North End and England

The best player I played with or against, the Preston lad who spent his entire career with his boyhood heroes was one of the nicest men I've ever met.

I don't know if anyone would agree with all of my selections, but I reckon this team would have been a match for any club or international side in the history of the game. Pace, power, commitment, skill and guile – they had it all.

This section is one of the shortest in the book, but probably took the longest time to write. There were so many great players in the game at the time that it was so difficult to narrow the choice down to just eleven. I mean, as well as Jim Baxter, how could anyone possibly leave out legendary players such as Frank Swift, Tommy Taylor, John White, Lawrie Reilly, Denis Law, Len Shackleton, Willie Woodburn, Ivor Allchurch and John Charles?

The modern side is almost entirely made up of players from the last twenty years, most of them still playing. There is one notable exception. A player who came along just after I'd finished in the game. The man oozed sheer class, and I just had to include him in my team.

You'll note a Spanish bias throughout the line-up. World and European success may have a little to do with this.

Within an attacking 4-3-3 formation, my side would line up thus:

Goalkeeper: Andy Goram of Rangers and Scotland

The best shot stopper I've ever seen, Goram was worth at least fifteen points a season to Rangers in their march to nine league titles in a row during the nineties. A series of great saves against Eric Cantona's Leeds United during a European tie and one incredible stop from Celtic's Pierre van Hooijdonk stand out in my memory. Indeed, it was saves such as this that prompted the late Celtic manager Tommy Burns to publicly declare his desire to include the epitaph 'Andy Goram broke my heart' on his gravestone.

Right wing-back: Glenn Johnson of Liverpool and England

I've been watching this young man's career with interest. A product of the West Ham academy, Johnson hit the big time when he became the first signing of Roman Abramovich's tenure at Chelsea. I was astounded when Jose Mourinho released him to Portsmouth.

Three years ago Johnson was snapped up by Liverpool and he hasn't looked back. Big, strong and athletic, the lad is going to be an England legend. I'm sure of it.

Left wing-back: Roberto Carlos of Real Madrid and Brazil

Quick as lightning, Carlos possessed a cannon for a left foot. Not the best defender in the world, he didn't need to be in that particular Madrid side. In any case, he more than made up for it in an attacking sense with his lung bursting runs down that left wing.

Centre-back: Sergio Ramos of Real Madrid and Spain

This selection may be a bit of a surprise to many people as Ramos is a fairly recent addition to the Madrid side. Quite simply, he is one of the best centre-backs I have ever seen. Two footed and majestic in the air, I expect Ramos to become a legend for club and country.

Centre-back: Carlos Puyol of Barcelona and Spain

My son recently received an internet link to a fans' forum type of website. There, I got it out of my system. That's right, I haven't a clue what it's all about! Apparently, it's a site where fans from all over the world can air their views on anything and everything football related.

If, like me, you wouldn't even know how to switch on a computer, I'll explain: Dai Woosnam, now residing in South Africa, is a big Cardiff City fan and used to watch the team during my time there. Dai very kindly referred to me as a City legend and went on to compare me to Carlos Puyol in every way – minus the wacky haircut, of course! If only for that reason, I just had to include the big man in my side. And he can play a bit as well!

Midfielder: Xavi of Barcelona and Spain

A tiny midfielder who must be a nightmare to play against, Xavi has quick feet with a great shot in either. The Catalonian has been shortlisted on a number of occasions for World Player of The Year. Xavi came through the youth ranks at Barcelona and was named player of the tournament after the 2008 European Championships. A vital part of possibly the finest midfield trio the world has ever seen.

Midfielder: Andres Iniesta of Barcelona and Spain

Second of the trio mentioned above, Iniesta is another product of the Barca youth academy. He originally started out as a defensive midfielder, but soon began to show he was destined for greater things. A superb dribbler with fantastic vision and movement, his partnership with the other two Barcelona midfielders borders on the uncanny.

Midfielder: Lionel Messi of Barcelona and Argentina

Arsene Wenger described the little man as 'the greatest player in the world ... by some distance.' It's hard to argue with that viewpoint and I'd even go further than Arsene and describe Messi as the best player of all-time ... by some distance. Sublime skill, lightning pace, poise, balance, vision, movement – he has all of these in abundance. And, like all great players, he can handle himself. He comes in for some rough treatment at times, but I'm convinced he must be made of rubber as he just gets up, shakes his head and dusts himself down.

Would Messi have been as effective during my time in the fifties and sixties? In a word – yes! The pitches were like gluepots most of the time and the full-backs could have kicked you into the stand, but a great player is a great player, whatever the conditions.

Striker: Ronaldhino of Barcelona and Brazil

Definitely in my top five of all time, the Brazilian was considered by most to be the best before Messi arrived. King of the spectacular, his free kicks, passing and ball control were out of this world. If I have some criticisms there were, at times, questions against his attitude and work rate. But what a talent!

Striker: Ronaldo of Real Madrid and Brazil

Okay, I know the big man also played for Barcelona but it was his spell at Madrid that convinced me to include him in my top eleven. A World Cup winner, Ronaldo actually reminded me of a British-style centre-forward. He was good in the air, big and strong with a rocket shot in either foot. He'd a tendency to put on a little weight from time to time, but my goodness, it didn't hold him back in the slightest. He was as quick as anyone over twenty or thirty yards.

Striker: George Best of Manchester United and Northern Ireland

As I mentioned before, the Northern Irishman was the best player I'd seen until Messi came along. But then, who knows what magic

George would have been able to weave on today's pitches, using modern equipment and operating within a 4-3-3 or a 4-4-2.

Now you may be entitled to ask after the likes of Maradona, Pele, Cruyff, Beckenbauer, Stoichkov, Zidane and Figo. The truth is I didn't feel I could leave out anybody from the above side in favour of any of these great players. I'd probably include them in my second side along with Cristiano Ronaldo, Gazza, Gordon Banks and Ruud van Nistelrooy.

Playing positions? Who cares? They were all so good I'm sure you could have played any of them in a choice of positions.

10

Life After Football

My daughter, Linda, arrived on 28th March, 1964 and the family was complete.

I considered a few coaching positions around the country, and even began to help out a little at local side, Dunipace Juniors. However, I soon began to feel like I was merely going through the motions and didn't want to short change anybody, so I decided to call time on the football.

The game had been my life for so long that I hadn't even thought about what I was going to do next. There were no millionaire footballers in those days and I was under pressure to find a job. I still had most of the money I'd received from the FA when I'd finished up in England. Five hundred pounds was a lot of money then and I was glad of it. It would tide me over for a few months.

We settled in Denny, Stirlingshire and I got myself on the job ladder. Nothing fancy, mind you. The sixties definitely weren't the boom times for this country and beggars couldn't be choosers. You just had to take what you got. I was approached by the manager of Pearl Assurance in Falkirk about a vacancy that had come up in the Denny area. He reckoned I would do well there selling insurance as most people would know who I was. Ironically, my son would choose that particular employment path more than twenty years later, eventually working his way into a managerial position in Coatbridge, Lanarkshire, but the job wasn't for me.

No, I started in a distillery – in the warehouse – before spending a little time working in the local paper mill. My brother James was a tradesman with a building firm and I went to work with him for some years, latterly getting into lorry driving which was to see me through to retirement.

My dear wife, Margaret, died from heart complications on 19th October, 1993, and I felt as if my world would collapse. It was only through the love and support of my family that I survived the most traumatic time of my life.

I'm still fit and active. I have my car to get around and love walking my wee Scottish terrier dog, Kirsty.

Over the past few years I've been invited to a number of what used to be called 'smokers' evenings', where invited guests would entertain the audience with funny stories. I was lucky enough to witness some great banter from the likes of Craig Brown and ex-Rangers full-back, Bobby Shearer at the local social club a few years ago. People like Frank MacAvennie, Alan Rough, Mark Hateley and Dick Campbell have all delivered first class entertainment.

Ex-Celtic and West Ham player MacAvennie wasn't afraid to have a laugh at his own expense. During a high profile court case he was reported to have asked the judge if he could plead the Fifth Amendment, stating that he did not want to make an arse of himself. The judge quickly advised Frank that, if he were in the US, he could take advantage of said amendment. Unfortunately, the option is, as yet, not part of the British legal process.

Goalkeeper Alan Rough spent a brief spell at Celtic under Billy McNeill towards the end of his career. McNeill explained to Roughie that he had bought him purely as a back-up keeper to new signing, Ian Andrews.

Andrews's signing came on the eve of an Old Firm match at Ibrox. In those days the Old Firm reserves played at the other ground at the same time and as Rough and Andrews wished each other good luck as they parted, Andrews mentioned something to the tune of, 'wondering what all the fuss was about.' Alan knew that Rangers were a much stronger side at that time and, to be honest, wasn't too disappointed to be running out at Celtic Park for the reserves. It turned out to be a good call as Rangers ran out 5-1 winners with Andrews finding out exactly what all the fuss was about! Incidentally, the Rangers fans later cruelly dubbed the keeper, Cinderella, as he could never get to the ball!

The first thing I said to Mark Hateley when I met him at a club some years ago was, 'I'm sorry for kicking your father!' Mark went on to wow the crowd that night with a rather dubious story involving fellow Rangers striker Ally McCoist and midfielder, Ian Ferguson. The team were flying out to prepare for a high profile European tie and tee-totaller Fergie was sitting directly in front of Hateley and McCoist as he ordered fresh orange juice from the stewardess. 'If you need a top-up, just press this,' she said, pointing at the call button above the seat. Ten minutes later Mark and Ally nearly choked on their drinks when they witnessed Fergie holding the glass up to the panel above him and pressing the top-up button! No? I don't believe it either! It's a good story, though!

Dick Campbell was one of the funniest I've ever heard at this type of event. Dick, ex-assistant manager of Dunfermline, and manager Bert Paton, were invited to a press conference to promote Sky Sports' first ever live match, a game at Ibrox against Rangers.

Apparently, there was a mix-up between them – each thought the other was attending the press conference – and they went into the game oblivious to anything the TV people had said. Evidently, the main reason for the meeting was to point out it was Sky's policy to install as many cameras and microphones as they could, including in and around the dugout areas. Now Dick believed very much in calling a spade a spade, and didn't hold back with any accompanying expletives. So when he and Bert spent the first half hour of the match effing and blinding at everything that moved, little did they know they were also giving the viewing public an ear-bashing. Dick felt his mobile phone vibrate in his pocket, the name 'mother' shone in the display. Mrs Campbell had been watching the match on TV and decided she couldn't listen to any more of her son's bad language. He had to stand there sheepishly as she tore strips off him.

The nearest I get to a game of football nowadays is watching it on television. There was a time in the mid to late sixties after I'd finished playing football, when I did go regularly to Ibrox. Of course there were no season tickets in those days and large sections of the ground were standing only. I've seen crowds of over 100,000 at some games.

The Ibrox disaster of 1971, where sixty-six people lost their lives, along with further tragedies at Heysel, Hillsborough and Bradford, switched the clubs' and football associations' focus squarely to safety, with the major grounds being converted to all-seater stadiums. This drastically reduced crowd numbers, making it a whole lot safer when leaving grounds.

I had my own brush with death following a match at Ibrox in the mid-sixties. In what was a mirror image to the 1971 tragedy, and on the same stairway – number thirteen – I was involved in a terrifying crush. A couple of minutes from the end of this particular match, large sections of the crowd were pouring down the stairways, heading for trains and buses. Suddenly, an almighty roar went up from the people still inside the ground. Everyone thought a goal had been scored and dozens of people stopped dead in their tracks and tried to turn and go back into the ground. The momentum of the majority carried them on top of the ones turning back. Luckily, I was on the very edge of the crush but still managed to lose one of my shoes during the almighty scramble. People just started piling on top of others. A man called out to me to try and get him out of the crush. I tugged and hauled at him with all of my might but I just couldn't budge him. He was bent over, his back straining hard against the barrier. The look of terror on his face is something that has stayed with me ever since. I comfort myself with the fact that nobody lost his or her life that day. It had been a close shave for all of us and I hoped that nothing like it would ever happen again. I decided at the last minute not to attend the infamous New Year's Day match of 1971. I still feel physically sick when I think back to the moment when I heard the first news report of the disaster on stairway thirteen.

As you will have realised from my greatest modern team selection, I like to watch Spanish games on the box. I think the standard of football in Spain is the best in the world at the moment and I often dream about moving there, especially when the winter weather in Scotland is at its worst. A season ticket for the Bernabeu Stadium in Madrid would suit me just fine.

Andrew and I enjoy watching Rangers matches and like to see them win. As with most teams these days, the Gers are beset with money troubles and I can only see this situation getting worse. I fear many clubs are going to go to the wall in the next few seasons; years of reckless spending and the economic climate ready to take their toll.

My old club, Dundee, were docked twenty-five points in the 2010-11 season for going into administration. When it would have been easier to throw in the towel, the team fought like tigers to finish mid-table and would have easily gained promotion back to the top flight without the deduction. I was delighted for manager Barry Smith and the lads that they managed to stay in the first division. The team were then invited to join the SPL when Rangers were dropped to the third division and I would dearly love to see them kick on from that position. It's where the club deserves to be.

As for Cardiff, they have been knocking on the door of the

Premiership for the past few years. I felt Dave Jones was really unlucky to lose his job as he got the team so close so often. They just couldn't get over the finishing line, the defeat to Blackpool in the play-off final at Wembley in 2010, deeply disappointing.

The previous year, Andrew and I were invited down to Ninian Park for the final league match at the old ground, against Ipswich Town. As soon as I walked into the stadium memories of the old days flooded back: the promotion-clinching game against Aston Villa, especially that wonderfully warm reception I received as I addressed the massive crowd at the end; that incredible match against all-conquering Spurs when we won 3-2. On the flip side, I also recalled the deflated feeling when I walked out the door for the last time in 1962.

That famous Bob Bank enclosure, the Grange End, the Canton End; I couldn't believe I was actually there, witnessing the very last match at Ninian Park. Richard Shepherd met us inside the main door and kindly treated us to a truly memorable day. Everything passed in a blur as I found myself giving radio and TV interviews, speaking to hundreds at special lunches in the various lounges in the main stand, and meeting a succession of fans old enough to remember me playing.

The highlight of the day was my introduction to the fans at half-time and the reception I received from both sets of supporters as I enjoyed a lap of honour will remain with me forever. And, I was tickled pink when my son told me about one touching moment on a stairwell on the way up to one of the lounges.

Former player Roger Gibbins and I were walking up the stairs when we came across a couple of young stewards. Roger introduced me to the lads and I stopped to shake hands with them before carrying on to the next level. Andrew was following behind and overheard one lad excitedly say to the other as he passed, 'I can't believe I just shook hands with Danny Malloy!' Now the boy couldn't have been more than twenty but he knew who I was. Those are the Cardiff fans for you. They love their football and their love for the club crosses generations.

My nephew, Andrew, who still lives in Cardiff, recently told me a story about walking up to Wembley on his way to watch the FA Cup Final between City and Portsmouth a few years back. He couldn't believe his eyes when he noticed a young City fan up ahead wearing a replica top with the number five on the back ... and the name **MALLOY** etched above it.

Dave Forbes at Dundee and Richard Shepherd at Cardiff couldn't have been more helpful, not just with providing vital information to assist in the writing of this book, but also with their kind invitations for Andrew and me to attend future matches. And Richard very kindly agreed to compose the foreword. I'm sure you found it very interesting.

*****

That just about wraps things up as far as my story is concerned. I hope you enjoyed reading it as much as I did the writing process. I wanted to provide an insight into, not only my time in football terms, but also my life in general. I wanted to give readers snapshots from the full story; from my working class roots and upbringing, to my views, thoughts and opinions on a variety of subjects.

My recollection of each and every event described in the book is pretty much how I remember it. If there are any discrepancies I can only apologise and trust they are minor ones. Unfortunately, the memory of this octogenarian is not quite as sharp as it once was.

Tributes

Tommy Docherty (Preston North End and Scotland)

Big Danny could trap the ball further than I could kick it! No seriously, I remember Danny as a 'formidable' opponent. Strong, fearless, good in the air, and deceptively quick, he was a winner. The kind you would want beside you in the trenches.

Craig Brown CBE (Former Scotland Team Manager)

When I arrived at Dundee in 1960 Danny had already left years before for Cardiff City, but the supporters and staff at Dens still spoke in admiration of his prowess and durability. In an age when there were many hard men around, Danny was THE hardest. Had I been Scotland boss at that time, I would have found it extremely difficult to leave him out of the national team because men of his attitude and ability were the kind of players I very much favoured.

Graham Moore (Cardiff City, Manchester United, Chelsea and Wales)

My abiding memory of Danny took place in a London hotel when fellow young player Steve Gammon and I came up against a jobsworth barman who refused to serve us a couple of shandies after dinner, even though it was before closing time. A huge hand passed between us and grabbed the barman by the collar. 'The lads asked for two shandies,' Danny said in his distinctive Scottish accent. Needless to say we got our drinks in double quick time!

The young kids had the utmost respect for the experienced players who would go out of their way to look after us on and off the pitch. Danny Malloy was one you could always count on to be in your corner.

Doug Cowie (Dundee and Scotland)

Danny was made for the centre-half position; strong, quick, fearless in the tackle, and good in the air. But for all he was big and strong, he was never a dirty player. Due to financial reasons Dundee allowed Danny to move south. Not only had we lost a very good player, but I had to say goodbye to a great friend. I often thought about Danny after his move, but I had absolutely no doubt he would be a huge success at Cardiff City.

Alan Harrington (Cardiff City and Wales)

Danny was one of the best centre-halves I played with or against. I always found him to be inspirational and encouraging as both man and team captain.

Colin Baker (Cardiff City and Wales)

Danny really was Captain Fantastic, leading the club back to the top flight in 1960. During his time in Wales, Danny became a permanent fixture in the side, well liked by the players and staff, and idolised by the fans.

Barrie Hole (Cardiff City, Blackburn Rovers, Aston Villa, Swansea City and Wales)

I remember going on a pre-season tour of Switzerland with City around the same time we won promotion to the top flight. During a match there, manager Bill Jones and trainer Wilf Grant were standing beside me near the touchline when Danny came across for some treatment following a blow to the stomach. Both stood open-mouthed before Bill turned to Wilf saying, 'Christ, he must really be hurt!'

I must have only been around 17 or so, and ten stone dripping wet, when I broke into the City side, but I well remember that big, burly, uncompromising Scottish centre-half. Yet for all Danny was a tough guy – and a tough guy he certainly was – he had a heart of gold and a soft spot for the kids at the club. He would go out of his way to make sure we were all right. Danny Malloy was a great captain and an inspirational leader.